THE
HIDDEN
MALPRACTICE

How American Medicine
Treats Women as
Patients and Professionals

Gena Corea

THE HIDDEN MALPRACTICE

HOW AMERICAN MEDICINE TREATS WOMEN AS PATIENTS AND PROFESSIONALS

WILLIAM MORROW AND COMPANY, INC.
NEW YORK   1977

RG14
U6
C67

Grateful acknowledgment is made for permission to quote from the following:

"Why Would a Girl Go into Medicine?" by Margaret A. Campbell, M.D. (pseudonym for Dr. Mary C. Howell), copyright 1973 by Mary C. Howell.

" 'What If You Were Married to a Cab Driver?': Medical-School Admissions, Interviews with Women Applicants," unpublished paper by M. C. Howell, C. C. Tentindo, and J. B. Walter.

"An Open Letter to the Women's Health Movement," by Mary Howell, M.D., *Health Right*, May 19, 1975.

A "Frankly Feminist" column of August, 1973, about the women's health movement from *The New Republic*.

"SpeakoutRage," *Second Wave*, Vol. 2, No. 3, p. 11.

"The IUD's Unnatural Birth," by Barbara J. Katz, *The National Observer*, September 8, 1973.

Printed in the United States of America.

2   3   4   5   6   7   8   9   10

Library of Congress Cataloging in Publication Data

Corea, Gena.
    The hidden malpractice.

    Bibliography: p.
    Includes index.
    1. Women's health services—United States—History.
2. Women in medicine—United States—History.   3. Sex discrimination against women—United States—History.
I. Title.
RG14.U6C67   362.1′9′8   76-53556
ISBN 0-688-03148-X

BOOK DESIGN   CARL WEISS

TO

T. E. M.

ACKNOWLEDGMENTS

I am greatly indebted to:

—Lia Coulouris Pavlidis whose comments on various drafts of the entire manuscript and whose constant support enabled me to complete this book.

—Tom Marlin for (among many other things) frequently telling me to get back into my office.

—Hillel Black and Bonnie Donovan for their patience and considerable editorial skills.

—Kris Glenn and Flora Davis for suggesting that such a book be written.

—Teresa Barbuto, Peg Beals, Fran Boronski, Ginny Caple, Betty Corea-Cohen, Flora Davis, Jan Harayda, Dr. Jane Hodgson, Dr. Mary Howell, Rosemary Maconochie, Dr. James Morris, Dr. Alice Rothchild, Mary Sanford, and Dr. Judy Tyson who were kind enough to read various chapters and make valuable comments. (Any errors in the manuscript are, of course, solely my responsibility.)

—John Van Doorn for help with the title.

—Kay Weiss, who generously shared with me the letters she had received from DES mothers and daughters.

—Librarians at the Sophia Smith Collection, the Francis A. Countway Library of Medicine at Harvard Medical School, the New York Academy of Medicine and the Rudolph Matas Library at Tulane Medical School who were very helpful as I searched for certain books and documents.

—The many people—too numerous to be named individually—who took the time to answer my questions and provide me with various material.

—Ed and Marie Corea for most everything.

CONTENTS

((10))

PROLOGUE

FOR TWENTY MINUTES ONE DAY IN 1965, AN INTERN AND A MIDDLE-aged woman argued over whether he would examine her pelvis internally. I, a nurse's aide in a Boston hospital, stood near the patient's bed, waiting to assist the intern.

Again and again, the patient refused the examination. The young man, embarrassed but determined, clutched the foot of the bed and looked directly at the woman's evasive eyes. He insisted that the exam must be performed, that all women entering the hospital must have one, that it was part of the standard admissions procedure.

"All right. Do it!" she finally snapped, anger thinly covering her fear.

To elevate her pelvis for the examination, I slipped an upside-down bedpan under her bottom. That was an indignity other women usually tried to joke about. She didn't joke. Instead, she grabbed a newspaper from her bedside table. It was something she could hide behind. Throughout the exam, while she lay with her bottom on the bedpan, her legs spread apart, and the intern's fingers in her vagina, she read that newspaper.

At the Peter Bent Brigham, a teaching hospital for Harvard Medical School, I often saw such scenes of a woman's discomfort. It surprised me that older women, who had delivered five or six children and who should be used to pelvics, were as embar-

13

rassed by them as young women. I assumed they were wrong to feel such an old-fashioned emotion. They ought to get over their embarrassment, I thought. These exams, after all, were a part of medical science. (My courage in the face of their ordeal may have sprung from the fact that I, a nineteen-year-old, had never had a pelvic.) The women, too, assumed that their feelings were illegitimate. As I prepared them for the doctor's visit, they would laugh nervously and say something like, "I know it's silly of me, but I always dread these exams."

In 1975, ten years after my stint as a nurse's aide, I sat in a Harvard Medical School building behind the Peter Bent Brigham. Medical writer Barbara Seaman was speaking during a conference on women and health. The portraits of twelve dignified white men, all former medical professors, looked down on Seaman as she proposed that, from then on, male medical students be barred from obstetrics and gynecology.

"It sounds a bit radical at first," she said, smiling, "but you get used to it."

Our Constitution, Seaman told us, guarantees us the right to privacy. Ever since the male incursion into midwifery in the 18th century, women haven't had it.

Listening to Seaman, I recalled the pelvic examinations I had witnessed at the Brigham and I wondered:

Why were all the men right to be looking up vaginas?

Why were all the women wrong to be embarrassed?

Why didn't the men acknowledge that whether or not women "should" be embarrassed, the fact was that they were? Why didn't women insist that the medical system be changed to accommodate their feelings? *

Such questions had never occurred to me as a nurse's aide, but in the decade between my nursing and Seaman's speech, I had discovered much that disturbed me about woman's health care.

So I listened, shocked and intrigued, when Seaman declared, "On a gut level, I am now convinced that it is a most basic violation of our civil rights for the group that is not at any risk from reproduction (male) to control the group that is at risk (female)."

As a reporter for the Holyoke, Massachusetts *Transcript* in 1971, I had learned myself how that violation of civil rights

* A female physician who read this manuscript for me penciled in at this point, "Pelvic exam as a form of rape?" A second female physician, reading the same copy later, scribbled next to the question, "Yes!"

harmed women. For eighteen months, I had investigated locally the charges feminists were making nationally. Medicine was one of the institutions I examined for sexism. (When I began my investigations, I was not a feminist. By the time I had finished, the evidence I had gathered forced me to become one.)

First, I read health articles in the archives of the local women's center. Several items in the files troubled me. For example, one newspaper clipping informed me that the contraceptive Pill had been approved on the basis of a study involving only 132 Puerto Rican women who had taken the Pill for one year or longer, and 718 other women who had taken the drug for less than a year. Five of the women died during the study, three with symptoms suggesting blood clots. No autopsies had been performed. This information jarred me because I had always assumed that the American Medical Association, the Food and Drug Administration, and the individual physician, or someone, somewhere, was protecting us from inadequately tested drugs. I had also assumed that the well-being of his patient was the doctor's only motivation in prescribing for her. Later, after reading documents of the eugenics and birth-control movements, I realized that population control could be the overriding motivation for some—certainly not all—doctors. I also learned that a physician often knows nothing about a drug except what the sales-conscious drug manufacturers choose to tell him.

Another newspaper story increased my uneasiness. Dr. Joseph Goldzieher of the Southwest Foundation for Research and Education, I read, wanted to see if the nausea, headaches and depression Pill-users often experienced were real or "psychological." So, in 1971, he experimented with 398 Chicano women in San Antonio, Texas. Of these women, seventy-six who thought they were getting contraceptives were given placebos instead. Ten became pregnant within four months.

The contempt Dr. Goldzieher had for those women revealed itself in a statement he made in defense of his experiment. "If you think you can explain a placebo test to women like these, you never met Mrs. Gomez from the West Side," he told *New York Post* reporter Barbara Yuncker.*

* *New York Post*, April 22, 1971. Barbara Seaman has reported elsewhere that the National Institutes of Health Center for Population Research granted Goldzieher $93,290 in 1973 and $83,155 in 1974. So, as Seaman observes, we are financing his experiments.

Dr. Goldzieher had undertaken his study, I realized, because he suspected women's complaints were due, not to the powerful hormones in the Pill, but to women's psychological deficiencies.

In the archives, I read of many incidents in which doctors, labeling women as hysterics, refused to take their complaints seriously. I particularly remember one woman whose severe case of peritonitis, caused by a botched sterilization, was at first dismissed by doctors as "psychosomatic guilt-induced" pain.

Could the view of women as hysterics be a common one among male doctors, I wondered? If so, how did that view affect their treatment of female patients? Later, in current gynecology textbooks, I saw that doctors were taught to view many of women's ills as psychosomatic and therefore, "unreal."

The October 23, 1970 issue of *Medical World News* gave me another jolt. I read there that at a cancer conference the previous year, surgeons had agreed that they rarely hesitate to remove an ovary but think twice about removing a testicle. "The doctors readily admitted that such a sex-oriented viewpoint arises from the fact that most surgeons are male," the *News* reported. "Said one of them wryly, 'No ovary is good enough to leave in, and no testicle is bad enough to take out!'"

Did this mean women might be undergoing unnecessary surgery?

More doubts arose from the material in the files. I read that women had had to sob hysterically and threaten suicide while pleading with doctors for legal abortions. Then I came across a statement by Dr. George S. Walter, Maternal and Child Health Consultant to the Indian Health Service in Fort Defiance, Arizona. In the September 1970 issue of *Journal of Obstetrics and Gynecology* he wrote: "The pregnant woman symbolizes proof of male potency and if the male loosens his rule over women and grants them the right to dispose of that proof when they want to, the men then feel terribly threatened lest women can, at will, rob them of their potency and masculinity. This flaunting of traditional subservience may . . . function in the frequent professional insistence upon sterilization as a 'package deal' with abortion. In this way, the male physician can maintain control."

I was becoming alarmed. Maybe there were a number of instances in which the doctor's motive in treatment was something other than the woman's well-being, something connected to his view of woman's function in his world.

Next, I read stories of early American female physicians. It surprised me to learn that their male colleagues had showered them with obscenities (and even, on occasion, with spit) when they tried to attend medical lectures. Some institutions, I learned, had halted women before they could even enter the lecture rooms. In fact, Harvard Medical School, which provides many of the interns who now examine ladies on upside-down bedpans, had declined to admit Harriet K. Hunt to lectures in 1847 on the grounds that it was "inexpedient" to reconsider its ban on women. (It didn't become expedient until 1945, nearly a century later.)

As I read in the archives, it was not the individual facts alone that disturbed me. I began to see that these facts might be inter-related. I learned, for example, that from 1900 until 1975, dis-crimination in medical school admissions had kept female physi-cians at between 4 and 9 percent of all physicians. The discrimi-nation that created an almost entirely male medical profession, I saw, might have something to do with female-focused contra-ceptive research, with unnecessary female surgery, with the in-accessibility of abortions and sterilizations, and with the lack of attention to menstrual and menopausal disorders.

So two questions arose from my preliminary reading: How did men get the power in medicine? What effect does that male domination have on the health care women receive?

I learned some answers while writing my articles on health care in Holyoke. Others escaped me until a year later when I decided to explore the subject in a book. I then began reading historical documents at the Sophia Smith Collection in North-ampton, Massachusetts, at the Elizabeth Bass Collection at Tulane Medical School in New Orleans and at Harvard Medical School. I found that doctors had changed childbirth from a natural event into a doctor-centered operation. I also discovered that early physicians had operated venereal disease-control pro-grams designed to preserve male health by locking up infected women.

The more I read in history and in current gynecology text-books, the more I realized that safeguarding a woman's privacy was the least benefit female physicians provide. Gynecologists, I understood, could control women through medical theories that were assumed to be scientific discoveries but which were, in fact, permeated with stereotypes about woman's nature and role. Consider what gynecology books written by men taught me about woman:

—That her hormonal system makes her utterly unlike men in her ambitions and abilities.

—That menstrual pains often merely reflect her psychological shortcomings.

—That she tends to invent symptoms so physicians must not take her complaints too literally.

—That she becomes repulsive at menopause. (In a 1966 book, one gynecologist referred to the menopausal woman as "living decay.")

—That her sex drive is inferior to man's and relatively unimportant.

Would these theories be the same if female physicians had access to the same medical information from which those theories were derived, I wondered?

I also wondered what would happen if, in a female-controlled medical system, men demanded male urologists. Suppose men explained that they found it awkward to have female doctors examining and performing operations on their penises. What if they said, "Look, when we're sick and in pain, we don't want to be embarrassed, too."

Would we consider men's demand for doctors of their own sex so unreasonable if men questioned the following medical theories women had devised about them?

—Man's supreme function in life is the impregnation of women. If he spends his energy in reading, writing or working outside the home, he will injure his reproductive capacity and therefore threaten the survival of the species.

—Woman's sex drive is much stronger than man's. Men who demonstrate an unnatural zest for intercourse or who maladjust to their housekeeping function can often be cured through castration.

—The monthly change in the man's testosterone level so upsets his emotional equilibrium that he is unqualified for professional jobs.

—Failure to accept the male role causes many of men's abdominal pains.

As we will see in chapter five, women can question the comparable theories that male doctors devised about them.

We can observe, moreover, that men and women have been brought up to esteem different kinds of behavior. We have received the medical care provided by men who often value toughness and aggressiveness and who sometimes see a disease as an enemy to be vanquished with drugs and surgery. In reading the history of gynecology and plowing through endless descriptions of "bold," "daring" surgeons possessed of "ruthless courage" who "attack" and "tackle" ailments by cutting out most of the female sex organs, doctors began to sound like warriors to me, and women's bodies, like conquered lands.

Might women, who come from the gentler female culture, bring a less military approach to healing? Perhaps they would emphasize the maintenance of health rather than the defeat of disease.*

Women might also feel more empathy for patients suffering from disorders to which they themselves are vulnerable. Taught to openly share feelings rather than repress them as men so often do, they might even be able to show their sympathy and give comfort to ailing women.

The information I first gathered seemed to indicate: Male villains victimized female patients. Only women physicians could rescue them.

But then a growing belief in the responsibility of each person for her own life made me look again at the male doctor/female patient relationship. I realized that we women, to a greater extent than men, fail to take responsibility for our own lives, our own health. We have been groomed to lean. Sex role stereotypes condition us to look to men for direction. Meekly and sometimes gratefully, we cede the male doctor (as well as the lawmaker and priest) the "right" he claims to control our bodies.

Yet taking responsibility for your health, I had learned during my research, was often essential to maintaining it. As I saw

* The International Conference of Women Physicians was convened in New York City in 1919 for this reason: "Increased numbers of female doctors were becoming dissatisfied with the method of waiting until the patient is sick and curing her by surgery and drugs." They decided to work for a program of health improvement through health education and the prevention of disease. See the preface to the conference proceedings in the Elizabeth Bass Collection, Tulane Medical School.

in the case of drugs like the Pill, you endanger yourself when you assume that every physician, clinic, drug company and federal regulatory agency places your welfare above all other considerations.

* It is safer to assume that no one cares about your life quite as much as you do.

When I am tempted to entrust my health to a doctor now, I ask myself these questions: If the operation or drug prescribed by the doctor produces serious complications, who feels the pain? Who loses the time? Who pays the bills? If the treatment fails, does the doctor die or do I?

As I take responsibility for my health, my research and gut feeling lead me to demand a female gynecologist for myself. (A friend recently recalled a *Candid Camera* episode in which men were asked to take off their clothes and prepare for an exam by a female doctor. It is considered outrageous to ask men to do that, I realized, but when women object to exams by men, we are made to feel pathologically prudish.) Since 95 percent of gynecologists are men, my chances of finding a female ob-gyn are low. As of 1971, Alaska, Nevada, New Hampshire and Wyoming each boasted only one. Five or fewer worked in eleven other states. In order for me to have female gynecologists then, I may have to work politically to increase their number.

In the following chapters, I present the information that finally led me to take command of my health care. First I explain how men dominated American medicine and nursing. Then, in Part II, I deal with the effect of that domination on the health care women receive. Chapters on venereal disease, birth control, abortion, childbirth, menstrual disorders, vaginal infections, menopause and cancer all concern the consequences of letting male doctors take responsibility for female health.

Finally, I describe the current efforts of female popular health activists to supervise their own health care and regain control over their bodies. The Epilogue is dedicated to the woman in the Peter Bent Brigham Hospital who, in 1965, read a newspaper on an upside-down bedpan.

PART

I

HOW WOMEN
HAVE BEEN BARRED
FROM HEALING

Chapter / **ONE**

FEMALE PHYSICIANS

"Nothing is impure and nothing unclean," the Sorceress proclaimed, stealing a corpse from the graveyard. She then dissected it and examined its anatomy. She studied, too, the chemistry of poisons and learned which ones, in what doses, cured.

Jules Michelet, author of a classical history of witchcraft, credits the Sorceress of the Middle Ages with making true medicine possible. She learned from her observations. This practice contradicted the antiempirical spirit of her times when physicians believed in the 4th-century Galenic theory as an article of faith. According to that theory, an imbalance of the body's four fluids—blood, phlegm, black bile and yellow bile—caused illness.

Philippus Aureolus Paracelsus, the great Renaissance physician who established chemistry's role in medicine, would have agreed with Michelet for he had attended the witch's pharmacology "classes" in the woods. In 1527, at the University of Basel where he was a professor of medicine, Paracelsus publicly burned his medical books, declaring that everything he knew he had learned from the Sorceresses.

Witches were often the only doctors who troubled to care for females and the poor. Physicians belonged to the upper class. They attended only the rich. The female healer, sometimes called a "saga" or "wise woman," must have cured better than the learned physician who bled his patients according to the signs of the zodiac and prescribed such remedies as "moss from the skull of a hanged thief." The saga offered herbal remedies and did the manual work, like lighting a fire, needed to make the ill comfortable. The poor felt at ease with her because she belonged to their own lower class. It is probable then that she, unlike the wealthy physician, could give them the emotional support conducive to healing.

But if a woman could heal without having studied, the Catholic Church declared in the 14th century, she was a witch and must die. The most reliable estimates indicate that about nine million people were executed as witches from 1479 to 1735.* Most were women. Many were healers and midwives.

Midwives were especially suspect because churchmen feared that they would steal placentas or umbilical cords for use in witchcraft rites. The regulations for midwives in Würzburg in 1553 and in Brandenburg in 1711 both specifically forbade the theft of such birth by-products.

It was also feared that midwives would destroy infants before baptism or offer them to Satan. Two Dominican friars, Jakob Sprenger and Heinrich Kramer, made just that accusation in their *Malleus Maleficarum*, a 15th-century instruction manual for witch detection. Witch-midwives, they added, "surpass all other witches in their crimes."

But these criminals, these witches, are the ancestors of the modern physician.

In the history of female healers, let us move to Colonial America. Medical institutions and full-time doctors hardly existed then so many women saw to the community's health. These part-time healers were called domestic practitioners.

A medical elite began to form in the colonies after 1765. Men who had served in the Continental Army's medical service or had studied in Edinburgh, then the world's medical center,

* See William Woods' *A Casebook on Witchcraft* (New York: G. P. Putnam's Sons, 1974), p. 26.

became full-time doctors who wanted to create a medical profession. So states began to pass laws that excluded the unlicensed from medical practice. (Before, licenses had merely marked certain healers as especially competent.)

Only allopaths received the new licenses. They were members of the orthodox, and exclusively male, medical sect and they belonged to the same class as the legislators who made the licensing laws. Still subscribing to the fourth-century humoral pathology, allopaths viewed disease as an imbalance of body fluids. With heroic doses of drugs like nitre and calomel (a mercurious laxative) and with leeches and surgical knives, they bled and purged their patients to restore the proper fluid balance. Unfortunately, allopathic treatments often caused more damage than the original ailment.

Women joined the "irregular" medical sects competing with Allopathy: Thomsonianism, Eclecticism and Homeopathy.

Thomsonians prescribed gentle herbal cures. Many were feminists and they insisted that females had a right to be treated by members of their own sex. Women attended Thomsonian meetings and formed "Ladies Physiological Societies" to share health information with each other.

Homeopathy emphasized treatment of the patient, rather than the ailment. The doctor tried to build up the patient's strength through rest, healthy food, microscopic doses of medicine, and the power of suggestion so that his or her constitution could resist the sickness.

Under the Eclectic system, doctors adopted what seemed to them the most sensible treatments from various sects.

The unorthodox doctors of these sects resembled the domestic practitioners of the 18th century and comprised the forefront of the Popular Health Movement of their own 19th century. This movement of radical activists championed the rights of lower-class people to control their own bodies without dependence on upper-class physicians. Some extremists even endorsed birth control. Most, emphasizing prevention rather than cure, advocated health foods, fresh air, exercise, bathing, and health courses for the common people. They passionately denounced harsh drugs and were equally eloquent in condemning tight corsets. (Women occasionally laced themselves to death, leaving pitiful, deformed skeletons, they reported.)

The "irregulars" opposed special privileges for the allopathic aristocracy. An elite class of doctors was undemocratic, they proclaimed, and in the 1830s and 1840s, they worked to repeal the medical licensing laws.

They succeeded because the public shared their hostility to the medical profession. Many lay people felt that a medical system demanding certain standards of "professionalism" set by the allopathic doctors was simply a device to limit competition and thereby keep incomes high.*

Some also believed that the licensing laws favored the rich. In the pages of a popular health journal, this argument was delivered before the Vermont state legislature: "The rich man's son is sent to your medical institutions—he pays his fees for lectures that he hears or does not hear—'tis all the same—money buys him a diploma—he is licensed to draw blood, to puke and purge mankind, at such price as he is pleased to demand."

A poor man's son, no matter how capable, could not afford to become a physician, the legislator observed. (He might have added that blacks and women were excluded from medical schools just as poor men were.)

Once the licensing laws were revoked in the 1830s and 1840s, medical sects could get charters for schools. That is what made it possible for women to regain their ancient role as healers. From 1850 to 1870, they established their own institutions.

When the Female Medical College of Pennsylvania opened in 1850, the all-male State Medical Society voted to expel any member who taught at the college or consulted with a female doctor.

Eighteen years later, Philadelphia's Pennsylvania Hospital proved more tolerant. It decided to admit woman into clinical training. Male medical students rebelled. At the first co-ed lecture, they hooted and jeered the young women who were taking

---

* A poem I came across in an 1835 issue of a popular health journal, *The Botanic Sentinel,* expressed that view:

> The Faculty (alleopaths) with dreadful hate,
> To ease their fears and check our cause,
> Cry Quackery both loud and late;
> They see its cures, but feel quite sure,
> By Latin terms and tyrant laws,
> The peoples pockets they'll secure.

seats in the hospital amphitheater. While their professors stood impassively, they threw paper wads at the women and spit tobacco juice on their dresses. Next, as the *Philadelphia Bulletin* reported the following day, they "assailed the young ladies with insolent and offensive language and followed them into the street where the whole gang joined in insulting them."

A week later, professors from neighboring medical schools and several hospitals voted to "solemnly protest against the admixture of the sexes at clinical institutions." The hospital board, however, declared that women would continue to be admitted. In protest, chief surgeon D. Hayes Agnew resigned.

Nineteenth-century documents at Tulane reveal that, like Dr. Agnew, most male physicians bitterly opposed the admission of women into medicine. So the men erected multiple barricades, many of which still stand, against females.

A Philadelphia County Medical Society's resolution against female doctors included several reasons often cited to discredit them. The society doubted women could bear up under the physical and mental strain of medical practice. Alluding to menstruation, the doctors noted, "The physiological peculiarities of woman even in single life, and the disorders consequent on them, cannot fail frequently to interfere with the regular discharge of her duties as physician in constant attendance on the sick.*

If a woman married and became a mother, the society continued, her professional duties would be interrupted even more: "The delicate organization and predominance of the nervous system render her peculiarly susceptible to suffer, if not to sink, under the fatigue and mental shocks which she must encounter in her professional round. Man, with his robust frame and trained self-command is often barely equal to the task."

Moreover, domestic life would be destroyed if women became physicians. What would be the condition of children, deprived of their "natural guardian" who would be working all day? "Nor when at home, can the mother, worried and

---

* If the standard of health had been female rather than male, menstruation would have been the norm and men's failure to menstruate the "physiological peculiarity." If the health standard had been a human one, neither menstruation in women nor the lack of it in men would have been peculiarities.

fretted and anxious about her patients, give healthy milk to her infant, or be in a fit frame of mind to interchange endearments with her beloved little ones, to receive their confidence and offer advice."

In her response to the Philadelphia County Medical Society, Dr. Ann Preston, a professor at the Women's College and one of its first graduates, observed that probably half the country's women had to support themselves. "Some mothers leave their young children day by day, and go out to labor, in order to be able to bring them bread at night," she informed the men. "Others sew away their strength for the pittance which barely keeps famine from their doors and, exhausted with their labors, they are indeed not in 'a fit frame of mind to interchange endearments with their beloved little ones.'"

A physician's work would be less exhausting and better paid than the work these women were obliged to take, she pointed out.

The medical society noted what it considered still another unfortunate consequence of medical education for women: They would treat male patients. "It is sufficient to allude merely to the embarrassments which would be encountered on both sides, in her visiting and prescribing for persons of the opposite sex."

Dorothy Reed Mendenhall, one of the first female students at Johns Hopkins Medical School, encountered that attitude in 1900. A top student in her class, she won, and eventually served, an internship at Johns Hopkins. But when she first came to assume her duties, the hospital supervisor told her it was impossible for a woman to take charge of a male Negro ward.

He informed Mendenhall that he had had experience with a female physician like her. She recalled, "He told me of her abnormal sex interests and of what he considered sex perversions. He said that of course he thought, and all my classmates and the medical staff would think the same thing—that only my desire to gratify sexual curiosity would allow me or any woman to take charge of a male ward."

Vigilant about "perverted" female doctors, such men never seemed to doubt the decency of the male physicians who attended women. Careful of the sensibilities of male patients, they were less concerned about the "embarrassments" of their female charges. While in the early days of Johns Hopkins, female doctors were reportedly allowed to examine male patients only from the neck up, pelvic exams of women in charity hospitals were conducted before groups of male interns and students. (That phenomenon has not passed into history. As *The New York Times* reported in July 1974, a female intern at the University of Michigan was not allowed to be present during a recent exam because a man's genitals would be exposed. At that same time, the woman's husband, also an intern, was giving a woman a pelvic exam.)

Other doctors argued that female physicians would excite male patients sexually. In 1881, the *London Lantern* observed that if, while listening to a man's heart, the female doctor's "eyes and rosebud mouth would be looking right in his face and her wavy hair would be scattered all around theirs, getting tangled in the buttons of his nightshirt, don't you suppose his heart would get in about twenty extra beats to the minute? Rather!"

Though they would excite the passions of male patients, women would lose their femininity by practicing medicine. If female doctors consulted with male doctors about male patients, their protectors feared, they would become hardened to discussing *anything* and would lose their gentleness, purity and refinement.

The State Medical Society of Pennsylvania inquired: "Will woman gain by ceasing to blush while discussing every topic as it comes up with philosophic coolness, and man be improved in the delicate reserve with which he is accustomed to address woman in the sick room?"

Dr. Ann Preston, who had led the female students into the Pennsylvania Hospital amphitheater the day male medics had spit tobacco juice at them and called them obscene names, found this argument astonishing. Earlier, in an 1855 lecture to students, she had brushed it aside impatiently. She warned the women not to violate proprieties "in your disgust for that mawkish affectation of sentiment which, shrieking at a shadow and ever ready to 'die of a rose in aromatic pain,' so often usurps and profanes the sacred name of delicacy."

(The delicacy argument is not without irony because from

woman's first appearance in the American medical classroom until today, a favorite harassment technique of male doctors has been the attempt to embarrass her with lewd stories.)

The medical profession's basic argument against female healers, of course, was that woman's place was in the home, not in competition with men. If God didn't intend woman to play a subordinate role in life, *The Ohio Medical and Surgical Journal* asked in 1848, why wasn't Adam given to Eve instead of Eve to Adam?

A resolution passed by the 1851 Women's Rights Convention in Massachusetts neatly expressed the sentiment female doctors used to dispose of the "home sphere" contention: "Resolved, that it is the duty of the women of our day to study enough of that obstruse science of surveying, to define, if possible, the boundaries of 'their own sphere,' that men be no longer compelled to keep them informed of its limits."

But people would never employ female physicians, opponents declared.

"Very well, then," Dr. William Cornell, a professor at the women's college, shrugged, "let them employ others."

He knew the real fear was that people would very readily employ female doctors.

As Dr. Ellwood Harvey, another professor at the women's college, told female medical students in 1855, they could expect opposition from doctors who were afraid of fair competition. "They will raise the cry, 'She is out of her proper sphere' because they are afraid they will be pushed out of places they are not fit to fill; 'A woman can't practice medicine,' because they are afraid she can."

Some feared woman's success in medicine not only because it would drive some men out of it, but because it would also make women economically independent. In 1885, King Strange, a Michigan legislator, opposed a bill to set up a department of medicine and obstetrics in a female college because, he explained, he didn't choose that females "should be in an upstanding, that is to say, independent position."

There was ground for that fear. Take Dr. Carrie Simpson Burr. She graduated from the University of Michigan medical school in 1889 and then earned her own living. When she married, her husband forbade her to practice medicine. She finally divorced him because, she explained, "I could not stand always being the underdog."

Sadly, she admitted being "spoiled for marriage."

In the late 19th and early 20th centuries, two events severely crippled the woman's medical movement.

First, women's schools merged with male medical schools or closed down as the latter accepted women. Some female medical leaders, like Dr. Emily Blackwell, sister of Elizabeth Blackwell and co-founder of the New York Infirmary and College for Women, actively sought such mergers or closures. They must have assumed that co-ed schools would treat male and female students equally. Such assumptions proved incorrect.

Secondly, many co-ed medical schools which had been especially hospitable to women shut down. The closures came after Abraham Flexner of the Carnegie Commission conducted a national survey of medical schools for both the Commission and an organization of "regular" doctors, the American Medical Association (AMA) Council on Medical Education. Flexner's 1910 report publicly condemned the "second-rate" schools, cut off vital foundation funding for them, deprived them of the support of state legislatures and licensing boards, and so, closed the schools. Many were indeed inadequate but others happened, by the way, to be the black medical schools and the sectarian ("irregular") schools which most readily admitted women and poor students.* From 1904 until 1928, the number of medical schools dropped from 154 to 79. Of the seventy-nine surviving schools, only five were sectarian. The remaining schools raised their admission requirements and only the relatively wealthy could afford to meet them. They made no effort to open doors for the displaced black, female and poor students. Instead, in the name of "professional" standards, such students were largely barred from competition with middle-class white males. At the same time, "irregular" physicians were effectively prevented from competing with allopaths, a situation that remains unchanged today.

With their own schools and the sectarian schools closed, women found the road to a medical career an obstacle course.

* Between 1910 and 1923, six of the eight schools for black physicians closed. See Rosemary Stevens' *American Medicine and the Public Interest*, p. 71.

As we will now see, that course still requires of women un-common athletic skills.

Today, psychological factors prevent many women from even training for the obstacle course. Lack of role models, dis-couragement from family and friends, fear of having to give up a family life, and concern that medicine is incompatible with femininity, keep many women out of medicine.

It simply didn't occur to girls who had never seen a woman doctor that they themselves could become physicians. Dr. M. Gene Black, chief of anesthesiology at Holyoke Hospital in Massachusetts, told me she had planned to be a nurse until she saw a female physician while in high school in 1920.

"That was it. I decided I wanted to be a doctor. In my youth-ful ignorance," she laughed, "I hadn't known that such a thing as a woman doctor existed."

By 1974, women composed only 8.7 percent of all U.S. physi-cians so girls still lack role models.

If they decide to become doctors anyway, their families are not apt to be supportive. Many of the 41,000 female college graduates questioned in a 1968 government survey said that their parents discouraged medical careers because it was not "the best field for a girl."

Sometimes women must also survive the accusation that they are entering medicine because no men would ever marry them. In 1971, Dr. Estelle Ramey, professor of physiology at George-town Medical School, described the stereotype of the female doctor as "a horse-faced, flat-chested female in Supp-hose who sublimates her sex starvation in a passionate embrace of *The New England Journal of Medicine.**

Today, several medical school deans have said, a crisis in female identity is one of the greatest problems for a female medical student. A well-known experiment that Dr. Matina Horner, president of Radcliffe College, performed in 1968 in-dicates why. It showed that women are in a double bind because

---

* In an astonishing editorial in the August 1974 *New England Journal of Medicine*, Dr. Franz J. Ingelfinger discussed four women who did not fit that stereotype. He referred to his medical colleagues, not as physicians, but as "four married ladies with M.D. degrees" and described them as "handsome in coun-tenance, dressed with elegant simplicity" and "far from shapeless." Later, he referred to one physician as "Mrs." rather than "Dr." Garrison.

they worry not only about failure but about something which unsexes women: Success. In the experiment conducted at the University of Michigan, college students completed a paragraph which began, "After one semester, John finds himself at the top of his medical school class." Another group completed the paragraph with the name "Anne" substituted for John. Students wrote that John had a wonderful personality, an active love life, and an outstanding academic and professional career. But both male and female students described Anne as "neurotic," "lonely," and "a grind." They assumed she was dateless and despised. That she could be both successful in medical school and a normal female was inconceivable.

After hearing about Horner's experiment in 1973, a social studies teacher in Oakland, California tried it in her high school class. In one class, two boys working independently wrote that Anne happily left the classroom where the grades were posted, walked out into the street and was run over and killed by a truck.

Living with such hostile attitudes, girls attracted to medicine learn to lower their aspirations. As *Medical World News* reported in 1964, one third of the high school National Merit Scholars interested in medicine were women but three years later, when it came time to apply to medical school, their goals had changed. Women counted for less than 8 percent of the applicants.

When comparing the barriers female healers confront today with those set up against them in the 19th century, an astonishing fact reveals itself: The obstacles are essentially the same.

If a woman today survives the discriminatory admissions policy of co-ed medical schools she, like her medical foremothers, must endure baiting and ostracism from professors and male students. If she survives that, she, like her predecessors, may fail to secure an internship of her choice, and later, a residency, and later still, a teaching position in a medical school. (Her foremothers had also been denied admission to medical societies, consultations with and referrals from male doctors, and hospital staff affiliations.)

The medical school admission barrier blocks women more effectively now than it did in the 19th century when women could attend a female medical college. By 1900, only one women's school—the Women's Medical College of Pennsylvania*—remained and a 5 percent quota seems to have been established for women in the previously all-male schools. In 1905, women totaled 4.1 percent of all doctors; in 1925, 5 percent; in 1935, 4.7 percent; in 1955, 6 percent. A 1965 survey of thirty-eight countries found that only three—Spain, South Vietnam and Madagascar—had a lower percentage of female doctors than the United States. Today, women number not quite 9 percent of our physicians.

Why has our percentage of female doctors remained so stable for so long?

Dr. Harold I. Kaplan of New York Medical College investigated the attitudes toward female applicants in 95 percent of American and Canadian medical schools over a seven-year period beginning in 1962 and found that discrimination is "a significant factor in the low number of female doctors." Some of the replies from medical schools, Kaplan noted, "were too outrageous to be published."

Kaplan's study showed that while no U.S. school officially refused to accept women, many simply were not willing to take in single women, married women and, especially, married women with children. That seems to cover all possible categories.

One Western medical school informed Kaplan that it would

* In 1969, male leaders opened the college's doors to men. The word "Women's" was removed from the college name. Around this time, the Anatomy Department sent a letter, signed by all department members, to the Committee on Admissions Policies, recommending that the college routinely accept 90 percent male and 10 percent female applicants. (That recommendation was not accepted.)

Dr. Glen R. Leymaster, president and dean of the college during this transitional period, discussed an alleged need for more female physicians in an interview with *Medical World News* writer Melva Weber in 1970: "Who says we need them? There's a shortage of places in medical school. If an effort were successful to get more women, it would mean that more men could not get in."

Women drop out at a greater rate than men, he added, and medical schools choose candidates they think are most likely to graduate.

As Dr. Leona Baumgartner, professor of social medicine at Harvard Medical School, pointed out, the dropout rate for academic reasons is equal between males and females but there are slightly more women than men who, for non-academic reasons, do not complete medical school. If medical schools had arrangements which allowed women to fulfill their family obligations, she believes, the dropout rates would be equalized.

(See "Women M.D.'s Join the Fight," *Medical World News*, Oct. 23, 1970; also, "Reasons for the Petitions of the Alumnae Association, Women's Medical College," *Discrimination Against Women*, Hearings before the Special Subcommittee on Education of the Committee on Education and Labor, House of Representatives, in Section 805 of H.R. 16098, Part I, June 1970, pp. 562–563.)

not admit a childless married woman unless she were an outstanding student and it added, "Up to the present we have refused to admit married women with children."

Another school told Kaplan that it screened female applicants carefully "to be as certain as we can concerning their motivation for studying medicine."

A female faculty member quoted in a July 17, 1974 *New York Times* article, observed that the special screening of female applicants is often handled with a standard "marriage-versus-career" admission question. It is used to deny admission to women whichever way they answer it, she noted. If the applicant says she does not want children or will hire someone to care for them, the male interviewer will conclude that she is an unnatural woman. If she says she will have children, he concludes that she is not committed to medicine.

In 1972, Dr. Mary Howell, pediatrician and former Associate Dean of Students at Harvard Medical School, examined the screening of female applicants. In her study, conducted with two associates, female students reported on eighty-seven interviews held by representatives of thirty-four different medical schools for admission to the classes of 1977. In more than a third of the interviews, Howell found, interviewers made "stop statements"—prejudicial comments about "woman's place" which allowed no correct answer. If the woman agreed with the statement, Howell explained, she would demean herself and if she argued with it, the interview would go badly. Such statements included:

—I like women doctors—too bad so few are really motivated.

—Women doctors are unattractively aggressive.

—Your career may jeopardize your marriage.

Interviewers asked some students in the study about such "problems" as reconciling their high status as physicians with the status of potential husbands. One student wrote: "Many times he insisted on my making a statement as to whether I would marry and how many children I would have specifically and when I would have them. I replied that I had no plans and didn't know . . . Later he asked, 'What if you were married to a cab driver?' "

In a 1971 *Centerscope* article, Dr. Felicia Liu and Dr. Alice

Rothchild, then students at Boston University School of Medicine, described the effects of such special screening: "Our medical school interviewers, with their frequent probing into motives, marital plans, and the usual reminder that women have to make great social sacrifices as medical students, were very discouraging."

The assumption underlying many of the interview questions is that a medical education is wasted on a woman because she will only marry and leave the profession. Medical school officials in Dr. Harold I. Kaplan's study frequently made that contention. At least six studies have refuted it. Conducted in 1881, 1900, 1938, 1942, the 1950s, and in 1965, the studies have all found little variation in the number of years male and female doctors practice. The latest study, sponsored by the Association of American Medical Colleges, reported that fewer than 9 percent of female medical graduates since 1931 are not employed. Female doctors did tend to take several years out for child-rearing, it found, but because they also tend to retire later than their male colleagues, their total years of medical practice were about the same as men's.

Sex discrimination in medical school admissions is now outlawed by Title IX of the Higher Education Amendments of 1972 and by regulations of the Public Health Service Act which went into effect in August 1975. Enforcement of those laws rests with the U. S. Department of Health, Education and Welfare. HEW has a deplorable enforcement record on women's rights legislation, but at least women can now sue discriminatory schools themselves.*

By 1974, after the feminist movement had reemerged and the expectations of many women had risen, the percentage of female doctors in the United States had jumped to 8.7 and that of

* In November 1974, five national feminist and education groups filed suit against officials of the U. S. Department of Health, Education and Welfare and the Department of Labor accusing them of failure to enforce antisex-discrimination laws. See "Government Accused of Laxness in Enforcing Sex Bias Statutes," *New York Times*, Nov. 27, 1974. For details on that laxness, contact the Center for Law and Social Policy in Washington, D. C.

At the same time, the Civil Rights Commission charged five U. S. agencies with failure to act against job discrimination. See "The Federal Civil Rights Enforcement Effort—1974," Vol. 1, A Report of the U. S. Commission on Civil Rights, November 1974.

female medical students, to 15.4. As girls grow up in a society where sexism is recognized and challenged, those percentages will ascend.

Once women are admitted to medical schools, the next obstacle they face is hostility.

"I think the male students harbor a tremendous amount of resentment toward female students," a respondent replied in a 1973 survey by Dr. Margaret A. Campbell of women in medical schools.* "One student said he didn't think girls should be admitted to medical schools as long as one male had to go to Europe."

"The terms 'castrating' and 'hysterical' are used surprisingly often on us," another student observed. "We often hear, 'I would never marry a woman doctor.'"

A third respondent told this tale: An histology professor demonstrating the digestive system asked for two female assistants. He added HCl to some food and ended up with its by-product, "shit," in the beaker. Asking the women to clean up the "shit," he said, "And that's the place of women in medicine!" The men laughed.

From questionnaires filled out by 146 female students at 41 medical schools, Dr. Campbell concluded that discrimination against women is widespread. Some of it—the baiting and belittling of women—was overt. Single women were sometimes accused of husband-hunting and married women were told to "Go home and bake cookies where you belong." Instructors would turn the questions women asked into jokes.

But some discrimination—ostracizing and stereotyping women —was subtle. Men ostracized women by treating them not as colleagues but as daughters, wives or "playmates," or they talked down to the women, smiled condescendingly, and answered questions simplistically.

At other times, women felt invisible. They would make an interesting point in a discussion and it would be ignored, as though no one had said anything. But later, when a man made a similar comment, it would be eagerly discussed. In classes,

* "Margaret A. Campbell" is a pseudonym for Dr. Mary Howell. She did not want publication of this survey to jeopardize her position as a Harvard Medical School administrator and thus, curtail her ability to help female students. She has since resigned her post and revealed her pseudonymous identification.

lecturers would ignore females who raised hands to ask or answer questions.

As Campbell's respondents noted, women also suffer from stereotyping. They are, of course, domestic. "In one class," a student reported, "all analogies were directed to the men and if a woman asked a question he related it to baking bread or to milk cartons."

Women were expected to act in a stereotypically "female" way—that is, to be flirtatious, admiring or servile at various times. If they did not act this way, they were "bitchy" or "castrating." If they did, they were "unprofessional."

As medical school graduates, female healers face the hurdle their predecessors confronted a hundred years ago: Admission to internship and residency programs.

To get clinical training, early female doctors had had to open their own hospitals or endure the reception male students gave them at the few city hospitals which would admit them. Even as late as 1941, only 14 percent of general hospitals approved for intern service admitted female interns. There are more internships than American candidates for them so women will eventually find *some* position. But do they have an equal chance at the best training programs? Dr. Leah M. Lowenstein, associate professor of medicine at Boston University, does not think so. Many excellent internship services today do not choose women because women are considered a sign of the hospital's failure to attract men, she stated in a 1971 article.

Indeed, women applicants are primarily compared against each other rather than the entire applicant pool, an internship selection committee officer told Dr. Felicia Liu and Dr. Alice Rothchild, "because having more than a few women interns was not considered desirable or good for the prestige of the department," the two women wrote in 1971.

(I found it very difficult to get any statistics on placement of women in training programs. Alice Skarzynski, executive secretary of the National Intern and Resident Matching Program, wrote me in July 1975 that the program could not tell me the percentage of male and female medical students who, in the previous year, got their first choice of internships. The program does not collect information on sex in its statistics, she stated.)

The female doctors I interviewed noted the sexist selection procedures and assumptions often encountered by women applying for internships: The "stop statements"; the assertions of hospital officials that women are not serious about medicine and might get pregnant; interview questions about the applicants' methods of contraception; and crucial letters of recommendation riddled with sex stereotyping.

In the August 1974 issue of *The New England Journal of Medicine,* a female physician who had served on an intern selection committee in California in 1973 cited several examples of such letters. One described an applicant as an "attractive" woman "who has no 'hang-ups' sometimes associated with female physicians." Another stated, "Her intelligence and aggressiveness are such that she stands out among, but does not antagonize, her male colleagues." (Who worries about a male medical student antagonizing his female colleagues?, the committee member wondered.) One physician wrote that he found the applicant "completely unintimidating despite her obvious fine intellect . . ." (This and similar letters portrayed the male writer's uneasiness about being in the presence of an intelligent woman, observed the female committee member.)

Sexist letters, she noted, do not help an intern candidate.

What is harder to combat is the subtle discrimination involved in discouraging women from entering certain specialties, Dr. Mary Howell told me, her voice a bit weary.

Dr. Morris Fishbein, former editor of the *Journal of the American Medical Association* and one of the most respected medical writers in the world, demonstrated such subtle prejudice in a 1974 *Medical World News* editorial. After acknowledging that women are virtually excluded from such specialties as urology, gastroenterology and aviation medicine, Dr. Fishbein stated that medicine should yield to some of women's demands. But he added that certain specialties "are by their nature not constituted to be practiced by women. For example, there are few women in orthopedic surgery, which is physically strenuous."

That is not far removed from the argument of 19th-century doctors that women are physically unable to heal because they menstruate. But the weakness of such arguments is no comfort to women who are tired of struggling. As Dr. Carol Nadelson and Dr. Malka Notman, both assistant professors of psychiatry at Harvard Medical School, wrote in 1974, the female medical student wants to feel accepted and needed. She hesitates to continue a fight for recognition in a specialty, like surgery, where hostility to women, by all accounts, appears great. In deciding on her specialty, the psychiatrists pointed out, the student weighs her own interests against the reality of obtaining internships and residencies.

In that way, subtle discrimination narrows her choice of fields. Tired of struggling, then, it is no wonder that women tend to go into fields where they are least objectionable: Pediatrics, psychiatry, anesthesiology.

A doctor does not usually finish her education until she is thirty and her healthiest childbearing years are over so she may want to have a child during training. Yet when interns or medical students become pregnant, many school officials react as though pregnancy were unprofessional. (After all, *they* had never become pregnant during training.) Using a male standard of health against which women are always found wanting, they make women feel guilty about their fertility. Instead of establishing programs to accommodate pregnant students, medical schools tend to treat each individual pregnancy as a violation of academic standards for which the student should be ashamed.

While women are made to feel they are not measuring up to the high male standard, medical schools quietly allow students like Tom Casanova, Tom Lyons and Malcolm Snider to play football with, respectively, the Cincinnati Bengals, the Denver Broncos and the Green Bay Packers. Though childbearing is not compatible with medical education, professional football is. Military leaves, too, have been considered normal and not something for which male students should apologize.

Yet the University of Florida at Gainesville, like many others, informed Dr. Harold I. Kaplan it has made no concessions to pregnant students. Most pregnant students return to school from three days to two weeks after bearing their children. This shocked Dr. Kaplan, who noted that such a short recovery period may endanger the women's health. The unstated reason for the quick return, Kaplan observed in his study of female medics, is usually that "there has been no provision made for their absence and they fear that they will lose the academic year's credit if they stay out longer." Almost every foreign country, he stated, provides a safer, longer postpartum recovery period.

Making women adhere to a training schedule created on the assumption that all doctors would be men, of course limits the recruitment of women into medicine. Minor modifications, as Kaplan points out, would allow medical students to be mothers too.

Hospitals could offer the kind of flexible training programs Carol Lopate describes in *Women in Medicine*. Instead of interning for twelve straight months, for example, four mother-students could share two twenty-four-month internships with three months off each year. At any one time, Lopate explains, two women would work only week days, one would work weekends and two out of three nights, and the fourth would be off duty.

But female interns have apparently accepted the validity of male standards and agreed that such programs are second-class internships. Most have not taken advantage of flexible training schedules in the few hospitals where they exist. (In 1973, only twenty-five women served part-time internships, according to the 1974–75 AMA Directory of Approved Residencies.) Women have generally felt, Lopate reports, that if they don't take exactly the same internships men do, they will be demonstrating their unfitness for medicine.

It seems obvious to me that for women to have real alternatives, part-time programs must no longer be confined to students who supplicate hospital officials for special schedules. Instead, regular part-time positions, for which both men and women may apply, should be established. (In 1974, 124 years after American women reentered medicine, the Medical College of Pennsylvania began a project to evaluate the feasibility of such programs.)

Training schedules are not the only problems of female interns. They find that hospitals commonly ignore them when planning athletic facilities, locker arrangements and sleeping quarters. Dr. Myra Shayevitz, a young Massachusetts internist, recalls that during her training, no sleeping quarters were provided female interns waiting for obstetrical patients to deliver.

"Sometimes you had to wait two days in the hospital," she told me. "There were sleeping quarters for the male interns but the women sat up in the hall. We weren't even allowed to throw a sheet over a bed in an empty room reserved for gynecological emergencies."

In many hospitals now, male interns regard the doctors' lounge as a men's club and resent the presence of women. This has effectively ostracized women from the lounge. Not surprisingly, women, frozen out of the camaraderie their male classmates enjoy, often find medical training a lonely period.

For a female medic who is a mother, it may also be a time of guilt. Her society often views her as an "inadequate" absentee mother and she may too.

"I did feel constantly torn between home and hospital," Dr. Judy Tyson, staff physician at the Women's Medical Center in Vermont, recalled of her recent medical school years. "When I was at work I wondered about and felt drawn to the kids at home. When I was at home, I felt I should be with my patients, on duty with my peers, or in the library. Frustrating and draining!"

Men are free of such pressures, Dr. Nadelson and Dr. Notman point out in their paper on female medics. The careers of men are not blamed for disrupting family life. (Of course men have other crippling pressures on them. Medical educators assume, for example, that families consist of mothers and children and that fathers, while bound to support their loved ones financially, are not required to spend any time with them. Though the careers of male physicians may bloom under such assumptions, their personal lives tend to wither.)

When she completes her residency, a female doctor finds another barrier guarding faculty positions in medical schools. In 1971, only 4 percent of female faculty members were full professors. Dr. Margaret P. Sullivan, then president of the American Medical Woman's Association, pointed out in 1974 that while men serve as professors (full, associate and assistant), the usual rank for women with M.D.s and Ph.Ds is research assistant. Men use the assistantship as a stepping-stone but, she noted, women tend to stay in it—with increased responsibilities but not pay—for years.

Very few women reach high administrative positions in medical schools. In 1972, Dr. Mary Howell became the first to do so at Harvard. Her appointment as Associate Dean for Student Affairs, she notes, was made in response to demands by activists for representation of women at that level.

In May 1975, Dr. Howell resigned, charging that she had been allowed no decision-making power and had merely been cast as the token woman. "The school's administrators have used me—by widely advertising my presence—to ward off complaints about their unwillingness to recognize the needs of the underrepresented in health affairs," she stated.

Squeezed out of the more desirable positions in medicine, women often take the salaried jobs—in hospitals, medical schools, industry and government—that men shun.

In 1972, while women were only one percent of general surgeons, medicine's biggest money-makers, they were 26 percent of the modestly paid public health doctors. It is not surprising then that in 1974 the median income of female doctors was about two-fifths that of equivalently educated male doctors.

The female physician's lack of power is more upsetting than her income status. Few women have been appointed to the scientific advisory groups of the National Institutes of Health. As Dr. Judith Pool and Dr. John Bunker point out in a 1972 paper, fewer than 3 percent of the some two thousand committee members shaping research projects have been women. Those projects, of course, affect the health of both sexes. Less than a third of NIH advisory committees deciding on research and training funding have had any women as voting members, they add.

In medicine, women are still pioneers.

"There are still too few of them for their own reassurance and security," Dr. Phoebe Krey Lanzoni, an instructor in medicine at Boston University School of Medicine, believes. "Each is basically lonely and isolated. Like the old settler in the West, she feels surrounded by real or imagined hostility."

In one way, the female doctor is more deprived than her 19th-century counterpart. Women like Dr. Marie Mergler who, in 1869, struggled for internships, did not struggle alone. Together, women eagerly watched developments and "mourned over each defeat and rejoiced with each success," Mergler wrote, "for with [us] it meant much more than success or failure for the individual, it meant the failure or success of a grand cause."

Those women knew that in medicine they were a colonized minority. In resisting their colonization, they shared a camaraderie. But today's female medical student often does not know that she is colonized. Grateful to have been admitted to medical school at all, torn by the "femininity crisis," and guilty at not fitting neatly into the male training program she mistakes for a fully human one, she often suffers alone.

Faced with discrimination, the student commonly protects herself from it by denying it exists, Dr. Howell found in her 1973 survey of women in medical schools. Thirty of Howell's respondents reported no discrimination at their schools but nineteen of these then proceeded to describe three or more discriminatory incidents. Of the remaining eleven, Howell noted, nine came from the same schools as other respondents who had reported discriminatory incidents.

In newspaper stories about female doctors, I often see that same denial. The woman says she has never been discriminated against and then adds, "Of course there was that time when . . ." After describing several such incidents, she dismisses them as insignificant.

Responding to allegations that female medical students were discriminated against, one woman physician gave a classic example of denial. In a 1974 letter to the editor of *The New England Journal of Medicine*, she asserted that women "are discriminated FOR." Yet she wrote:

> It is true that I had some difficulty getting into medical school, back in 1939. I had a polite letter from the dean of the Harvard Medical School reading: "Dear Miss ( ), If, due to the exigencies of war we are unable to obtain male medical students, we shall reconsider your application, Sincerely yours," but eight years later they let me teach their third-year boys.
> . . . In medical school, both the boys and the profs went out of their way to be nice to me. To be sure they let the air out of my bicycle tires every night for three months . . . and they spent four years trying to make me blush, but it was all in fun and both they and I enjoyed it.

Denial is not the only mechanism for dealing with discrimination. Some students share the woman-hatred that underlies discrimination and count themselves exceptions to the generally inferior race of women. As childbirth crusader Doris Haire found when she attended medical school recently, some of the worst male chauvinists are women.

"The female students looked uneasy at my presence and passed me by," she noted. "They looked on me as a problem. They thought it was audacious of me to be there."

To feminists, sexism in women is not surprising. Woman, they explain, has internalized man's negative image of her and so, she undervalues herself and other women. Women, then, become some of the strongest apologists for sex discrimination.

But some female students, supported by the country's second wave of feminism and determined to regain their ancient role as healers, are challenging sexist practices in medicine. What Dr. Ann Preston said of her students a century ago could as well be said of these students now: "On behalf of a little band of true-hearted young women who are just entering the profession, and from whose pathway we fain would see annoyances and impediments removed, we must protest, in the sacred name of our common humanity, against the injustices which place difficulties in our way—not because we are ignorant, or pretentious, or incompetent, or unmindful of the code of medical or Christian ethics, but because we are women."

Chapter / TWO

FEMALE DOCTORS DIVIDED: ELIZABETH BLACKWELL AND CLEMENCE LOZIER

IN THE 19TH CENTURY MALE PHYSICIANS HAD INDEED PLACED "annoyances and impediments" in the way of female healers but women had also impeded their own progress. They had turned on each other.

To gain acceptance, the few women who were finally admitted to allopathic ("regular") medical schools took on the values of their powerful male colleagues and looked down on women who joined more hospitable sects. These women believed that "irregular" female doctors were quacks, just as male allopaths had labeled them.

Anxious for the respectability orthodox medicine conferred, some female institutions, including the Women's Medical College of Pennsylvania, dismissed any "irregular" doctors from their faculties. Instead of joining together to improve woman's health care, female physicians divided according to medical sects and formed separate professional societies. Only in 1915 did they come together to build what is now the American Medical Women's Association.

I saw the split between orthodox and heretical medical

45

women in the careers of two contemporaries: Dr. Elizabeth Blackwell, the first female to secure male medical credentials, and Dr. Clemence Sophia Lozier, a fiery homeopath.

Early in her career, Blackwell worked with Lozier. Later, because of the antagonism between orthodox and unorthodox doctors, a deep rift developed between the two women. They argued publicly over medical treatments and refused to hold consultations with each other. To their deaths, their relationship remained chilly.

Elizabeth Blackwell graduated from Geneva Medical College in 1849, the same year the Eclectic Central Medical College in Syracuse, from which Lozier would graduate in 1853, began its co-education policy. While Blackwell's graduation was an isolated event—Geneva did not admit other women—Lozier's signified a trend. Many more women would obtain a medical education at "irregular" schools.

Blackwell, in fact, had been admitted to Geneva as a joke. A friend with a pelvic disease had urged her to study medicine and open up the field to women. Referring to the embarrassing examinations, her friend told her, "If I could have been treated by a lady doctor, my worst sufferings would have been spared me."

So Blackwell applied to twelve medical schools. They turned her down. When she inquired at Geneva (now Hobart College), the faculty didn't want responsibility for rejecting her on account of her sex so it decided that if the freshman class accepted her, the college would. But it added a stipulation that it assumed would guarantee her rejection: If even *one* freshman voted against her, she would be turned down.

When the dean explained the situation to the freshmen, they thought it was hilarious. As freshman Stephen Smith recalled, the prankish students received the dean's announcement "with the most uproarious demonstrations of favor." They met that night to vote. Students made many extravagant speeches favoring Blackwell's admission and they were enthusiastically cheered. When the vote was taken, all shouted "Yea!," except one man who uttered a timid "No." The others rushed toward him and advised him to reconsider his vote. He quickly did. The vote was unanimous.

"The faculty," Smith reported, "received the decision of the class with evident disfavor."

Two weeks later, when the students had almost forgotten their prank, Blackwell arrived. They treated her well but the medical press did not. Blackwell, *The Boston Medical Journal* sniffed, "is a pretty little specimen of the female gender reporting her age as 26. She comes into the class with great composure, takes off her bonnet and puts it under the seat, exposing a fine phrenology." *The Baltimore Sun,* it added, had advised Blackwell to confine her practice "to diseases of the heart."

Her colleagues outside of Geneva were as hostile as the press. At Blockley Almshouse in Philadalephia where she worked one summer, the resident doctors would walk out of the wards when she walked in. To make her work more difficult, they stopped writing the diagnosis of patients on cards on each bed.

Despite this treatment, Blackwell sometimes seemed to identify more with male physicians than with other women, whom she scorned. She never had any trouble relating to her male classmates, she wrote, but found "the lower classes of women" in Geneva often "worthless" and the upper, "fastidious and exclusive." (Yet when she graduated, the women of Geneva came to see her receive the diploma.)

Later, Blackwell advised her younger sister, Emily, who also became a physician, to study obstetrics at France's École de Medicine. However, she warned Emily that "the association would be unpleasant from the character of the women."

Did Blackwell see herself as a Superwoman? Did she feel that most women were indeed inferior but that she herself was an exceptional woman, fit to associate with that higher species, man?

Note Blackwell's report of her commencement. The speaker, a male doctor, "gave it pretty strong to Homeopathists, Hydrapathists, Mesmerists, Thomsonians etc. and gave the ladies of the audience quite a lecture for their encouragement and circulation of quack medicines, informing them that they had better study a little the principles of medicine before attempting to practice what they were profoundly ignorant about."

Blackwell does not object to this speech though she knew the speaker was scolding women for the medical ignorance which he and his colleagues steadfastly tried to maintain in them. She also knew how inadequate was the medicine these orthodox doctors taught. When "facts, scientifically accurate observations" were needed, she later complained, medicine offered "vain thought."

At the commencement, college officials urged her to walk in procession with the other students but Blackwell, saying "it wouldn't be ladylike," went to the ceremony with her brother and sat humbly in a side aisle. Her decision endeared her to her brother and classmates who were impressed with her feminine demeanor.

But a Boston medical journal was not impressed. It regretted that Blackwell had aspired "to honors and duties which, by the order of nature and the common consent of the world, devolve alone upon men" and that Geneva had been "the first to commence the nefarious process of amalgamation."

The journal had little to fear. After Blackwell graduated, Geneva—its four-year joke ended—closed its doors to other women.

Blackwell studied in Europe for the next two years. Because she was a woman, she was obliged to join a maternity hospital in Paris, not as a doctor, but as just another apprentice-midwife. At St. Bartholomew's Hospital in London, she wrote, every department was cordially opened to her "except the department for female diseases!" (Though one would expect female doctors to experience the least discrimination in obstetrics and gynecology, often that is where they experienced the most.)

Back home, her first seven years practice in New York City were hard. People gossiped about her. She had trouble finding someone willing to rent an office to a female doctor and when she finally did, all the other tenants moved out. Few patients came at first.

"It is hard," she wrote, "with no support but a high purpose, to live against every species of social opposition . . . I should like a little fun now and then. Life is altogether too sober."

Her practice began to pick up after she gave physiology lectures to groups of women, many of whom were Quakers. The Quakers soon supported her work and employed her as their family physician.

When Blackwell's application for a staff position in the women's department of a city dispensary was rejected in 1853, she formed her own and treated the poor there three afternoons a week. A proponent of preventive medicine, she trained "sanitary visitors," workers who gave poor mothers health instructions in their homes.

The next year, she obtained a charter for what was to become, in 1857, The New York Infirmary for Women and Children. Her sister Emily and Dr. Marie Zackrzewska of Germany helped found and staff the infirmary.

In 1865, the infirmary trustees (all men) applied to the legislature for a charter to make the infirmary a female medical college as well. They did so at the urging of leading physicians who warned that the medical education of women might otherwise fall into the hands of the "irresponsible people" who were then trying to establish a woman's college in the city. Since Dr. Clemence Lozier, an irregular doctor, opened her medical college in 1863, it is very likely the doctors were talking about her.

Clemence Lozier was no stranger to healing. Her mother had been a domestic practitioner in the territory that later became Kentucky. Even Indians hostile to white trespassers had accepted her as a medicine woman.

Lozier was no stranger to death, either. She married at sixteen and watched five sons die, one after another. Accidents killed two. Referring to harsh drugs and blood-letting, Abraham, her one living son, recalled that three others were "victims to the severity of the medical treatment of the time." Lozier's husband, moreover, was an invalid for many years. After he died, she studied medicine in self-defense.

"My poor mother," Abraham noted, "was driven to study physiology and hygiene, to save her life and my own from sickness and the doctors."

Lozier then, never respected "regular" medicine.

She became one of the first females at the Eclectic New York Central Medical College in Syracuse and graduated at the top of her class. A small woman with curly brown hair, she was then forty.

She began a practice. It soon became a large one. (In 1864 her professional income was $25,000, an enormous sum then.)

Her success, her son believed, was a vindication of her belief that in the name of common sense and modesty, women had to replace men in obstetrics and gynecology.

Lozier saw suffering among the patients who thronged her office and believed much of it was caused by the women's ignorance of physiological and hygienic laws. So she gave her patients weekly lectures on these subjects in her own parlor. She also organized a library association to circulate medical literature among the women. Her patients soon told their friends about the lectures and they came too until scores of women were flocking to the lectures, the 19th-century precursors of self-help meetings.*

Medical men watched Lozier closely, her friend, feminist Elizabeth Cady Stanton recalled, "to see if, by some legal quirk, she might not be arrested and forbidden to practice." Male doctors would not recognize her as a member of the profession.

Undeterred, Lozier, seeing how eagerly women sought medical information at her lectures, decided to found a woman's medical college. In the midst of organized opposition, she struggled to secure passage of a legislative act granting her a charter. She succeeded in 1863. So the New York Medical College and Hospital for Women—the third woman's medical college in the country—opened in New York City with seven students.

Lozier was the first to introduce the study of hygiene in a medical school, an innovation that, her son wrote, excited "considerable opposition" from conservatives. (He did not explain why.)

As soon as her efforts brought success, Stanton recalled, men determined to dominate Lozier and the funds she raised for the college. When the college opened, no female medical professors were available so Lozier was obliged to appoint male professors. Later, when capable female graduates existed and the female college trustees wanted to put a woman in the chair of obstetrics, Stanton noted, "it took us a whole year to oust the male professor."

After five years, Lozier bought a building on Second Avenue for the hospital.

". . . Sick and sorrowful women were not slow in finding their way to our little hospital," Dr. Phoebe J. Wait, the school's

---

* American women began holding self-help meetings in 1971 to learn about and regain control of their bodies.

dean, recalled, "and went away not only cured but comforted with the knowledge of a hospital where women might be treated by members of their own sex."

Half the hospital and all the dispensary work was done for free. Lozier gave the institution an initial $25,000 and then maintained it for seven years out of her own purse.

Knowing that her students, like all those at accredited medical colleges, had a right to attend clinical lectures in state hospitals, Lozier got tickets for the admission of her class to Bellevue Hospital lectures.

Stanton accompanied that first class of thirty women and recalled their reception: "We were greeted by a thousand students with shouts of derisive laughter, and, ever and anon, during the lecture, were pelted with chewed balls of paper. The professor selected the most offensive subject and disease for the day, thinking thereby to end the experiment."

He took pains to be as coarse as possible and the male students applauded him enthusiastically, Stanton observed.

"As we left the building," she continued, "the students had formed themselves into a double line, through which we passed, mid jeers and groans, coarse jokes and shouts, pelted with bits of wood and gravel." The lecturer could have stopped all that harassment, she noted, "but as he encouraged it, we had no appeal."

When Lozier heard of her students' reception, she called a "public indignation meeting" to denounce the outrageous conduct. Horace Greeley, Henry Ward Beecher and other well-known citizens addressed the rally. The press and churches quickly sided with Lozier and public opinion was so strongly roused in the women's favor, that the mayor sent a marshal and a police force to the next lecture at Bellevue "to protect the ladies in their rights."

As Abraham noted, "The Faculty whose voice had been strangely paralyzed til then, found strength enough to declare that they would thereafter enforce order and see that the ladies were undisturbed in their privileges."

After that, Lozier's medical school prospered. Students and patients abounded. The $70,000 building was finally mortgage free. But, Stanton reported, some of the male professors in the school wanted a larger building uptown and, by promising financial aid, persuaded the women to sell the present building and buy others. Lozier strenuously objected but was overruled.

The new buildings were heavily mortgaged. The male professors reneged on their promised aid. In the panic of 1872, real estate values fell. In 1878, when Lozier was sixty-four, the college went bankrupt.

Lozier might have concluded what Dr. Johanna Baltrusaitis did about 'her alma mater, the Women's Medical College of Baltimore. It had opened in 1882 and ten years later, men ran it. Only one woman was a trustee. Of its premature closing in 1910, Baltrusaitis commented: "The greatest mistake made in the founding of the college was to have men man and steer the craft on which women expected to reach the shore. What has been inspired and produced by us, we must always nurture and promote."

Like Harriet K. Hunt and other irregular doctors, Lozier denied the validity of the sexual caste system under which men and women had unequal access to jobs, goods and prestige. She challenged that system by heading the New York City Suffrage League and by calling six meetings to protest various wrongs against women.

Rejecting men's "right" to set the health-care standards, she set her own. It stressed health maintenance. She spurned the warrior-doctor model of the allopaths and adopted the gentle-healer ideal set by her medical foremothers. Her aim was not to flagellate diseases, but to make the sick well. Often that could be achieved by strengthening the patient and thus, her recuperative powers.

Blackwell challenged men's standards much less vigorously than did Lozier. Though she realized that many of the treatments she had been taught were nonsensical and that she, perhaps, would have to "commit heresy with intelligence" in her own practice, both she and her sister nonetheless seemed to equate male medical standards with high ones.

As Emily explained, "When Harvard took the lead in lengthening its medical course, (our) College followed suit. Whenever any of the large schools . . . raised their requirements either by lengthening their term, or by widening their curriculum, the College followed upon the same line."

Similarly, Dr. Marie Zackrzewska, their friend and colleague, persuaded the New England Female Medical College trustees to declare Latin a prerequisite for admission. That way, she explained, well-educated women could "take a proper place in the medical profession." But only women who had attended one of the scarce female colleges could then hope for a medical degree.

When standards were thus "raised," it meant, of course, that it became more difficult for lower-class women to attend medical school. But Zackrzewska and the Blackwells seemed to see nothing wrong with that.

If students spent an extra three months studying the four humors of the body and learning when to blood-let, were they really better healers? Around this time, remember, orthodox doctors like John Thompson were telling TB patients to soak their feet daily in soup "to restore the equilibrium of the system." Such doctors left highly esteemed medical schools and began practice without ever having seen a broken leg set or a baby born.

Meanwhile, "ignorant woman practitioners" like Harriet Hunt and Clemence Lozier were stressing preventive health care and the need for establishing sound habits of exercise, diet, cleanliness and rest. Hunt was also advocating the formation of medical parishes that would hire a doctor to keep parishioners healthy. For the ill, both doctors preferred moderate treatments to blood-letting and massive drug-dosing. Yet Hunt and Lozier were "quacks" and Elizabeth Blackwell did not question that label.

Identifying more closely with the upper-class medical profession than with women, Blackwell also joined her male colleagues in their campaign to outlaw midwifery by lay women. Obstetricians, Blackwell agreed, must take full medical courses. Yet she knew that, with few exceptions, only white males were admitted to "regular" medical courses.

Unlike Lozier, Blackwell disassociated herself from the feminist movement. When asked to participate in the Women's Rights convention in Worcester, Massachusetts in 1851, she declined: "I cannot sympathize fully with an anti-man movement. I have had too much kindness, aid and just recognition from men, to make such attitude of women otherwise than painful, and I think the true end of freedom may be gained better in another way."

This, from the woman who, recalling her first seven years

practice, wrote, "I had no medical companionship. The profession stood aloof, and society was distrustful of the innovation. Insolent letters occasionally came by post and my pecuniary position was a source of constant anxiety."

By contrast, Dr. Hunt enthusiastically attended the convention to see what she could do to alleviate the social conditions that caused such suffering among her female patients. Her friends tried to dissuade her from attending. She would "lose caste," they told her, if she identified herself with "such a motley crew." Hunt scorned their warnings: "What was all this to one who, for 15 years, had been the confidant of woman, who had known that her diseases resulted in great measure from her position?"

The warning that she would "lose caste" by advocating woman's equality is a fascinating one. Hunt responded by challenging the right of the caste system to exist.

Blackwell accepted caste. When she decided to become a doctor, two male physician friends advised her to don men's clothes and study medicine in Paris. She rejected the proposal. She wanted to study as a woman, not as a pseudoman. Yet her actions suggest that while wearing female clothes, she often donned men's values.

In divorcing themselves from each other, Blackwell and Lozier, along with other "regular" and "irregular" female physicians, caused a debilitating breach in the nineteenth-century woman's medical movement.

That breach interests me because I think it could reappear today. Now it would divide female physicians and feminist "self-help" women, members of the modern Popular Health Movement.* It could hobble the centuries-long effort of women to regain control of their bodies.

Rifts seem to result when some female physicians take on the values of the powerful medical caste which they long to join. As Ozzie G. Simmons of the Harvard School of Public Health noted in 1955, value-adoption is a problem common to upwardly mobile people. To consolidate their new positions, such people must sever their emotional ties with the lower-status group from which they come and take on the attitudes of the higher-status

* See Epilogue.

group. ("Oreos" do that. They are blacks who are white inside.)

This explains why some female doctors are as sexist as male ones. Their sexism helps them survive in a male world.

But it threatens other women.

Dr. Mary Howell who, in 1972, became the first high-level female administrator in Harvard Medical School's history, pointed out that problem when she resigned. In a 1975 letter to the woman's health movement, she noted that token jobs like hers harmed woman's interests.

"It is especially damaging to our cause," she wrote, "when visible positions are filled by persons who appear to be members of under-represented groups but who are in fact 'honorary' white, middle-class males, by their own identification with the values of that empowered group."

How often do female doctors become honorary white males, I asked Dr. Howell in a recent telephone conversation.

"Very, very often," she told me. "To men choosing someone for a high position, a 'male' woman is most acceptable. These men don't want anyone reminding them of the other half of the world. A 'male' woman can't represent women but her presence makes it look as though they are being represented."

Female doctors who are "honorary white males" don't defend female patients against harmful obstetrical practices, unnecessary surgery, unsafe contraceptives, and forced sterilizations. But, Dr. Howell told me sadly, the effects of identifying with the upper caste are even more serious than this failure to safeguard women's welfare.

"If you're a member of an oppressed group, and you don't see it, you block the ability to see other kinds of oppression too," she explained. "These women may be even less feeling than men about patients' rights, and the rights of blacks and poor people."

From Dr. Howell and her nineteenth-century colleagues, Dr. Blackwell and Dr. Lozier, we learn this: It is not enough to have more women physicians. We need female healers who remember where they came from and who, like the ancient wise women, identify with their lower-caste patients.

Chapter / THREE

FEMALE HEALTH WORKERS

IT IS 1877. LINDA RICHARDS, THE FIRST AMERICAN PROFESSIONAL nurse, begins her advanced training at King's College in England. She wants to go downstairs so she descends the nearest staircase. Her superior gently rebukes her: "You went down the front stairs, which are used only by the doctors." Richards promises never again to use that staircase. Like the other nurses, she will take the back stairs and the back exit.

"Here I learned what was meant by yielding an absolutely willing as well as implicit obedience," she recalled. "This lesson once well learned, hospital life goes much more smoothly."

Dr. Edward Cowles, who established the Boston City Hospital School of Nursing with Richards in 1878, must have agreed. Praising her, he wrote: "She saw no reason against subjecting the head of the department of nursing to the larger coordinating medical control. There was no pride of authority, no thought of personal insight."

This, then, was what female healers had come to. Most had been barred from medical schools. Others, like Richards, yielded all "pride of authority" to doctors and became handmaidens.

Even today, nursing is a female-dominated occupation controlled by men outside that occupation. These men—physicians and hospital administrators—decide whether a nurse gets hired or promoted, what her duties and priorities are, how much money her department can spend, how much time she can devote to patients.

As lay healers in earlier times, women never submitted to such domination. The domestic practitioners in Colonial America and the witches and wise women of medieval Europe had been independent healers who both nursed and doctored.

But, as health activists Barbara Ehrenreich and Deirdre English point out, when scientific medicine developed, healing split into two functions: Curing and caring. Doctors (male) cured and nurses (female) cared. Because he participated in the mystique of Science, the doctor got all credit for the patient's recovery. The servant-nurse could claim none.

Yet for the better part of history, nursing was the better part of healing. If anxiety and fear could cause physical disorders like ulcers and colitis, then the compassion some nurses radiated may well have been a healing force. At any rate, the ill probably recovered faster by having nurses massage their bodies, change their bed linen, and hold their hands than by having doctors place leeches on their bodies to suck out their blood.

The women of the family usually attended the ill at home until the 19th century when nursing developed as a profession under the leadership of England's Florence Nightingale. A few full-time nurses had practiced before Nightingale, but they were considered a drunken, immoral lot. Nightingale, an aristocrat herself, turned nurses into respectable ladies.

The doctor's fear of the nurse as a potential competitor and his consequent efforts to keep her in her place as his handmaiden, appear as constant themes in nursing's history. That fear first manifested itself during the Crimean War of the 1850s when doctors at Scutari refused to let nurses work. Nightingale won over these physicians by demonstrating that nurses would be completely subservient to their authority.

In Nightingale's book, *To Her Nurses*, she stressed obedience: "With the nurse, as with the soldier, whether we think it right or not, is not the question. Prompt obedience is the question. We are not in control but under control.*

Nightingale did not want nurses to govern themselves or to learn too much medicine—positions that further reassured doctors. (In view of these stands, it is hardly surprising that Nightingale was, as she put it, "brutally indifferent to the rights and wrongs of my own sex.")

Nursing developed in America shortly after Nightingale began her work in England. The first three nursing schools opened in 1873. By 1900, the number had jumped to 432. Hospitals, which were becoming increasingly important, found that if they opened nursing schools, they had a ready supply of cheap labor. The desire of nursing educators to train students well conflicted with the wish of doctors and hospital administrators to staff hospitals cheaply. Nurses lost. As Adelaide Nutting, the first professor of nursing, reported in 1896, it was quite common for nursing students to work 105 hours each week at the hospital. During that week, the school would offer them only one lecture.

Barred from most jobs, women eagerly attended the exploitative schools. They found nursing attractive because it did not present the agonizing "femininity crisis" medicine did. Serving and nurturing were the roles of all women so nursing was feminine.

But once hospitals had gotten free labor from student nurses they had "trained," they failed to provide jobs for many of them. New students did the work of potential job-holders. Women, no longer independent healers, were now used as cheap, obedient health workers.*

* See Florence Nightingale, *To Her Nurses,* London: Macmillan and Co., Ltd., 1914, p. 137.

* In the decades before World War II, hospitals made it difficult for a nurse who was middle aged, married or black to find work. While the median age of employed nurses was twenty-nine, that of employment-seeking nurses was thirty-six and many older nurses had undoubtedly given up job-hunting in despair.

Most hospitals and institutions and some industries and public health agencies discriminated against married women. If Army and Navy nurses wed, they had to resign. In pre-World War II days, a 1945 Labor Department bulletin explained, "marriage did not combine well with the practice of nursing." Since over a third of nurses married within three years of graduation, the marriage restriction kept thousands of nurses from annoying hospitals with pleas for work.

Black women fared worse than married white women. Black nurses were only

From the beginning, doctors and hospital administrators controlled nursing. Many physicians at first opposed any schooling for nurses because they feared educated workers would not accept the doctor's "right" to discipline them. As Linda Richards recalled, the thirteen doctors at Boston City Hospital radiated hostility at her efforts to set up a nursing school there.

The doctors soon learned they had little to dread for nurses were easily ruled. Physicians themselves lectured nursing classes and wrote nursing textbooks. The doctor knows infinitely more than the nurse and must be accorded the greatest respect, doctors taught.

When nurses took over instruction, they too emphasized the doctor's authority. This allayed the physician's fear that women were really being given a shortened medical course so they could compete with him for patients.

Fearing that the nurse's knowledge would undermine their stature and authority as well as threaten their jobs, doctors tried to keep her ignorant by forbidding her to read the medical histories of patients. At The New England Hospital for Women and Children where Linda Richards graduated in 1873, they also placed numbers rather than names on the drug bottles. "Great care was given that we should *not* know the names of the medicines given," Richards recalled.

To further ensure that the women served as order-takers rather than independent thinkers, nurses were taught *how* to do things, not *why*. Even now, nurses have told me, instructors

---

2 percent of the trained and student nurses. None served in the Army or Navy Nurse Corps.

Then the war came. The country needed more workers so, patriotically, hospitals sacrificed racist, sexist and ageist hiring practices.

The Army Nurse Corps raised its maximum age from thirty to forty-five. The National Nursing Council for War Service asked all nurses, regardless of age, to work. Women over seventy were given refresher courses and jobs.

While only twenty-nine nursing schools admitted blacks in 1941, three years later, in the midst of war, forty-nine schools welcomed them. Moreover, the Navy Department declared there would be no discrimination against black nurses.

The married nurse was urged to reenter the hospital. Though in 1927 only 20 percent of active nurses had been married, the percentage doubled in 1943. "Some hospitals in which the shortage has been especially severe," the bulletin noted, "have opened nurseries to care for the children of nurses while they are on duty in the hospital." See: "The Outlook for Women in Occupations in the Medical and Other Health Services," U.S. Dept. of Labor, Women's Bureau, Bulletin 203, No. 3., 1945. Elizabeth Bass Collection at Tulane Medical School.

sometimes answer students' questions with, "That won't be on the exam."

Today many doctors disapprove of collegiate training for nurses. Dr. June Rothberg, nursing school dean at Adelphi University, told me that a partial explanation for this disapproval may be that college-educated nurses "have a strong sense of independence and self-worth. They ask questions. They're professional practitioners."

Doris Haire, an obstetrics reform crusader, put the case more bluntly: "Doctors prefer the diploma school nurse because she's more easily intimidated."

Doctors controlled nursing effortlessly because it was a largely female occupation. The women had been programmed from childhood to esteem themselves lowly, to assert themselves rarely, to fear power, to shun leadership, to slight their careers. Their minds had been throughly conditioned for domination.*

Until recently, doctors did not have to contend with nurses who were committed to, and took responsibility for, their field. Many entered nursing by default; they did not want to be teachers or secretaries and they knew of few alternate careers for women.

Others saw themselves as potential wives and mothers who were only working until they married. Training-school recruiters and some advertisements in nursing publications still foster that attitude. They emphasize that nursing is an excellent preparation for motherhood. One ad in the November 1970 *American Journal of Nursing,* for example, pictures a young woman sitting by a fire with a son at her side and a dog at her feet. As Dr. Virginia Cleland, nursing professor at Wayne State University, notes, the text's clear implication is that this woman caught a good man while working at X institution.

Once married, nurses tend to accept dead-end jobs that fit in with their families' needs, Dr. Cleland found in a 1970 study. Trained to see their families as their first responsibility, they

---

* The literature on female conditioning is so extensive I can suggest only samples: *The Second Sex,* Simone de Beauvoir; *On the Subjection of Women,* John Stuart Mill; *Woman in Sexist Society,* Vivian Gornick and Barbara K. Moran; *The Feminine Mystique,* Betty Friedan; *Sisterhood Is Powerful,* Robin Morgan; *Sexual Politics,* Kate Millett; *Sexism in School and Society,* Nancy Frazier and Myra Sadker.

often change or quit jobs when home problems arise.

Poor working conditions and low status and pay also contribute to the nurse's lack of commitment, the National Commission for the Study of Nursing and Nursing Education observed in its 1970 report. While starting salaries for nurses have improved in recent years, the Commission stated, those salaries rise very little with experience. In 1969, 75 percent of community hospitals in the United States paid nurse practitioners less than $7,500 per year.

All these factors explain why one third to one half the nurses in this country do not practice and why a phenomenal 70 percent yearly turnover rate exists among nurses.* (The rate for teachers is only 20 percent.)

Feminine conditioning explains not only the lack of commitment to nursing but the lack of leadership within it. Leadership, like success, has hair on its chest.

Few nurses want to direct others, observed Angela McBride, assistant professor at Yale School of Nursing, during a 1971 conference. Some think they would have to become mannish, aggressive and unattractive.

Nurses occasionally attack colleagues who do prepare themselves to lead. In fact one woman felt obliged, in the *American Journal of Nursing,* to defend her right to fulfill her career potential. Ever since she had returned to school on a U.S. Public Health Service traineeship, Joan M. Fenske wrote in 1972, retired nurses have asked her how she could possibly accept government money while the poor needed educational funds.

Behind this question lies the feminine conditioning which dictates that a woman must place the needs of everyone else before her own. To assert the validity of her own needs and desires is considered contemptible. With such attitudes pervading nursing, how could it be anything but a powerless occupation?

Women have been trained to look to men for direction, rather than make decisions themselves, so the nurses who have filled leadership slots have often been weak. Most nursing directors

* See *An Abstract for Action,* report by the National Commission for the Study of Nursing and Nursing Education; Jerome P. Lysaught, director, McGraw Hill, New York, 1970. Pp. 35, 53 and 132. The Commission was organized by, but independent of, the American Nursing Association and the National League for Nursing.

do not even control their departmental budgets. When dealing with male hospital administrators, Dr. Virginia Cleland observes, they often act "like housewives asking for grocery money."

Dr. Cleland sees the "acquiescing, submissive, overly-cautious" nursing leaders who have developed as "Uncle Toms." She explains it this way: Nursing gave women one of the few paths to upward mobility not closed to them by sex discrimination. Only women approved by the male physicians and hospital administrators could become nursing leaders. To be acceptable to these men, the nursing leaders take on their values. (Like female doctors, then, they adopt the attitudes of the higher-status group with which they begin to identify.) Nursing directors fight collective bargaining, written contracts, grievance procedures and other provisions that would help nurses because they accept the guidance of male administrators.

Afraid of losing her special favors—a good salary and prestigious position—the director often works for the administration and against nurses, Gloria Donnelly, a faculty member at Villanova University's nursing college, told me.

"It's like the days of slavery," she said. "One slave was picked as the leader of the group and given special favors. His job was to keep the other slaves in line. This has been the role of the hospital nursing director."

Because of the conditioning of both participants, the doctor-nurse relationship mirrors the male-female one. In fact Martha Fowlkes, a medical sociologist at Smith College, finds it identical to the interaction between boss-secretary, principal-teacher and husband-wife.

"In all cases," she explained in a 1972 interview, "it is a relationship between a dominant person (the male) and a submissive person (the female). The nurse is there to supplement and assist the doctor in his primary skills."

The doctor's handmaiden, the nurse calls him "Dr. Jones" while he calls her "Susan." She obeys his orders, sets up equipment for his performances in the examining or operating rooms and cleans up after him. Only a few years ago, she was even expected to open doors for him, stand when he entered a room and offer him her chair.

"Male M.D.s tend to look upon nurses as dumb, or sex objects but definitely necessary to do all the small-time, boring work," according to Dr. Judy Tyson, staff physician at the Vermont Women's Health Center.

Even though the nurse observes patients all day while the doctor sees them for only minutes, she can not imply that she knows something the doctor does not. Yet, because of her observations, she often guides the doctor's treatments. She does so indirectly, however, so it seems as though the idea were the doctor's.

"One hundred milligrams of Demerol knocked Mr. Smith out when he had this pain last week, but 75 milligrams seemed to work well for him," the nurse will mention to the intern. She will then humbly take his order: 75 milligrams of Demerol for Mr. Smith.

In a 1968 paper, Dr. Leonard Stein, a psychiatrist at the University of Kentucky College of Medicine, described this process, the doctor-nurse game, as a "transactional neurosis." In the game, the nurse makes recommendations to the doctor while both pretend she is doing no such thing. Every nurse Dr. Stein interviewed felt that to make a direct suggestion to a doctor, thus questioning his infinite knowledge, was to insult and belittle him.

Since about 1970, I have seen the calling cards of the health revolution regularly in *American Journal of Nursing* (*AJN*) articles: "Sex Discrimination: Nursing's Most Pervasive Problem"; "Nurses' Rights"; "Power: Rx for Change"; "Patient Advocacy or Fighting the System."

In articles like these, nurses have begun preaching this message to their colleagues: As the largest group of health professionals in the country, we have enormous power. If we use it, if we finally take responsibility for our own occupation, we can radically change and improve our health care system.

"Nursing is going through its own process of 'consciousness raising' and . . . we are learning of the need to liberate our practice from male domination," Dr. June Rothberg, the nursing school dean at Adelphi, wrote in 1973 in *Nursing Outlook*.

Lucille Kinlein led her own liberation parade. An R.N. who had taught nursing for twenty-two years, she became so frustrated by the doctor's power to control and limit nursing care that in May 1971, she became an independent nurse practitioner, the first in the country. At her office in Hyattsville, Maryland, she emphasizes health maintenance and charges her patients low fees.

Other women joined together to free nursing from male control. At the National Organization for Women convention in Washington, D.C. in 1973, I watched fifteen feminist nurses draw their chairs into a circle, give a dollar dues each and announce that they had just formed the Nurses Task Force of NOW.

As they discussed their training in subservience, they leaned forward, straining to hear each other. Another NOW task force had met in the room during the previous hour and two members of it, both men, had stayed on and were talking loudly.

After a half hour, one woman finally burst out, "Is it because we're meek little nurses that we allow this to go on?"

The women turned to the men and firmly told them to leave. They did.

Nurses asserted themselves again in May 1974, when the American Nurses Association established the Nurses Coalition for Action in Politics. Its purpose, according to *AJN* editor Thelma M. Schorr, is "to promote the improvement of the health care of the people."

The next month, four thousand nurses struck forty-three hospitals in the San Francisco area. Their primary demand was not a pay increase; it was the right to help determine patient care. They would not tolerate the staffing of intensive and coronary care units with inadequately trained personnel, the nurses declared.

The American Hospital Association protested: The "fragmentation of responsibility" that would result from the nurses' demands "violates principles of sound management."

Nurses rejected that contention. They would no longer accept the "unity of institution control" principle (i.e., nurse impotence) that Dr. Edward Cowles had advocated and Linda Richards had bowed to in 1878.

"We in nursing have lived long enough with powerlessness," Schorr, the *AJN* editor, wrote the month of the strike. "Our acceptance of it, as a given, has led to our acceptance of sub-

standard health care as a norm. Our acceptance of powerlessness has cost us our self-respect and that was too high a price
to pay."

Nursing self-respect blossomed in Philadelphia in 1975.
There, for the first time, nurses declared that they were the
equals of physicians, that their work was vital, that they were
the patient's advocate, not the doctor's handmaiden, and that
they refused to play the demeaning nurse-doctor game any
longer.

Nurses made the declaration at St. Agnes Hospital in Philadelphia where conflict with doctors had been brewing since
mid-1974. Thomas Daley, R. N., the university-educated nursing director, saw nurses as the colleagues rather than the subordinates of doctors. He disapproved of the game in which
nurses pretend that their knowledge is the doctors'. According
to Gloria Donnelly, former nursing school director at St. Agnes,
many nurses Daley hired would call up a physician and politely
say, "Doctor, I think your order for Patient X should be
changed for these reasons: A. B. C."

"Some of the physicians went crazy when this began to
happen," she told me.

Tempers also flared when Daley refused the doctors' demands
to participate in the hiring, transferring and promoting of
nurses.

"I don't think I should have to clear my choice of nurses with
a doctor," Daley explained. "He doesn't clear his choice of
physicians with the nursing director."

Open warfare erupted in December. A nurse questioned a
doctor's mineral-oil order for an elderly burn patient because
she feared that the oil, in combination with another drug the
doctor had prescribed, could cause oil emboli in the liver and
spleen. According to Daley, pharmacology literature upheld the
nurse's judgment.

"The physician rescinded the order but still complained to
me about it," Daley told the *American Journal of Nursing.*
"I defended the nurse because it is her obligation to question
treatment when she thinks it is detrimental."

"Nurses are supposed to be dum-dums," Daley said in a
recent telephone interview. "The doctor is the authority who
knows all. Well, that's not so. Believe me, if it weren't for

nurses questioning doctors' orders, patients would have many more problems than they do now."

Daley refused to reprimand the nurse. A month later he was fired. Sister Anthony Consilia, hospital administrator, said that Daley was dismissed "because of his inability or unwillingness to cooperate with other department heads."

That, Daley asserted, simply meant that the physicians had not gotten their way.

Every year, many top nurses are fired over this nursing-control issue, Kathryn J. Grove, executive director of the Pennsylvania Nurses Association (PNA), told me.

"Top echelon nurses who attempt to adhere to standards of practice get in trouble with doctors or hospital administrators and they're fired summarily, right on the spot," she said. "It's happening all over the nation. I think it's always happened."

But this time, nurses picketed the hospital carrying signs with such messages as "Nurse Patients, Not Doctors," and "Doctors Are Not Gods." They told their story to television, newspaper and radio audiences. Thirty-three nurses from a staff of 140 also resigned in support of Daley. Gloria Donnelly, the nursing school director, Andrea Mengel, director of nursing practice, and Eunice King, psychiatric clinical nurse specialist, were among them. The three wrote an article for a journal, *Supervisor Nurse,* in which they stated that doctors in administrative positions at St. Agnes "seemed baffled by independent, thinking women and uncertain of their relationship with them."

PNA Director Grove wrote to Sister Consilia supporting Daley and objecting to his dismissal. The Pennsylvania Nurses Association was totally committed to supporting the efforts of nursing to retain control over the practice of their own profession, she asserted in January 1975.

Doctors insist on their orders being followed to the letter, they often explain, because they are legally responsible for the patient's welfare.

"There's one captain to the ship," Dr. Frank Tropea, president of the St. Agnes medical staff, told the *Philadelphia Inquirer.* "Ultimately, the doctor is the most responsible, informed member of the team."

The "captain" theory, though frequently invoked by doctors, has been successfully challenged in the courts.* It holds only in very special circumstances.

In every state in the country, a nurse is legally liable for her actions even if she is following a doctor's order. Nurses can be and have been sued in such cases. According to the *Philadelphia Inquirer*, at the end of 1973 there were 680 unresolved suits against nurses for their actions in hospitals.

"Clearly, the nurse is entitled to no consideration in a malpractice case because she alleges that she was ordered to perform that function," attorney Milton J. Lesnik and Bernice E. Anderson, R. N., wrote in *Nursing Practice and the Law*. "No order may contravene the inherent obligation to secure the patient's safety." †

The nurse at St. Agnes who believed that the doctor's order could harm a patient was faced then with these alternatives: Reprimand or dismissal if she disobeyed the order and a possible malpractice suit if she obeyed it.

The uprising at St. Agnes was one of the nurse's first battles in controlling her own profession. When nurses themselves do define nursing, this is what many think it will become:

Nurses will promote health, not just take care of those who have fallen sick. Instead of meekly allowing physicians to define health care as medical care, they will develop health education and maintenance programs for the public.

The nurse will become a gatekeeper in the health-care system. In other words, she will assess the patient's problem, provide nursing care if that is called for or refer the patient on to the appropriate doctor.

"The only entry into the health-care system now is the physician," Daley said. "This is ridiculous. A good nurse could screen patients and say, 'You go to Clinic X.' There's no need to pay a $20 fee for the doctor to screen you."

The Professional Nursing Law passed in Pennsylvania in 1974 does allow nurses to refer patients and to engage in health

* "Recent Cases: Captain Theory at Issue," *Journal of Legal Medicine*, July/August 1974, p. 9.

† For further discussion of the malpractice liability of physicians and nurses, see the following pages in the Lesnik and Anderson book published in 1955 by J. P. Lippincott Co., pp. 224–231, 260–261, and 272–283.

counseling and teaching. Connecticut, New York and California have similar laws.

In some places, like Kentucky's Frontier Nursing Service, nurses already screen patients. Mary Breckinridge established the service in 1925 to provide health care to poor people in the Appalachians. The nurses give the primary care and they hire physicians to work for them.

"Doctors are technicians," Andrea Mengel, former nursing practice director at St. Agnes, told me. "They're highly trained, but they're technicians. Nurses are the humanists."

Doctors see a patient for a few minutes a day. They are sometimes concerned only with the condition of one organ—a liver or a heart.

"Now, a patient receives fragmented care," Dr. June Rothberg of Adelphi's nursing school, said in an interview. "Different people file into his room to do different parts of his treatment. He needs one person who is concerned about him as a person. That's the nurse's role."

Good nursing means caring for the well-being of the total person, not just performing a series of tasks like giving injections and pills, she added.

Many nurses believe that nursing care now centers around the convenience of the doctor, rather than the needs of the patient. When nurses do indeed become the patient's advocate, that focus will shift.

If the empowerment of the nurse means that the physician is dethroned as king of the hospital hierarchy only to be replaced by a queen, hospital workers will hardly rejoice for while doctors often see nurses as stupid underlings, nurses treat lower-paid practical nurses (LPNs) and aides just as contemptuously.

One aide explained to *Ms.* magazine in October 1975: "The doctor thinks he's God; the nurse thinks she's an angel; and everyone thinks the aide is shit."

The low status of the aide is spelled out for her every day. For example, a new nurse will be introduced to the staff during the morning report but a new aide will often not be given that courtesy.

"Almost every oppressed group has turned on someone 'lower,'" Kathleen McInerney, chairperson of Nurses NOW, a task force of the National Organization for Women, told me. "We've been oppressed and we oppress others down the line."

Rather than challenge the healing hierarchy doctors established, then, nurses quietly take their place in it. They mimic doctors by setting up their own hierarchy in which the class falls lower and the skin grows darker as the jobs drop in status and pay.

In 1946, there were 6,280 hospitals (compared to 149 in 1870) and they needed large nursing staffs. To cut labor costs, hospitals created the lower-paid practical nurse (LPN) category. Studies by the American Nurses Association had recommended such an increase in auxiliary nursing personnel and an upgrading of the R.N.'s status.

Within their own ranks, nurses began differentiating between "professional" and "technical" nurses. The former, who have bachelor degrees, are more apt to be middle class and white and the latter, who hold nursing school diplomas, are likely to be working-class blacks. If a two-year diploma nurse wants to become a baccalaureate degree nurse, she must start the program from the very beginning. Few nursing programs provide part-time or evening programs for such working nurses. These obstacles solidify class and race differences between the levels of nurses.

The various nurses—diploma, associate degree, and baccalaureate degree—play the "Mine Is Bigger Than Yours" game. They argue about whose pedigree is best and who, therefore, should escape dirty work, get more pay or be promoted. Pamela Levin, R. N. and Dr. Eric Berne, psychiatrist, note that the game is prevalent in nursing organization policy-making decisions.*

With increasing technology after World War II, the number of health jobs proliferated. New health workers, like inhalation therapists and cardiopulmonary technicians, also followed doctors and nurses in setting up their own "professions" and in trying to raise their status above those of other workers. A hospital hierarchy developed and ossified.

Almost no career ladders were built into it. Rigid job definitions froze workers at each level of the hierarchy. Ward girls changed water pitchers but were not trusted to empty bed pans.

* Pamela Levin and Eric Berne, "Games Nurses Play," *American Journal of Nursing*, March 1972.

Nurse's aides took temperatures but not blood pressures. Licensed practical nurses changed dressings but did not dispense pills. Regardless of her ability, each would be taught more complicated duties only if there were a shortage of workers at the next level.

Are nonprofessional health workers as stupid as many professionals assume they are? Or do they, like most human beings, live down to the limited expectations others have of them?

Dr. Donald Ostergard's experience suggests that the latter is true. He runs a training program for paramedical personnel in family planning and cancer screening at Harbor General Hospital in Torrance, California and finds that R. N.'s, LPN's, medical assistants and persons with no prior medical experience can all "perform in a satisfactory manner."

During the twenty-week course, women learn to give pelvic exams, screen for abnormalities, insert intrauterine devices (IUDs), fit diaphragms, give local anesthesia and perform other procedures usually done only by physicians. Ostergard and his colleagues conclude that after the training program, the women are as skilled as similarly trained doctors in recognizing normal and abnormal pelvic findings. On IUD insertion, Ostergard reports, paramedics perform at least as well as physicians.

But Ostergard's program is unique. Most female health workers, their capabilities constantly underestimated, have never been allowed to develop new skills.

Seventy-five percent of America's four million health workers are women so the hierarchy that keeps people locked at various levels mainly harms women. In 1971 at a typical institution, Holyoke Hospital in Massachusetts, only 9 percent of the top decision-makers (directors, administrators and medical staff) but 85 percent of the workers were women.

While doctors (92 percent male) are the very highest paid workers in America, these female health workers are among the lowest paid. They take home such meager wages that, a 1972 Labor Department study showed, some, *while still working full-time,* are periodically forced on welfare rolls.* Drs.

* The study concerned welfare careers and low-wage employment in Detroit. Commissioned by the U. S. Labor Department, researchers Joe A. Miller and Louis A. Ferman found that there were not two separate groups—welfare poor and working poor—but one group—low-wage workers—some of whom must occasionally go on welfare to supplement wages that provide no security. Despite

Bonnie and Vern Bullough, a nurse and historian respectively, pointed out in a 1975 paper that the paycheck of an aide earning a median salary falls $700 below the poverty line of $3,743 (for a family of four) established by the Social Security Administration in 1969. If the aides had children, the Bulloughs noted, they would be better off to quit work and apply for welfare.

Poor, nonwhite women often get these low-paying jobs. They do not have the money or encouragement for further training so they become the aides, hospital cooks, attendants, practical nurses and office clerks.

White, middle-class parents expect their daughters to enter training schools and they can afford the tuition. So these women become R. N.'s, dietitians, physical therapists, x-ray technicians, medical technologists and medical social workers.

The two groups of women do not support each other in struggling for decent pay, training programs and decision-making power.

"Racism and classism work against that mutual support," NOW's McInerney explained. "When women are trained as nurses, they become 'ladies.' They're taught that they're better than the lower-class aides and LPNs who must be kept in line."

Because of that feeling of superiority, professionals and technicians often refuse to belong to the same union as "lower"-class workers. In the last decade, unions finally began organizing hospital employees. Local 1199 Health and Hospital Workers Union at first succeeded in recruiting blue-collar workers but failed to attract white-collar workers.

"The problem was that once workers got a certain amount of skill, they were called 'professional,'" Arlene Ezratty, a vice-president of 1199, explained. "For some, that term substituted for bread and butter. They believed that 'professionals don't

---

a screening procedure used to get more males in their study, Miller and Ferman ended up with 85 percent females. What stood out clearly in Detroit, they noted, was that the low-wage labor market is essentially a woman's labor market. The female nondomestic service workers who were welfare recipients, the study showed, were 50 percent of all service workers in health care institutions. Their mean hourly wage was $1.98.

A personal note: As a nurse's aide in Charleston, S. C. in 1966, I took home $34.50 for a forty-hour week. My co-workers, many of whom were black, supported their families on that salary. I never could figure out how.

join unions,' and they didn't want to belong to the same organization as unskilled workers."

Nurses, she added, "are absolutely hung up on being professionals." The union has been so unsuccessful with them that it has reduced its recruitment efforts.

In 1964, the union formed a "guild" especially for clerical, technical and professional workers so they would not have to associate with unskilled workers.

Hospital workers destroy each other through such divisiveness. The "professional" nurse feels superior to the "technical" nurse who lords it over the radiology aide who outranks the kitchen worker, so they do not join together to challenge the hospital structure which keeps them all powerless, ill-paid and underutilized.

Kathleen McInerney is convinced there is an alternative to the petty rank-pulling prevalent among the powerless. Concerned about *all* women in the health labor force, Nurses NOW wants the hospital organized horizontally rather than vertically, she said. "The work I'm doing is as valuable as the work a doctor is doing. It's the same with an R. N. and an LPN and an aide," she added.

When she was a head nurse in a California hospital, McInerney arranged for aides, R. N.'s and LPNs to take turns giving seminars to each other. Each one had special talents and shared them with the others. Morale increased, she said, and workers requested transfers to her floor.

"We must begin to relate as peers and draw the best out of each other," she said. "We need to learn from and support each other."

PART

II

HOW THE MALE DOMINATION OF MEDICINE AFFECTS THE HEALTH CARE WOMEN RECEIVE

Chapter / FOUR

PATIENT-DOCTOR RELATIONSHIP

THE MALE DOMINATION OF MEDICINE DOES NOT JUST DENY female healers an opportunity to practice. It compels women to receive medical treatment from members of the more powerful sexual caste. Because of the stereotypes males and females hold about each other, differences in the sexual stratum of doctor and patient can harm the healing relationship.

We already know that gulfs in social class can affect the way patients and doctors interact. Studies conducted mostly in the 1950s suggest that the greater the social distance between participants, the worse the therapeutic relationship.* Mutual respect, trust and cooperation seem to dwindle as the social distance widens. The doctor and patient become so preoccupied

---

* For details on those studies, see "Social Status and Public Health," by Ozzie G. Simmons. Pamphlet #13 of the Social Science Research Council, 1958. Available from Kraus Reprint Co., Route 100, Millwood, N.Y. 10546. In one study Simmons cites, staff members at a Veterans Administration hospital, who were themselves middle class, gave more time and attention to middle-class patients. Another study reported that psychotherapists "liked" nine out of thirteen higher-class patients and "disliked" nine out of twelve lower-class patients.

with their positions in the social hierarchy that they give less attention to the goal: Healing.

When male physicians too frequently dismiss women's complaints as products of neurotic imaginations (a charge both female patients and doctors have made), we can speculate that the sex of doctors also affects the quality of health care.

Dr. Estelle Ramey, endocrinology professor at Georgetown University School of Medicine, believes that some male physicians today, even those of good will, do view women as hysterical, emotionally unstable children.

"If a busy doctor assumes that a menopausal woman who complains of a gastrointestinal disorder is imagining the disorder, and if—without examining her thoroughly—he sends her away with a 'There, there, little girl, you'll be all right,' and the woman really has something grim, then she's in trouble," Dr. Ramey told me in a telephone interview. "This means that the menopausal woman is at risk because some doctors will ascribe anything she complains of to menopause."

Pregnant women and the mothers of young children are also at risk because they, too, are considered particularly hysterical, she observed.

Medical schools seem to fuel the belief that emotional conflict causes many female disorders. Dr. Mary Howell, the Maine pediatrician, points out that lecturers refer to patients exclusively as "he," except when discussing a hypothetical patient with a psychogenic disease. Then they automatically shift to "she."

In a 1973 survey of female students in forty-one medical schools, respondents reported that their lecturers frequently refer to women as "hysterical mothers," "hypochondriacs," and "old ladies" whom doctors must "manage."* ("Douche bag" and "crocks" are other common terms medical professors use for women.)

Gynecology textbooks, too, often condition doctors to suspect a psychosomatic ailment when a woman presents a complaint. In the 1971 edition of *Office Gynecology*, for example, Dr. J. P.

---

* Dr. Mary Howell conducted the survey of 146 students. See, *Why Would a Woman Go Into Medicine?*, 1973. Available from The Feminist Press, Old Westbury, New York. (The report is published under Dr. Howell's pseudonym, Dr. Margaret A. Campbell.)

Greenhill observed that "many women, wittingly or unwittingly, exaggerate the severity of their complaints to gratify neurotic desires."

He also suggested that doctors look for "personality factors" in the diagnosis of such conditions as menstrual disorders, the menopause, urinary difficulties, sterility, and low back and pelvic pain. To tell the difference between psychologic and physical pain, he lists questions doctors should ask themselves and ranks this as the most important one: "Does the patient accept herself as a woman?"

Later he notes that the inability to menstruate "may occur in women who consciously or unconsciously cannot accept womanhood. This condition is commonly noted in 'tomboys.'"

Functional dysmenorrhea (painful menstruation) "is generally a symptom of a personality disorder, even though hormonal imbalance may be present. Therefore a thorough study of the woman's attitudes toward femininity is often necessary."

Clearly, sex stereotypes influence how seriously a physician may take a woman's ailments. If she does not accept his definition of "femininity" and chooses to spend her life in a way of which he does not approve, her health may well be jeopardized. If she loves her job as a telephone repairperson and dislikes housekeeping, then any physical ailment she describes may be attributed to her failure to accept the female role. The physician might label her pain a "personality disorder" despite the fact that no scientific supporting evidence for this view exists and that organic causative factors *are* present.

Some doctors insist that besides dysmenorrhea (painful menstruation), several other exclusively female disorders are induced by the patient's emotional or psychological defects. They assert then, that a woman's inadequacy as a human being causes certain ailments—ailments which doctors cannot be expected to study or to treat.

In the February 1973 *New England Journal of Medicine*, Dr. Jean Lennane, a psychiatrist, and her husband, Dr. John Lennane, Senior Registrar of the Renal Unit at Prince Henry Hospital in Australia, examine four such disorders, including the nausea of pregnancy. Although 75 to 88 percent of pregnant women experience this condition, it is classified with the neuroses. Morning sickness appears to be related to the estrogen hormone which pregnant women secrete in larger quantities than nonpregnant women. Yet the 1972 textbook, *Gynecology and Obstetrics, Current Diagnosis and Treatment,* states that the nausea "may indicate resentment, ambivalence and inadequacy in women ill-prepared for motherhood."

Women on oral contraceptives containing estrogen often suffer from the same type of nausea as pregnant women. Are these women "resentful, ambivalent and inadequate because they are *not* pregnant?" the Drs. Lennane ask.

Since morning sickness, dysmenorrhea and other conditions the Lennanes discuss all affect women and since most of the specialists and textbook authors are men, they wonder whether "an underlying sexual basis for this prejudice" exists.

Perhaps this is another example of sexual prejudice: When doctors were asked in 1971 to describe "the typical complaining patient," 72 percent referred spontaneously to a woman.* Only 4 percent referred to a man. (The remaining 24 percent did not mention the patient's sex.) Men describe symptoms, it seems, but women "complain."

Sexist assumptions affect not only the perception of female ailments but the willingness of physicians to give patients vital information. That became evident at the 1970 Senate hearings on the oral contraceptive. Several physician witnesses, clearly holding the woman-as-featherbrain stereotype, implied that most women were not bright enough to understand information on the Pill's adverse effects. For example, when Dr. Joseph Goldzieher of the Southwest Foundation for Research and Education was asked to comment on the "informed consent" issue, he said that while some females were indeed intelligent enough to understand data on the Pill, there were "vast numbers of women" who did not have inquiring minds or enough education to comprehend more than the simplest biological facts. He continued:

"A misguided effort to 'inform' such women leads only to anxiety on their part and loss of confidence in the physician . . . They want him (the doctor) to tell them what to do, not to

* See Ruth Cooperstock's "Sex Differences in the Use of Mood Altering Drugs: An Explanatory Model," *Journal of Health and Social Behavior,* 1971, 12, pp. 238–244. Ms. Cooperstock, a sociologist, is a research associate with the Alcoholism and Drug Addiction Research Foundation in Toronto, Canada.

confuse them by asking them to make decisions beyond their comprehension . . . The idea of informing such a woman is not possible." *

By their behavior, women sometimes appear to confirm the sexist views of male physicians. They come from a social caste foreign to men. There are cultural differences. Women have been conditioned to freely acknowledge their emotional difficulties and express their feelings. To men trained in the stoicism of the masculine stereotype, this may appear to be hysterical behavior.

Women have also been trained to look up to men as protectors. So while some women object to the condescending way doctors relate to them—the pats on the head, the slow baby talk, the gentle refusal to explain the diagnosis or treatment—other women like it. For this reason, Dr. Estelle Ramey, the endocrinology professor, thinks it is a mistake to identify doctors as the villains in the doctor-patient relationship.

"Both doctors and patients have been acting as they have been trained to act and the interaction between them is mutually reinforcing," she told me. "It's difficult to have villains without a fair number of willing victims. Many doctors are taken aback when they find it is no longer acceptable to call their patients 'dear' and 'honey.' Their patients have *loved* it, have worshipped them, have wanted them to play daddy."

Dr. C. Scott Russell expanded the doctor's daddy image to cosmic proportions in his 1968 book, *The World of a Gynecologist:* "If like all human beings, he (the gynecologist) is made in the image of the Almighty, and if he is kind, then his kindness and concern for his patient may provide her with a glimpse of God's image."

Through the physician mystique that such men create, the godlike doctor becomes all-knowing and all-powerful. The doctor creates this myth of omnipotence by shrouding his work in mystery. He uses big words to render his field incompre-

---

* For testimony on the issue of informed consent to Pill usage, some of which reveals a breathtaking underestimation of woman's ability to think, see the following pages in "Hearings before the Subcommittee on Monopoly of the Select Committee on Small Business," Oral Contraceptives: 5932-33; 6081-82; 6466; 6484-85; 6518-22; 6568; 6610-11; 6614; 6626-27; 6644-45. Ask your congressperson or public library to obtain a copy of the testimony for you.

hensible to patients, though small words would do as well. (For example, diaphoresis simply means sweat.)* The doctor tells patients, through his monstrous words, his authoritative manner and his silence after their questions, that he is wiser than they. He never hints at puzzlement or admits fallibility. Patients should, therefore, be awed and obedient.

Whether or not some women welcome such an unequal relationship, it can harm them. As we will see in later chapters, a woman's reluctance to question the omnipotent doctor makes her vulnerable to unnecessary surgery, unproven drugs and population-control experiments.

It became obvious at the Senate Pill hearings that when the class biases of doctors are added to their sexual stereotypes, low-income females are at special risk here. Dr. Goldzieher, for example, said that whether a woman should be informed of the Pill's adverse effects hinged on the woman herself: "It depends on her socioeconomic status. It depends on her education. It depends on her cultural pattern."

Throughout the hearings, various physicians implied that lower-class women were not "educated" or "motivated" enough to use the safer mechanical means of contraception like the diaphragm and so had a special need for the Pill, despite its possible risks.†

Women with serious maladies visit the doctor. So, most likely, do women with ailments induced by the mind—ailments that cause real pain and are undeserving of the contempt with which they are often met.

In the first case, there is the danger that doctors, programmed to suspect psychosomatic afflictions in all women, may overlook a critical condition. (Everyone has heard stories of women who complained of blinding headaches, were dismissed with tranquilizer prescriptions and had strokes two days later. No one knows how often such incidents occur.)

---

* In 19th century America, popular health activists refused to be bullied by words. One asked, "If I were really to say that in consequence of the cirticular membrane of his digitals having been severed, the veinous and arterial cylinders had discharged their sanguinous fluid, would it be plainer than to say I had cut his fingers?"

† For testimony revealing certain assumptions physicians sometimes make about women in different social and economic classes, see pp. 6212-15 and 6482-83 in "Hearings before the Subcommittee on Monopoly of the Select Committee on Small Business," Oral Contraceptives, *op. cit.*

In the second case, a middle-aged woman suffering from the loneliness of a suddenly empty nest or feeling otherwise unhappy with her life, may well translate her sadness into physical symptoms hoping that the sadness will then become curable. When that happens, the woman obviously needs someone to talk with her sympathetically and identify the problem. It is difficult to imagine such a personal conversation taking place with a physician who has been trained to think of women as "douche bags" or as whining children. Nor can one envision the busy doctor exploring with the woman various alternatives to help her regain control of her life: A career counseling or assertiveness-training workshop at a local college or a meditation course to help her cope with her life while she is assessing her abilities and goals.

If, instead of referring her to a counselor, the doctor advises her to take alcohol or drugs, her problem will be masked rather than solved. But that is apparently what some doctors do.

In his recent study of alcoholic housewives, Dr. J. W. Bedell, a California sociologist, found that they often begin drinking when they are bored, lonely or depressed—sometimes after a divorce or at a child's departure from home. Bedell blames doctors for launching many women into alcoholism by dismissing their problems as trivial and by suggesting that they simply need a few drinks.

Other physicians respond to women's complaints by prescribing mood-altering drugs. Almost half of American women (45 percent) use such drugs regularly. That is more than twice the percentage of men doing so, according to a 1971 study by Dr. Carl D. Chambers, former director of research for the N.Y. State Narcotics Control Commission. Nearly all the women had these drugs prescribed for them by physicians. In other words, it would appear doctors are twice as likely to prescribe mood-altering drugs for women as for men.

Chambers also found that women are an astonishing 70 percent of the habitual users of minor tranquilizers and 72 percent of the antidepressant users.

Dr. Linda Fidell and Jane Prather of the California State University Psychology Department, conducted a drug-usage study in a California suburb in early 1975 and came up with findings similar to Dr. Chambers'. Fifty-three percent of their

465 female respondents had used psychotropic drugs during the past year.

Why do doctors prescribe more mood-altering drugs for women than for men? One explanation: The doctor misinterprets his female patient's symptoms as imaginary because she speaks in a cultural language that he does not understand.

A 1966 study on the way in which patients from two cultures describe their ailments suggests this possibility.* While the study concerned the Irish and the Italian, it is also relevant to all males and females. At the Eye, Ear, Nose and Throat Clinic of Massachusetts General Hospital, the Irish patients presented few symptoms and refused to admit pain. Italians with comparable ailments gave more symptoms, acknowledged their illness, and complained of pain. Doctors concluded that the Irish needed medical help more urgently than the Italians, even though the two groups had been matched for seriousness of illness.

Apparently, the more stoical the patient, the more seriously the doctor tends to regard him or her. The more expansive the patient, the less seriously the physician takes her.

In a 1974 update of this study, it was discovered that if no organic basis for the disease exists, doctors tend to describe an Italian as having emotional problems but they describe an Irish patient in more neutral terms.

Dr. Linda Fidell, one author of the California drug study, pointed out to me that in our culture men generally act like the stoic Irish and women like the expansive Italians.

From childhood, a female is encouraged to admit her pain, to freely ask for help and to expect and accept weakness in herself. As a male, the doctor is programmed to endure hardship rather than to ask for help immediately. When confronted with a patient from the female culture who describes vague symptoms at length, the doctor, already assuming that women's ailments are often psychosomatic, may consider her problem an emotional one. So he prescribes a tranquilizer.

An undervaluing of the housewife's work may also play a role in the overprescribing of mood-altering medicine. Doctors

* Zola, I. K., "Culture and Symptoms—An Analysis of Patients' Presenting Complaints," *American Sociological Review*, 1966, 31 (2), 615–630. Dr. Fidell discusses this paper in a 1973 speech. See source notes.

are far more likely to give these drugs to housewives, even for minor complaints, than to patients of high social or intellectual status, Dr. Carrol M. Brodsky, associate professor of psychiatry at the University of California School of Medicine, found in a survey reported in 1969. Apparently, he noted, this resulted from the idea that a housewife could always take a nap if the drug made her sleepy, and that "in any event, her work was dispensable."

Drug advertisements foster such sexist assumptions. An analysis of several leading medical journals over a five-year period ending in 1972 showed that the ads strongly tended to associate psychoactive drugs with female patients and nonpsychoactive drugs with male patients.* As one of the investigators observed, the advertisements gave this message to physicians: Men have "real" illnesses; women have mental problems.

Advertisements also tend to advise doctors to drug women who are unhappy with their "feminine" role and with the tedious jobs that sometimes go with it. In his ten-year study of drug ads in twenty-four medical journals, Dr. Robert Seidenberg, clinical professor of psychiatry at the Upstate Medical Center, State University of New York, found tranquilizers often recommended for women distressed by humdrum tasks. One ad portrayed a woman upset by a pile of dirty dishes. After medication, she was seen washing the dishes "happily." In another ad, a woman stood behind bars made of brooms and mops. "You can't set her free," the caption told physicians, "but you can help her feel less anxious."

Sometimes, Seidenberg observed, advertisements urge physicians to prescribe tranquilizers to manage patients who are annoying them. One such ad pictures an old woman. The text reads: "A Problem in Any Practice. Every time this patient comes in she has a different symptom—usually the result of a disturbed nervous system. She needs help to quiet her fears and anxieties."

Dr. William Smith, director of pharmacy at Long Beach (California) Memorial Hospital, told me that doctors often do prescribe such drugs to get rid of emotional women. "You

* Linda Fidell, "Put Her Down on Drugs: Prescribed Drug Usage in Women," Address to the Western Association of Women Psychologists, Anaheim, California, April 12, 1973.

have to understand that a doctor has tremendous pressures on his time," he explained. "This puts him in a bind. Prescribing tranquilizers is one way of getting rid of the patient."

In medical schools now, doctors often learn to view women not only as hysterics, but also as sexual objects rather than human beings. One clinician, for example, demonstrated an abdominal examination by first having a lab technician strip down to her bathing suit in front of the class. Many other professors customarily begin classes with sex jokes and break up lecture monotony by inserting slides of nude women amid those of diseased tissues.

At U. C. L. A. Medical School, the last slide in a presentation would sometimes be a picture of a naked female rump with "The End" written across it, one female student recalled in a letter to the feminist newspaper *Sister*. She was informed that there was an underground competition to see which professor had the niftiest slide collection.

That such slide shows take place in a context so close to human misery disturbs this student: "A dying woman's emaciated body and huge, swollen belly were presented, 'Now this is Bubbles, and as you look into her lovely eyes. . . ' "

Students laughed.

A 1973 survey of medical students found such presentations of women widespread.* Female patients were ridiculed by being referred to as "Matilda Menopause" or described as "female, forty, fat, fertile," medical students reported.

When doctors make women appear ridiculous, the U. C. L. A. student pointed out, they also make them seem somehow deserving of their misery: "Well, the prostitute's vagina . . . ha ha ha."

Some medical textbooks, as well as class lectures, portray women as sexual objects. In a new text, *The Anatomical Basis of Medical Practice,* lascivious pictures of women were used to liven up the pages and keep medical students interested. Leering asides and dirty jokes abounded.

The textbook was immediately withdrawn when women objected to it but the authors called chief protester Dr. Estelle

---

* Dr. Margaret A. Campbell (Dr. Mary Howell), "Why Would a Woman Go Into Medicine?" See source notes.

Ramey "a sour old maid who couldn't take a joke," she recalls.

That joke has disturbing implications for women who need medical care. Poor women at a health center in New York City found that out when they went for medical care in 1971.* A staff gynecologist examined them without gloves and manipulated them sexually. Shocked, patients said they wanted a different doctor. Attending nurses complained about him too. After the center's director had received several complaints from different persons, he fired the gynecologist.

No medical association took any action against the gynecologist, though professionals claim that they police themselves.

About a year after the center's director had fired the gynecologist, he wondered what had happened to him. He learned that the gynecologist had secured a job in a women's prison.

Another problem with the female patient/male doctor relationship quickly crystallizes whenever any group of women discusses health care: Many women do not like to discuss their vaginal infections, breast lumps, menstrual irregularities and sex difficulties with men, nor do they feel comfortable being examined by men.†

Though doctors now claim that they become sexless beings when they don white coats, and though professionals try to "educate" women into thinking that their embarrassment at these examinations is silly, for many women, that embarrassment remains. Rather than changing the patients to fit into the medical care system then, perhaps the system ought to change to accommodate the patients.

In the last few years, a change occurred on a very small scale at Harbor General Hospital's Family Planning Clinic in Tor-

* As a condition for verifying this incident, the center's director stipulated that I identify neither him nor the institution.

† This was particularly true in the nineteenth century when many women would not call on male physicians for any ailments of the sexual organs. Dr. Charles Meigs, a midwifery professor at Philadelphia's Jefferson Medical College from 1841 to 1861, thought the women were admirable to suffer in silence without hope of cure. He wrote: "It is perhaps best, upon the whole, that this great degree of modesty should exist even to the extent of putting a bar to researches, without which no very clear and understandable notions can be obtained of the sexual disorders. I confess I am proud to say, that in this country . . . there are women who prefer to suffer the extremity of danger and pain rather than waive those scruples of delicacy which prevent their maladies from being fully explored. I say it is an evidence of the dominion of fine morality in our society . . ."

rance, California. Female paraprofessionals there were trained in contraceptive fitting and cancer screening. After these women began working, the clinic experienced a 500 percent increase in patient visits. The questioning of eight hundred patients revealed that 83 percent preferred the paramedic and only 1 percent, the physician. Sixteen percent did not care.*

Today, cervical cancer is 100 percent curable if caught early enough through Pap smears. But even though this test was developed thirty-five years ago, an estimated 7,700 American women still die of cancer of the cervix every year. Many do not go for exams. As of 1970, only 12 percent of American women were having regular Pap smears. Sometimes Spanish-speaking men do not allow their wives to have the test because they do not want male doctors examining their wives' vaginas. In the twenty clinics of the Human Resources Administration Family Planning Program throughout New York City, some Spanish-speaking women prefer to see a female doctor, Project Director Ella McDonald told me. Their reluctance to be examined by a man, she said, stems from their concern about their husbands' reactions if they found out about the exam.

While fear of husbands, cost of exams and anxiety about malignancy also keep women from the doctor's office, gynecologists themselves concede that many women shun health care out of embarrassment. Laying the blame on women, doctors say they should be "educated" about the necessity for regular examinations.

Probably none of these doctors has consulted a member of the opposite sex about his own intimate ailments for, as of 1974, there were only nine female urologists in the entire country. Before doctors talk about "educating" women on gynecological exams, perhaps they should themselves experience examinations by female physicians.

* Ostergard, Donald R., et al. See source notes.

Chapter / FIVE

MEDICINE AND SOCIAL CONTROL

AFTER ELIMINATING WOMEN FROM MEDICINE, MEN WERE FREE to define female health and disease. They interpreted both in ways which safeguarded their privileges as members of the upper caste. Programmed from infancy to see women as "different," they undoubtedly believed the sexist medical principles they set forth.

To 19th-century doctors, upper-class women were natural invalids. These physicians fostered female weakness, helped train women to be sickly and then used woman's frailty and "nervous susceptibility" to declare her unfit for any occupation outside the home. As priests had blessed sexist practices by calling them divinely ordained, physicians validated those same practices by pronouncing them "natural." According to science, woman should be restricted solely to childbearing.

Women often helped perpetuate the frailty myth, for it gave them a kind of power, though, indeed, it was the power of manipulating slaves. They discovered that men smiled indulgently when they fluttered and fainted, and frowned when they showed their strength and boasted of their good health. They

86

learned how to suffer from "hysterics" and fainting fits (and forgot again as soon as both ailments went out of fashion). Femininity, they knew, was identified with weakness. In an 1840 journal, popular health activist O. S. Fowler of Philadelphia recorded the consequence: To be troubled with a liver complaint or a sour stomach were as indispensable to a lady as a tight corset.

"Good health," Fowler observed, "is a sure indication of want of refinement."

Truly bad health refined women into saints. In his 1870 newspaper column, Dr. Augustus Gardner, midwifery professor at New York Medical College, described the angelic cancer victim: "Suffering and agony have marbled that fair brow; pain and torture have sowed lilies where once were beds of roses, and the light of heaven gleams forth from the wondrous depths of those glorious orbs."

Worshipped for their weakness, upper-class women cultivated it.

As the dying heroines of both *La Traviata* and *Love Story* knew, however, whatever the lady's ailment, it had to be becoming.

Tuberculosis was good. (Pale cheeks with two charming red spots; a delicate cough; a fragile frame easily swept up, during a fainting spell, by a strong, protective man.)

Leprosy was bad.

Sometimes, in punishing their families with their illnesses, women used the myth of feminine frailty to rebel. While sick, the woman could not keep house. Through this slave technique—the passive aggression of illness—she could avoid the domestic work she had been compelled to undertake. A man could not rebuke her for this rebellion because the woman would meekly whisper, between fainting spells and sips of broth, how sorry she was to be such a burden to him and how she wished she could get well.

Women used illness in another way—as a contraceptive. Much as they wanted to fulfill their marital duty, they became too "sickly" for it.

Invalidism, moreover, could be turned into a career for a woman who had no other. It gave her status and made her interesting.

In view of all this, Dr. Kristin Mann believed, women would only be well when the desire for illness ended. Dr. Mann, a former instructor in hygiene at Smith and Wellesley colleges, concluded in 1919: "As long as it is charming to be weak and women believe unconsciously that they actually gain power thereby, through the control of men who are their supporters, they will not care to produce an environment for themselves in which they can be strong."

Only when women objected to ill health would they rebel against physicians who had profitably turned the stereotype of feminine frailty into a medical principle. These doctors discoursed on the lady's weak muscles and meager lung capacity and on her susceptibility to "the vapors," a fainting ailment never in vogue among uncorseted lower-class women. They would find her uterus slightly "misplaced" or too "flabby" and cure the problem by propping up the organ with a pessary or painting it every week with carbolic acid.

Dr. Mary Putnam Jacobi, a pioneer in women's medical education, thought physicians often encouraged women to magnify every little twitch and take to bed for months. The increased attention doctors paid to women, "especially in their new function as lucrative patients," helped explain the skyrocketing ill health among women, she theorized in 1895.

To doctors, women were so different from men as to constitute a subspecies. They used those differences to justify discrimination against the lower caste. Dr. Frances Emily White, professor of physiology and hygiene at Women's Medical College of Pennsylvania, pointed out in an 1880 address to her students that arguments against woman's advancement in work and study had previously been based on her alleged physical inferiority—her lighter skeleton, smaller muscles and lesser physical endurance. But now, she observed, woman's failure "is predicated chiefly on the score of a natural semi-invalidism inherent in her sex, which, though it has never stood in the way of her success in unskilled labor—as the washwoman, the cook, or even as the nurse—it is claimed will at once interfere fatally with any attempt in the departments of skilled labor or of professional work, in which the emoluments, both social and pecuniary, are also of a high order."

Laypersons eagerly seized upon medicine's woman-as-invalid pronouncement. Explaining why female librarians were paid so much less than males, one hundred library officials agreed, in 1904, that women were hampered by their "delicate physique" and "inability to endure continued mental strain." *

In his 1871 *Counsel to Woman in Health and Disease,* Dr. Walter C. Taylor gave institutions further medical rationales for sex discrimination. He discussed the female's body and concluded that since she has a distinctively feminine physiology, as well as emotional and intellectual pattern, she also has "her own social destination, entirely distinct from that of the other sex." She has muscles that "are molded for the gentler exercises of the domestic circle—for grace, rather than strength of movement." She even breathes differently—from the upper chest rather than, as men do, from the abdomen. This peculiarity enables her to breathe during pregnancy, a consideration which "shows how the woman is modeled and prepared in advance for the performance of that maternal duty which is the supreme end of her physical being." (It was left to Dr. Clelia Mosher, medical advisor to women at Stanford University, to demonstrate in 1894 that the difference in respiration was due, not to sexual physiology, but to tight corsets.)

Male doctors also asserted that menstruation, pregnancy, childbirth and menopause were illnesses. Healthy men certainly never experienced them. These functions were such severe disabilities that they, along with woman's general weakness, precluded well-paid work. For their health's sake, women would have to keep out of job competition, marry and remain dependent on men.

Before menstruation begins, Dr. Taylor warned, the girl is apt to become ill. He advised that she "not be permitted to

---

* We still occasionally see the medical myth of woman's frailty used to justify discrimination against her. Before admitting girls, under the threat of lawsuits, the Little League used a medical rationale for barring females: "We have a five-page medical report which points out that girls are incapable of competing on the same level with boys," Robert Sirrat, the League's public relations director, declared in 1973. "Their bones are more vulnerable, their reactions slower."
In 1974, New York City Police Department psychologist Dr. Harvey Schlossberg used similar reasoning in arguing that female police officers were inferior to males. According to *The New York Times* he said: "Physiologically, a woman's system is different. It's more complex, more delicate and therefore it has to be more in balance. Police work is on and off. The routine is suddenly interrupted by violence and women will have a difficult time adjusting."

period

study too much." Since the "monthly sickness" is very liable to derangement, Taylor recommended that at the first hint of irregularity, the girl be put to bed and confined to a room with a uniform temperature. At each period, every girl was to suspend her normal activities and avoid walking, dancing, shopping and partying.

(It was because of such advice that Bryn Mawr President M. Carey Thomas wanted a female doctor for her students: "She will prescribe sheer idleness as a remedy neither for the indisposition of girls in their teens, nor for the ill health of college students.")

Menstruation was such an all-consuming activity that "the female seems to live chiefly for this purpose," Dr. Frederick Hollick, author of *The Marriage Guide,* declared in 1850. Laying bare the use of medicine to control women, he asserted that "the existence of this function alone (menstruation) makes it impossible for women, except in a few peculiar individual cases, to pursue the same mode of life as man. It makes her, of necessity, not so continuously active, nor so capable of physical toil, while, at the same time, it causes her to yearn for sympathy and support from some being that she feels is more powerful than herself."

By cutting women off from employment, male doctors helped herd women into one of the few fields open to them: Matrimony.

"Marriage," Dr. Taylor asserted, "is, in many instances, a direct sanitary measure. It remedies complaints of long standing, and often restores a debilitated health."

Advising the "tonic" of marriage, Taylor assured women that it was unhealthy to remain single. "Speaking medically," he wrote, using the phrase that often precedes a value judgment, "(the single woman) has tendencies to certain diseases, especially mental ones, to a greater extent than her married sisters." She is, he noted, more exposed to digestive ills and womb displacements. Later, he observed that "pregnancy is also a preservative of female health." Failure to become a mother seemed to injure a woman's mind, he added.

Doctors viewed women as forever on the verge of popping babies. How absurd it was then for baby bearers to hold steady jobs. Buttressed by the facts their medical brothers provided them, New York *Herald* editors in 1852 ridiculed the desire of the "mannish" feminists to hold men's jobs. How funny it would be, they wrote, to read in the newspapers "that Lucy Stone, pleading a cause, took suddenly ill in the pains of parturition, and perhaps gave birth to a fine bouncing boy in court!"

Disabling as men made pregnancy, women were often denied the option of forgoing it. Once a woman conceives, Dr. Taylor stated, her body "no longer belongs to herself; she is the guardian of a new life." If she tried to gain control of her body, doctors like Augustus Gardner, professor of clinical midwifery at the New York Medical College, scared her into submission.

Referring to contraception as "detestable practices," Dr. Gardner asserted in 1905 that "all the methods employed to prevent pregnancy are physically injurious" and could cause, among other ailments, neuralgias and "degeneration of the womb." Any attempt to deceive and thwart nature in her life-creating function, he thundered, would result in "moral degradation, physical disability, premature exhaustion and decrepitude."

To women who sought abortions, Dr. George H. Napheys, author of *The Physical Life of Women: Advice to the Maiden, Wife and Mother,* delivered a warning in 1871 even more frightening than that issued against contraceptives: "If maternal sentiment is so callous in their [women's] breasts, let them know that such produced abortions are the constant cause of violent and dangerous womb disease, and frequently of early death, that they bring on mental weakness and often insanity . . . Better, far better, to bear a child every year for twenty years, than to resort to such wicked and injurious steps; better to die, if needs be, in the pangs of childbirth, than to live with such a weight of sin on the conscience."

The childbearing years passed but menopause brought no relief from men's commands. Then, as at menstruation and pregnancy, the woman had to retire to a quiet life. One doctor decreed that she should withdraw from the world "even in the midst of her legitimate successes" and unobstrusively wait out the rest of her life by performing charitable works.*

* Dr. Walter C. Taylor, the author of *Counsel to Woman in Health and Disease.*

Gynecologists helped keep woman ignorant as well as home-bound. They believed anything affecting woman's brain also affected her sexual organs and vice versa. Therefore, they warned, too much brain activity would cause the uterus to wither and die; likewise, any disturbance in the uterus or ovaries could cause a mental breakdown.

In 1875, Dr. E. A. Clarke argued that higher education damaged women's reproductive capacities. That theory provided yet another rationale for limiting women exclusively to child-bearing. Some men seized on it eagerly. Students at the Agricultural College of Pennsylvania, for example, argued in 1889 that woman "cannot afford to risk her health in acquiring a knowledge of the advanced sciences, mathematics, or philosophy for which she has no use."

Accenting the differences between men and women to justify different treatment, one physician asserted in 1883 that the ovaries "give to woman all her characteristics of body and mind." * He added imperially, "We need not explain how or why."

Physicians attributed most female ailments to excessive sexual excitement (which could cause uterine cancer, vaginal infections and inflammation of the uterus or ovaries), and to displacement of the uterus. They treated the latter ailment by propping the uterus up with one of the 123 different types of pessaries on the market or they cut and burned the uterus to such an extent that, one doctor feared, the old-fashioned womb would exist only in history.

Dr. Lillian Welsh, staff physician at Goucher College, pointed out that as a result of gynecological disease theories, there was scarcely a neurotic co-ed in 1894 "whose mind was not fixed upon her reproductive organs as the source of all her troubles." One of her students had been told by her male physician, Welsh reported, that "if women knew what dangers lurked in their pelvic organs, they would not step from the pavement to their carriages or vice versa."

Women subjected to such warnings were dismayed at the prospect of exercise or sports, Welsh observed. Often, she

* George L. Austin, M.D., author of *Perils of American Women, or, a Doctor's Talk with Maiden, Wife and Mother.*

added, gymnastics teachers could laugh women out of their "frailty."

What 19th-century medicine dictated then, was that, to safeguard their health, women marry, bear children, and refrain from studying and from developing their muscles.

Some women, cut off from work and study, confined to endless childbearing, put to bed at every menstrual period and to pasture at menopause, became bored, restless, unhappy. The medical treatment for such "nervous disorders" was further inactivity. To recover her health, she must take still longer naps, forbear from stimulating conversation, and not tire herself out with reading or letter writing.

Treatment, in other words, was imprisonment in an unlocked house.

Confined to life as only a sexual being, woman was not even allowed to enjoy sex and would, in fact, be punished for such a transgression against her peculiar female nature.

In the 19th century, England's William Acton held views on female sexuality typical of physicians: "The majority of women (happily for society) are not very much troubled with sexual feeling of any kind."

But behind the assertion that "love of home, of children, and of domestic duties are the only passions that they [women] feel," lurked a terror of woman's sexuality. In their oat-sowing days, many men first knew "vulgar" women whose sexual appetites seemed so great that men feared gratifying a woman was beyond their exhausted strength, Acton wrote. So they dreaded marriage. Acton reassured them. Since decent (i.e. upper-class) women did not like sex, men could simply attend to their own pleasure.

"No nervous or feeble young man need, therefore, be deterred from marriage by any exaggerated notion of the arduous duties required of him," Acton declared.

Female doctors viewed woman's sexuality differently. In America, Dr. Elizabeth Blackwell explained that childbirth injuries and "brutal or awkward conjugal approaches" hurt women and doused their libido. Refined women had been taught, moreover, that sexual feeling was a sin so shameful they would die rather than confess to it. Blackwell maintained, however, that woman's sexual drive was just as strong as man's.

But it was male doctors who decided what constituted normal female sexuality and they tended to share Acton's view, not Blackwell's.

If a woman did develop the illness of sexuality—called "nymphomania," "ovariomania," or "uterine madness"—physicians could cure her. As Dr. Charles Meigs recalled in 1859, he gave a nine-year-old masturbator severe purgative medicines until she became thin and weak. He also applied a nitrate of silver solution to her clitoris.

Other doctors cauterized (burned) the organ. Isaac Baker Brown, a London doctor who published the first surgical work on gynecology, had a more direct approach: He removed the clitoris with a pair of scissors. In his 1866 book, *On the Curability of Certain Forms of Insanity, Epilepsy, Catalepsy and Hysteria in Females,* Brown described innumerable cures by his operation. Masturbation, which caused various nervous ailments, was the chief indication for the clitoridectomy.

His records show that he diagnosed a case as a nervous disease and performed "my usual operation," when presented with almost any symptom: Indigestion, insomnia, fissure of rectum, pain in back or side, sterility, "an inability to look one straight in the face," painful urination, melancholy, headache, a desire to run away from home or to become a nurse, heart palpitation, anemia, swollen joints, failing eyesight, dry skin and clammy skin.

"Observation convinced me that a large number of affectations peculiar to females depended on loss of nerve power (due to masturbation)," Dr. Brown wrote.

Brown's clitoridectomy was a controversial operation but many physicians in both England and America adopted it in the late 19th century.*

Dr. Brown relates numerous case histories in which it is obvious that he used the operation to control rebellious females. One such case involved a thirty-year-old mother of three suf-

---

* Brown names fifteen doctors who adopted his operation and then asserts that "very many others" also employed it. Isaac Flack, author of *Eternal Eve, The History of Obstetrics and Gynecology,* agrees with Brown's assessment. See p. 435 in Flack's book. In my reading, Dr. Joseph Howe, a professor of Clinical Surgery at the Bellevue Hospital Medical College, Dr. William Alcott, author of the 1855 publication *The Young Woman's Book of Health,* and the English physician William Acton all referred to the operation quite matter-of-factly.

fering from a mental disease which caused her to dislike her husband and refuse to sleep with him. Dr. Brown cut out her clitoris. According to him, she "recovered" and became a happy, healthy and pregnant wife.

Commenting on this case, Dr. Brown wrote that many unhappy marriages might be saved "if medical and surgical treatment were brought to bear." When a physician suggests, as Brown does here, that marital discord can be solved by cutting out the sexual organs of wives, there can be no doubt that medicine is political.

Removal of both ovaries was another operation frequently performed to cure female sexuality and nonconformity. According to historian G. J. Barker-Benfield, assistant professor of American Studies at the State University of New York in Albany, indications for ovariotomy included "neurosis, insanity . . . troublesomeness, eating like a plowman, masturbation, attempted suicide, erotic tendencies, persecution mania" and "anything untoward in female behavior."

Dr. William Steward of Philadelphia described an ovariotomy case he handled around 1885. A twenty-six-year-old housewife continued to masturbate even after he had fixed a pad filled with sharp steel pins over her vulva. Dr. Steward had "no recourse," he recalled, "but to deprive her of her ovaries, hoping in that way to remove her perverted instincts." After the operation, she was "willing and anxious to return to the management of her home," he reported.*

The propriety of such operations was much debated in medical circles. When one physician began removing both

* In their excellent booklet, "The Politics of Sickness," Barbara Ehrenreich and Deirdre English argue that in the 20th century, the burden of female control shifted from gynecology to psychiatry. Certainly rebellion against the female role has often been defined as a mental illness. As a 1968 study demonstrated, standards of mental health differ from men and women and are dependent on sex stereotypes. (See: Broverman, Inge K., et al., "Sex-Role Stereotypes and Clinical Judgments of Mental Health," *Journal of Consulting and Clinical Psychology,* 1970, Vol. 34, No. 1, pp. 1–7.)

I suspect that psychosurgery, which is performed twice as often on women as on men, is the modern equivalent of the clitoridectomy and ovariotomy. (See: "Brain Surgery—Therapy or Tampering?", by Jean Dietz, *The Boston Globe,* April 17, 1972; "The Return of the Lobotomy and Psychosurgery," by Dr. Peter Breggin, *Congressional Record,* February 24, 1972; "New Information in the Debate over Psychosurgery," by Dr. Breggin, *Congressional Record,* March 30, 1972; "Psycho Surgery: The Final Solution to the Woman Problem," by Barbara Roberts, *Rough Times,* September 1972.)

Another important work is *Women and Madness* by Phyllis Chesler.

ovaries and the fallopian tubes, the *Lancet,* a British medical journal, indignantly termed the procedure a "spaying."

Controversial or not, these operations were common.

Nineteenth-century morality discouraged sexual activity in both men and women but while it generally defined eroticism in women as pathological, it called the same natural, though not commendable, in men. Late in the century, many doctors began to declare that men needed sex to remain healthy.

Since women abhorred sex and men (medicinally speaking) required it, doctors absolved husbands of any obligation to gratify their wives. It is not surprising then that those "brutal or awkward conjugal approaches" Blackwell mentioned are referred to much later in a 1920 study on sex education.* American doctors were asked how often maladjusted marital relations were caused by the husband's ignorance of woman's sexuality. While Dr. A. W. Stearns replied testily, "Rarely and only in psychopaths," 37 percent answered, "Very frequently." One amplified: "Many men married twenty years never knew women have orgasms and never try to give their wives satisfaction, thinking only of themselves."

The men who became doctors presented their opinions—not as the self-interested views they were—but as science. Their medical theory of female sexlessness gave scientific validity to the double standard. Women were forced to cripple themselves to fit the medical definition of "decent women." If they failed to do so, male physicians would do the crippling for them— cutting out their clitorises or ovaries if they exhibited the sexual feeling doctors said they could not have.

How could women, who had little access to the study of medicine, dispute its findings? They had only their individual experiences to go on and, since they probably did not discuss such matters with other women, concluded that they themselves were diseased and unnatural, and endured the mental distress such a conclusion must produce.

Dr. Kate Lindsay was one of many female doctors who, in 1875, advocated sex education for women to end this female

---

* See John B. Watson and K. S. Lashley, "A Consensus of Medical Opinion Upon Questions Relating to Sex Education and VD Campaigns," published by The National Committee for Mental Hygiene, Inc., New York City, 1920. Copy available in the Sophia Smith Collection, Smith College, Northampton, Massachusetts.

suffering. Dr. G. K. Johnson was one of many male doctors who opposed it, saying, "The less they (women) know of their sexual functions, the better." *

Female doctors often disagreed with theories devised by men to control, not succor, women. Physicians like Frances White, Lydia Sayer, Clelia Mosher, R. B. Gleason, Mary Putnam Jacobi, Kristin Mann, Emily F. Pope, Lillian Welsh and Kate Lindsay all registered their protests against and rebuttals to such medical ideologies. Study would not destroy female health nor would birth control cause insanity, they said. Woman's sexual feelings were as strong as man's. Women could and should be strong.

At the Medical Women's International Conference in New York City in 1919, Dr. Clelia Mosher described her study of the differences in muscular strength in men and women. They were caused, not by gender, but by the difference in muscle use "brought about by conventional limitations of activity or dress." (She was referring to the corsets, heels and cumbersome skirts which kept women immobile.) Dr. Mosher came to a highly political conclusion: "A woman who has had a normal development should be able to do any work that a man of the same size and weight may profitably do."

In a much-applauded speech at the same conference, feminist Beatrice Hale, author of *What Women Want,* told the female doctors that the woman's movement must be based on physical strength and health. If it were not, she declared, no amount of higher education or economic independence would do any good.

All the emphasis had been laid on male physical development, she noted, "until the women doctors got busy."

Gynecology, a specialty almost exclusively composed of men, still has the power to define women. As two University of Illinois sociologists found in a 1972 review of current gynecology textbooks, men continue to define women as childbearers. The sociologists, Dr. Pauline Bart and Diana Scully, read twenty-seven textbooks, or 84 percent of those on the market.

"Women were cast in the traditional sex roles, i.e., ana-

* Both doctors are quoted in "Women Physicians," an unpublished, undated essay by C. B. Burr, M.D., marked Vol. II, Chapter VI of *Medical History of Michigan.* The essay is located in the Elizabeth Bass Collection, Tulane Medical School, New Orleans.

tomically destined for motherhood and fulfilled only by reproducing, mothering and attending their husbands," they wrote.
Doctors also expected women to be passive and subservient to
their mates.

While such assumptions are apt to be challenged now by
feminists and by enlightened physicians, the fact that men, as
gynecologists, are in a position to proclaim these sex stereotypes
at any time in the name of "medical science," is an ever-present
danger for women.

Some physicians, like their 19th-century counterparts, still
assert that menstruation, pregnancy and menopause disqualify
women from prestigious jobs, that marriage and childbearing
are "healthy" for women, and that failure to conform to the
stereotyped feminine role is disease-producing.

As late as 1970, one physician cited the female hormones as
a reason for neglecting women's rights. Dr. Edgar F. Berman, a
retired Baltimore physician and then a member of the Democratic Party's Committee on National Priorities, disagreed with
U. S. Rep. Patsy T. Mink's suggestion that the Party give special attention to the advancement of woman's equality. If you
had an investment in a bank, Dr. Berman asked, would you
want the bank president making a loan under the "raging hormonal influences" of her period? *

In an interview in January 1976, Dr. Berman, who is now a
medical writer, said he had been misquoted. He clarified his
position. During menstruation, he said, hormones influence
every cell in the woman's body and over one third of all women
are affected physically, emotionally and mentally by this. Half
of these women will have difficulty even after medication.

"Menstruation may very well affect the ability of these women

---

* Others have used Dr. Berman's argument. In 1923, the all-male medical subcommittee of the International Air Conference voted to prohibit women from
competing for an international pilot certificate because, it explained, a men-
struating woman should not be responsible for the lives of airplane passengers.
That ruling barred women from participating in commercial flights. Female
pilots appealed to the Medical Women's Federation of Great Britain for help.
As Dr. Isabel Hutton reported, the female doctors studied the matter and concluded that there was no reason whatever why women should not make efficient
pilots.
    While using hormonal changes to justify the exclusion of women from desira-
ble jobs, male physicians have ignored the monthly fluctuations in hormone
levels men experience. See "Men's Cycles (They Have Them Too, You Know),"
by Dr. Estelle Ramey, endocrinologist, in the Spring 1972 issue of *Ms.*

to hold certain jobs," he told me. "Take a woman surgeon. If she had premenstrual tension—and people with this frequently wind up in a psychiatrist's office—I wouldn't want her operating on me."

To other physicians, like Dr. J. P. Greenhill, author of the 1971 textbook *Office Gynecology*, painful menstruation often "reflects the unhealthy attitude toward femininity that is so predominant in our society." He added that many women are no longer willing to be regulated by femininity, marriage and motherhood.

"The woman who is at odds with her biologic self develops serious conflicts, and tensions, often leading to psychogynecic (psychosomatic and gynecologic) symptoms," Dr. Greenhill concluded.

In 1965, gynecologist Thomas H. Green asserted that marriage and childbearing could cure nonorganic dysmenorrhea (painful menstruation). That ailment was sometimes caused by "rejection and misunderstanding of the feminine role," he wrote in *Gynecology: Essentials of Clinical Practice*. What banished the dysmenorrhea was—not any physiologic change—but the maturity the woman displayed in establishing a normal relationship with a man.

Dr. Robert A. Wilson, a gynecologist and author of *Feminine Forever*, held similar views. To him, he wrote in 1966, a woman who had experienced several pregnancies "is basically healthier, more infection-resistant, and more feminine than her barren sisters . . . I seem to detect a certain look or attitude in some women that one might call 'the birth-control look.' Women who have plenty of sex but no children somehow strike me as vaguely tense and unfulfilled."

In like vein, Dr. Ralph C. Benson, author of the 1971 *Handbook of Obstetrics and Gynecology*, stated that "an emotionally healthy married woman will welcome pregnancy as a step toward maturity. The 'reasons' for not wanting a child usually betray an underlying ambivalence toward the feminine role. They may be expressions of unconscious anxiety, conflict or inadequacy."

Once pregnant, as some doctors have decreed she must be to maintain her physical and mental health, her condition is used against her. In 1970, for example, Dr. Edgar F. Berman, the

Baltimore medical writer, expressed doubt that a "slightly pregnant female pilot" could handle a difficult landing.

More importantly, credit discrimination, the educational channeling of women into dead-end jobs, and employment hiring and maternity-leave policies all rest on the assumption that women are wombs and when they are not pregnant, they will become so momentarily. By defining pregnancy as a unique disability, doctors have helped provide business with the rationale for depriving women of the opportunity to earn a living.

"Girls have been taught early that childbearing is a disqualification for many of the challenges of life," Trudy Hayden wrote in the American Civil Liberties Union 1973 report, *Punishing Pregnancy*. Taught that their options are limited, that they cannot bear children without also bearing the sole responsibility for raising them, girls do not prepare themselves for careers in science, business, law or medicine. Most females do end up working—many for twenty-five years or more—but, for lack of preparation, they work in low-wage, nonunionized jobs.

When women apply even for these jobs, employers often ask them whether they might become pregnant.

Most company insurance policies still pay little if any of the hospital or doctor bills for childbirths, though they will pay medical expenses for exclusively male disabilities. As late as June 1974, the Supreme Court, using the same male health standard doctors have established, ruled that states can deny disability benefits to women incapacitated by pregnancy. Justice William J. Brennan, Jr., however, noted in his dissent, that such benefits are awarded to those incapacitated by prostate trouble, circumcision, hemophilia and gout—all of which are largely or exclusively confined to men. While men receive full compensation for their disabilities, he observed, limitations are imposed on the disabilities for which women can collect.

Nineteenth-century gynecologists warned women that abortions caused insanity. Today's physicians have asserted that women who abort suffer long-term psychological harm. In 1970, the Johns Hopkins Hospital Center for Social Studies in Human Reproduction conducted a study which, by comparing women undergoing abortions and women bearing children, showed that abortions are no more traumatic than births. Investigators interviewed and tested women before their abortions or deliveries and again thirteen to sixteen months after the procedures. There were no differences between the two groups of women in measures of self-esteem or social integration.

Furthermore, in a 1970 issue of *Obstetrics and Gynecology*, a physician reviewed thirty-six studies of the psychiatric consequences of abortion and concluded that while it is reasonable to suspect that abortion would be a damaging episode in a woman's life, this has not been the case.*

The reported incidence of guilt in the studies varied from none at all to 30 percent. No severe cases were reported. As time passed after the abortion, the guilt decreased until by one year, almost none remained.

The studies showed that the physical set-up of the abortion facility and the attitude of the people caring for the woman were critical factors in the degree of guilt she felt. Emotions experienced in "a cold, frightening, across-the-tracks type of abortion," then, could be quite different from those felt in a clean, safe setting where the health personnel were supportive and nonpunitive.

Medical pronouncements on menopause are also as political now as they were a hundred years ago.

"Having outlived their ovaries, they [menopausal women] may have outlived their usefulness as human beings," wrote Dr. David Reuben, author of the widely read book, *Everything You Always Wanted to Know About Sex*.

Dr. Robert A. Wilson is hardly kinder in *Feminine Forever*, a book advocating estrogen replacement therapy for menopausal women. He refers to menopause as "death of womanhood," "a serious, painful and often crippling disease," and "castration." Professing to esteem women, he calls postmenstrual females "neuters" and "living decay."

Despite the fact that women respond to the change of life very differently, with many hardly reacting at all, doctors often assume that all menopausal women are subject to grave emotional disturbances. This provides a rationale, once again, for excluding women from desirable jobs.

* See Dr. George S. Walter's "Psychologic and Emotional Consequences of Elective Abortion," *Obstetrics and Gynecology*, September 1970, p. 482. Also see Jane Brody's "Mental Effects of Abortion Called Mild," *The New York Times*, Jan. 21, 1974.

The menopausal female executive, with her disoriented and capricious mind, has many opportunities to take out her frustrations on her subordinates, Dr. Wilson declared in 1966. This disturbs employee morale and "may also lead to serious errors of executive judgment." The question he then raises is a familiar one: Should women really be entrusted with decision-making jobs?

Dr. Edgar Berman, the former member of the Democratic Party's Committee on National Priorities, asked that question in 1970. Wouldn't it have been terrible, he wondered, if we had had a menopausal president who had to make the decision of the Bay of Pigs? (How could it have been handled less competently than it actually was?)

Some doctors then, still say that menstruation, pregnancy and menopause are disabilities prohibiting women from enjoying the same social and economic opportunities men do.

While 19th-century physicians asserted that healthy women did not have sexual feelings—only diseased women did—20th-century doctors have discovered equally self-serving medical facts. In their 1972 review of gynecological textbooks, Dr. Pauline Bart and Diana Scully of the University of Illinois found that modern physicians, too, are writing "from a male viewpoint." At least half the authors dealing with the topic stated that the male sex drive was stronger than the female's and that women were interested in sex more for procreation than pleasure. Despite the findings of sex researchers Alfred C. Kinsey and William Masters and Virginia Johnson, physicians also maintained that the vaginal orgasm—in contrast to the clitoral one—is the "mature" response.

Women, the textbooks asserted, were sexually passive: "An important feature of sex desire in the man is the urge to dominate the woman and subjugate her to his will; in the woman acquiescence to the masterful takes high place." *

The bias in textbooks also appears in medical books for laypersons. Dr. Wilson proclaimed in *Feminine Forever*, for example, that "female orgasm just isn't that important," an assertion any woman who has experienced one will deny.

* Bart and Scully are quoting from Thomas Jeffcoate's *Principles of Gynecology*, London: Butterworth, 1967, p. 726.

Though doctors used to castigate women for having erotic feelings, now they blame them for lacking those sensations. As Dr. David Reuben declared in *Any Woman Can!,* female O.I. (orgasmic impairment) is due to "underlying emotional obstacles."

Reuben's cure for frigid women happens, by the way, to provide a medically approved method for keeping women in their place. "The only way for a wife to find true sexual fulfillment in marriage," Reuben asserts, "is to make it her primary goal. She must be willing to cast aside everything else in life that might come between herself and her husband."

That "everything," of course, includes her work. She can have a career but must be ready to drop it if it interferes with the main purpose of her life: making her man happy. Reuben finds part-time jobs like typing, filing and practical nursing acceptable for wives. Yes, he agrees, they are dead-end jobs but "that's the idea."

Now, as before, doctors provide a medical rationale for bolstering marriage and the family. Dr. Reuben informs woman that the primary thrust of her being "is to be fertilized, to conceive and to reproduce." Marriage is the best arrangement, he declares; living together is but a pale imitation.

Since physicians set themselves up as authorities, we might well ask, "What do doctors know about sex anyway?"

In 1973, Dr. Robert J. Cross, a medical professor at Rutgers, said the average American regards his physician as an expert in sexuality while that physician knows nothing about it.

For a field study, Diana Scully, the University of Illinois sociologist, observed in two obstetrics and gynecology residency programs during 1974 and 1975. She found that the residents in these programs received no training at all in female sexuality.

"Out of approximately forty residents, only a very few had even read Masters and Johnson," she told me in a recent interview.

Chapter / SIX

TREATMENT OF
VENEREAL DISEASE

VENEREAL DISEASE WAS INTERFERING WITH THE EFFICIENCY OF England's soldiers. The Contagious Diseases Acts (CDA) of the 1860's, which required the forcible cleansing of women for soldiers' use, aimed to restore that efficiency. Under the Acts, prostitutes in nineteen English garrison towns were compelled to register, submit to periodic examination and, if found diseased, be confined up to nine months in a "lock hospital," so named because the first one had been founded on the site of a house for shackled lepers.

Only women—not men—were subject to examination and arrest because the Acts' aim was to protect male—not female—health. Physician William Acton said so outright when, in 1869, he advocated the extension of the CDA to women in civilian towns "so as to protect our adult male population from the effects of syphilis."

Once again, this time in the treatment of venereal disease, physicians used a medical theory to control, not heal, women.

To male doctors, women did not themselves suffer from VD—they merely infected men with it. Women were "hosts," "dis-

104

ease distributors," walking germs who had to be controlled. Doctors disregarded evidence that the majority of women attending venereal clinics were wives who had been infected by their husbands. They ignored the miscarriages, stillbirths, sores, pains, paralysis and blindness from which venereal women suffered. They closed their eyes to the rich, promiscuous men spreading VD among mateless lower-class women who had been forced to take one of the few adequately paying jobs available: whoring. To doctors, VD victimized only men.

Though Acton noted an enormous increase in female sickness following the revolution of 1848, he never seemed to see the waste products of war—rape by soldiers, prostitution *for* them, and epidemics among refugees—as threats to female health.

It was the International Conference of Women Physicians, 1919, New York City. Dr. C. C. Pierce, director of the U.S. Public Health Service Division of VD, was patiently educating the female doctors on venereal disease control.

"Now," he was saying, "the difficulty of eliminating prostitution as compared with the elimination of the mosquito which spreads yellow fever, is that we are dealing with a human host in one case and an insect host in the other. The insect host can be destroyed, killed, and we are through, but we cannot destroy these poor misguided women who are now practicing prostitution."

His solution to venereal disease control, like that of his European colleagues, was "permanent custodial care" for prostitutes. We should "take care of them," he told the doctors solicitously, "because about 75 percent of them are feebleminded and should be in institutions."

Social worker Edith Hooker took the podium and refuted Dr. Pierce's arguments in a speech frequently interrupted by applause from the female physicians.

"It is a curious coincidence," she said, "that synchronously with the advent of women in medicine, reason instead of prejudice began to govern the treatment of venereal disease and the inclination on the part of the profession to excuse masculine promiscuity on the pleas of sexual necessity began to disappear."

Speaking of prostitutes not, in Dr. Pierce's words, as "foci from which venereal disease spreads," but as "women that are bought by men," she made this observation: Public health programs, with their compulsory physical examination of prostitutes, seemed most concerned with protecting the health of the prostitutes' male patrons.

Picking up a Baltimore newspaper, she read the headline announcing the arrest of one woman then being held at a government clinic: "COIFFURE FURNISHES CLUE: THE WAY LILLIAN'S HAIR DRESSED AROUSES PATROLMAN'S SUSPICIONS."

"It goes on to say," Edith Hooker continued, "that Lillian Simon was seen by the police upon the street and she was forthwith arrested, taken to the station house and presented at Mercy Hospital for examination. I looked into the case and found that the girl had been committed for three months to the House of Correction on the single say-so of one policeman. This is perhaps not a very safe thing, to give all the women of a community over for compulsory physical examination on the single word of one policeman."

Imprisoning prostitutes would never stop VD, she added, because, "The demand for prostitution is what causes the consequent infection."

A roar of applause halted her.

"If we annihilated these women as they did the mosquitoes," she declared, "if we hung by the neck until she were dead every prostitute in the world today, within a week we would have a new crop . . . If [men] want a thousand prostitutes and can pay for them, they will get them.

"Although we have had for a century the lock-hospital treatment of women and although we have found it has not done a particle of good, still we have at this moment included in he programs of all the thinking men of America the lock hospital and I think, until medical women rise up and demand that this particular measure should be given over, we shall continue to have this measure in operation.

"We do not wish to have forever a double standard of morality; we wish to have a single standard."

The entire culture held a double standard which viewed

promiscuous sex as roguish and natural in men but contemptible in women. When men from that patriarchal culture became physicians, they had the power to shape VD control
programs, a power that placed women at risk.

For centuries, doctors did not even acknowledge that women
suffered from VD. They believed that women with inflamed
pelvises merely had inflamed uteri. But in 1857 two doctors
performed autopsies and proved that the inflammation arose in
the fallopian tubes or ovaries and then spread. In many of the
women, pelvic inflammation seemed to be directly caused by
gonorrhea.

The information caused no stir in medical circles. "It was
realized that gonorrhea might affect women but it was not
regarded as important," one historian commented.*

At the American Gynecological Society's first meeting in
1870, Dr. Emil Noeggerath offended his colleagues by asserting
that 90 percent of sterile women were married to husbands
who were or had been venereal. The doctors were enraged at
his assertion that vaginal inflammation in women was caused
by their husband's gonorrhea. These doctors were accustomed
to viewing VD as something women gave to men, not vice
versa.

In a paper published two years later, Noeggerath concluded
that latent gonorrhea in husbands partially explained "the
prevalence of uterine diseases in large cities, and their increase
during the last twenty-five years."

Gonorrhea, which inconveniences men, maims women.

About 95 percent of men get gonorrhea symptoms promptly,
go for a reliable test, and then take a cure.†

Women often either get no symptoms at all, or symptoms
which both they and their doctors fail to recognize as gonor-

* Dr. Harvey Graham, author of *Eternal Eve, The History of Obstetrics and
Gynecology*. (Harvey Graham is a pseudonym for Isaac Flack.)

† For many years it had been assumed that all men get gonorrhea symptoms.
A study by Dr. King K. Holmes and colleagues between 1971 and 1973 proved
that assumption false. The physicians examined 2,628 sexually active soldiers at
Madigan Army Medical Center in Tacoma, Washington and found that 2.2 percent of them had gonorrhea. Dr. Ralph H. Henderson of the Center for Disease
Control explained to me that while most men do get symptoms, the number of
men with symptomless gonorrhea is growing because they tend not to go for
treatment. Women can no longer assume that a man without symptoms is free
of VD.

rheal. Physicians at the U. S. Center for Disease Control in Atlanta estimate that about 60 percent of female gonorrhea victims are asymptomatic. Dr. King K. Holmes, a VD researcher at the U. S. Public Health Service Hospital in Seattle, points out, however, that no reliable data on this issue exists. He believes, but can not yet prove, that women usually do get symptoms but because they are less specific than men's, they are probably more often ignored or misdiagnosed. Both women and their doctors, he explained to me in a letter, need to be educated to suspect gonorrhea promptly when women experience abdominal pain, pain in urinating, a discharge and menstrual abnormalities.

As it stands now, chances of a woman's gonorrhea being detected in a routine medical examination are almost nil because even though VD is epidemic, most doctors do not test for it routinely. Nationally, an estimated 700,000 women contract the disease each year and many probably are not aware of it. Even if, without warning signs, women ask for a gonorrhea test, the commonly used Gram stain test, which is 99 percent accurate for men, is highly unreliable for women.

"It misses half the cases," Dr. Michael Rein of the Center for Disease Control says, noting that it is used more than it should be for women.

The test involves staining a sample of cervical discharge and examining it under a microscope. A culture test, which is much more (though not completely) reliable, is a time-consuming, expensive procedure. It involves allowing a discharge sample to grow on a plate for several days to see if any gonococcus germs multiply.

Women whose gonorrhea goes undetected are likely to suffer from Pelvic Inflammatory Disease (PID). A 1972 study of gonorrhea complications in Memphis, Tennessee, indicates that an estimated 213,000 PID cases occur each year in the United States. PID can cause agonizing pain, lead to sterility, require surgical intervention and irreparably injure the fallopian tubes, ovaries and other pelvic organs. Chronic gonorrhea infection may result in urinary obstruction, arthritis, inflammation of the heart's lining and increased susceptibility to cervical cancer. It may also lead to ectopic pregnancy, a life-threatening situation in which a fertilized egg is trapped and grows in a misshapen fallopian tube.

Despite gonorrhea's threat to women, medical schools have decreased their already inadequate teaching of venereology, a 1965 survey found.

If gonorrhea is, as Dr. Michael Rein calls it, "a major health problem for women," and if gonorrhea is, as federal health officials declare, out of control, and if gonorrhea is, as venereologists explain, so hard to detect and, therefore, to cure in females, and if gonorrhea accounts for, as is estimated, the hospitalization of 3,200 female patients each day and 122,000 operations on women each year, then obviously physicians ought to be emphasizing VD prevention.

But to emphasize prevention is to accept nonmarital sex and to thwart punishment for it. People must fear VD so they will have only authorized sex. In the physician's value system, as in society's, chastity outranks health.

An article on the *American Medical News* editorial page in 1974 demonstrated that. It lauded a Bureau of Epidemiology report for commenting that control of VD requires the end of promiscuity. It praised the government for recognizing "that there is a moral problem here and that venereal disease cannot be brought under control by procain penicillin alone."

In view of that attitude, the AMA's 1974 policy on VD comes as no surprise. After acknowledging "the epidemic proportions of gonorrhea and the need for all practical and legal methods of prevention and spread of this most common reportable communicable disease," the AMA recommended:

1. "Fidelity and continence in married couples."
2. "Abstinence by unmarried individuals."

Its third recommendation is sensible: The display and sale of condoms where legal. But if the powerful AMA is sincere in this, why doesn't it publicize its advice and lobby for the repeal of any laws restricting the sale of condoms?

Historically, when physicians have advocated prevention of VD, they have instituted programs for men. In 1919, a group of eminent English doctors founded the Society for the Prevention of Venereal Disease through which they instructed all men on the use of disinfectants, but only the women who specifically asked.

Women objected. The Society condoned promiscuous sex for men by teaching them how to indulge in it safely but left women's safety dependent on the good will of men. It denied women control of their own bodies.

In a Society-approved pamphlet, a writer identified only as "A Woman," justified the policy: "A measure of reticence which is absurd for men is still desirable for women, a reticence which would be outraged by, for instance, posters set out in public lavatories."

As Ettie Rant, a Red Cross worker who had specialized in VD control during World War I, pointed out in a 1925 pamphlet, "Civilians refuse to prevent, cure or control disease among women." They refused even though VD's damage was much more severe in females than in males, she wrote.

Five years later, Dr. Evan Thomas, head of the Bellevue VD clinic in New York City, discovered a prophylactic property in a certain contraceptive jelly for women and eagerly informed its manufacturer. Here was a way to protect the health of millions of women. But here also was a way to help make women as sexually free as men.

The manufacturer did nothing.

At about the same time, a patent-medicine developer in Tulsa, Oklahoma invented Progonosyl, a VD prophylaxis for the vagina.* He gave it to four local doctors who performed some very limited tests on it with prostitutes and reportedly found the preparation effective. Certainly when the physicians announced their findings in 1938, researchers should have been given impetus to undertake a carefully controlled, ethical, long-term study.

The medical community did nothing.

The role of prophylaxis in VD control, researcher Dr. John C. Cutler noted in 1974, has been "dramatically demonstrated in two world wars . . . It is of interest, though, to note that these efforts were directed toward the males." †

* Frank Bickenheuser, Jr.

† Dr. Cutler made this statement in a paper entitled "Advantages and Disadvantages of Vaginal Prophylaxis Using Preparations Which Are Simultaneously Contraceptive." The paper was delivered before the First International Conference on Methods of VD Prevention, held in Chicago.

In the 1940s, while most researchers at the VD Research Laboratory of the U. S. Public Health Service were investigating ways to protect men from VD, Dr. Cutler and Dr. R. C. Arnold developed a prophylactic douche preparation for women. It was tested in 1948 and found to be highly effective. Work on the douche was not pursued because after the war, when penicillin had largely cancelled VD's threat to men (though not to women) and the health of soldiers was no longer such a concern, the government stopped financing VD prophylactic research.

Cutler and Arnold left their research.

VD multiplied.

The douche stayed on the shelf.

So did Progonosyl.

Finally, in 1971, about forty years after its development, Progonosyl was studied.

Dr. William M. Edwards, Jr., chief of Nevada's Bureau of Preventative Medicine, tested it on prostitutes in Nevada brothels. It was, as Edwards acknowledges, "far from a controlled study."

The prostitute turnover was enormous. (A third of the women in the study were only in the brothel one week.) Some physicians insisted on using the unreliable Gram stain test. The prostitutes were not all examined regularly. Researchers collected no data on other drugs and prophylactic measures the women might have been taking.

The one thing that was clear from Edwards' study was the women's dislike of the drug.

"It smells and tastes bad and dried them out. Of course, they each averaged at least five sexual contacts a day. I should think the work itself might dry them out," Dr. Edwards laughed. "The rejection rate was 15 percent and it was apparent after six weeks that it was going to go higher so we stopped the test.

"We found that Progonosyl is not the answer," he said. "We need a better product."

But the answers are not all in on Progonosyl. The women who need a prophylactic are not prostitutes so much as women who would use it just for casual sexual encounters. If Progonosyl were used only occasionally, would it have the same adverse effects it has when used five or more times each day?

Edwards' study did not answer that question because he was thinking only of prostitutes as potential users.

"Progonosyl is not for the high school girl and the housewife," he said. "It's for the really sexually active girl. For the professional."

Yet schoolgirls and housewives have a higher rate of VD than brothel prostitutes. The prostitutes examine their customers carefully and refuse to sleep with suspected VD carriers.

Edwards himself acknowledged that the VD rate for women aged fifteen to thirty-five in Nevada's general population is 4.9 percent, more than double the 1.8 percent VD rate in brothels. He also noted that no cases of syphilis had been found in the brothels in all of 1970 and 1971.

Why then use prostitutes for the Progonosyl study?

"Control," Dr. Edwards replied.

It is true that women in brothels can be used like animals in cages. They are always on hand for examinations. You do not have to worry about their returning for cultures. They are required by the state, as Edwards pointed out, to have a culture once a week.

While doctors have undertaken few controlled studies of any VD prophylactics, the studies they have done have usually used prostitutes—vulnerable women who can be required to do certain things in order to keep their jobs in a brothel. In Guatemala, in Japan, in Taipei, prostitutes were the "volunteers."

By 1973, several VD experts were making the same accusation Red Cross worker Ettie Rant had made in 1925: Doctors were refusing their patients prophylactic information.

While venereal disease germs still localized on surfaces are fragile and easily killed, even by soap and water, few doctors were willing to explain this to patients so they could protect themselves from VD, according to Edward M. Brecher, author of *An Analysis of Human Sex Responses* and a *Viva* article entitled "Women—Victims of the VD Rip-Off."

To escape VD, women could use the vaginal contraceptive foams and jellies and avoid the Pill which, by increasing the alkalinity of the vaginal tract, tends to make women more susceptible to venereal disease. They could learn a method prostitutes use for inspecting a man for VD before sleeping with him. They could insist the man use a condom. They could douche with an antiseptic after sex or wash themselves in an improvised bidet. These methods, though not perfect, are highly effective.

Prevention of VD seems to be just as possible as prevention of pregnancy. In a population with a thousand cases of gonorrhea, if prophylactic procedures only half effective were used just 30 percent of the time, there would be fewer than ten cases in five years. However, if no procedures were employed, the case load would jump to 1,860 in that same period.*

Yet, in a 1973 study for the U. S. Department of Health, Education and Welfare, Koba Associates, a private organization that undertakes socioeconomic research, found that half the patients interviewed at twenty-one VD treatment facilities received no VD information material while in the facilities. Despite the fact that over 50 percent were visiting the clinic for the second or subsequent time, they were not counseled on prophylaxis.

Government and medical authorities continue to recommend a curative, not preventative, method of handling VD. That recommendation, Edward Brecher observed, places generally less symptomatic women at much greater risk than men.

The notion that the venereally exposed person deserves punishment (rather than protection) still seems to live in the medical profession.

Some doctors ridicule or intentionally hurt venereal patients, Dr. Donna Cherniak and Allan Feingold maintain in "VD Handbook": "We have seen patients come once to a clinic and, embarrassed, hurt and insulted, they never return."

Unnecessarily long waits—sometimes for more than four hours —and violations of patient privacy and dignity also discourage people from ever returning to VD clinics, Koba researchers found. At VD clinics, patients told the researchers they resented being asked personal questions in earshot of other patients, being examined in front of medical students, and being exposed while staff members left examining room doors open.

---

* John C. Cutler, M.D., "Advantages and Disadvantages of Vaginal Prophylaxis Using Preparations Which Are Simultaneously Contraceptives," a paper read at the VD conference in Chicago sponsored by The Midwest Association for the Study of Human Sexuality, Nov. 16–17, 1974. Dr. Cutler was quoting a projection by T. Y. Lee, et al.

If not in clinics, then at least in laboratories, some progress is finally being made in shielding women from VD. Dr. John C. Cutler and Dr. R. C. Arnold, in a return to VD research, are testing existing contraceptives for their prophylactic value. Some foams and jellies, they have found, do exhibit an anti-microbic property, probably because of the spermicides they contain. A woman's protection from disease is now dependent on the "permissiveness" of her doctor but now these scientists hope to come up with a prophylactic women could get without a prescription, perhaps from a vending machine.

(The studies do not excite the medical profession. Generally, medical schools, medical journals and medical meetings avoid discussing research on prophylactics, Dr. Lonny Myers, a clinician and vice-president of the Midwest Association for the Study of Human Sexuality, told me.)

Other research indicates that while we may finally be close to a blood test for gonorrhea, we are still a long way from a VD vaccine. As the National Institutes of Health (NIH) noted in 1973, "One reason there is no vaccine or preventive medication is that, with the discovery of penicillin, research efforts virtually ceased."

Penicillin may have handled the male VD problem in which diagnosis is relatively simple, but certainly not the female one. The cure may be available but that is no help to the thousands of women who do not know they have the disease. They need a good screening test.

But are we allotting enough money for blood test and vaccine research? In fiscal year 1973, a mere $3.2 million was spent on VD research at the Center for Disease Control (CDC) and through federal grants to other researchers. Clearly, the American Social Health Association observes, research efforts on venereal disease are inadequate.

Could it be that men do not view gonorrhea as a serious health problem because they are not as seriously affected by it as women are?

"That could easily be the case," Dr. Ralph H. Henderson of the CDC replies. "A common idea among men is that gonorrhea is no more serious than the common cold. We don't think the male gets as many complications from it. But gonorrhea is a real hazard to the woman."

(Gonorrhea is more hazardous to women because it is more difficult to detect in them.)

Despite the fact that it does not work, the national strategy for controlling gonorrhea has almost always been the tracing of sexual contacts. It is ineffective because people resist such a "kiss and tell" method. As Koba Associates concluded, the high rate of asymptomatic patients, the failure of physicians to report VD cases and the staggering number of investigators needed to locate contacts, also make the practice futile.

Every VD control officer Koba researchers interviewed during their survey felt that even with the necessary number of investigators, gonorrhea, by its very nature, could not be controlled through contact tracing. Gonorrhea's incubation rate is too rapid and its incidence too high, to be controlled in such a way.

So Koba advocates shifting the responsibility from public health authorities to the gonorrhea patients. The patients must be persuaded of their moral responsibility to find and inform their own contacts. (Koba found that personnel at half the treatment facilities studied did not even bother to tell gonorrhea patients that they should inform contacts of their exposure to disease.)

Here, in brief, is the new gonorrhea-control strategy Koba proposes:

The doctor or paramedic asks the gonorrhea patients how many contacts they have had and explains how vital it is that they inform those contacts of their exposure to VD.

Then the medic gives them Gonorrhea Patient Information packets for themselves and an appropriate number of Gonorrhea Contact Information Kits. The patients give one kit to each contact.

The contacts read about the implications of their exposure to gonorrhea and about the procedures for getting a cure. To guard against an allergic reaction to the standard treatment, they then call a special public health department number and answer a health officer's questions about their medical histories.

The officer gives the contacts authorization numbers which are coded prescriptions for the druggist. The contacts take the numbers to a distribution center and pick up their treatment, along with information on follow-up.

This strategy eliminates the need for contact tracing by armies of epidemiologists and provides for the prompt treatment of massive numbers of gonorrhea contacts.

With this strategy, Koba challenges the assumption that gonorrhea contacts must be treated by medical personnel at medical facilities. There is a safe, effective, orally administered treatment for the disease—ampicillin with probenecid—and there is no need for contacts to go to a doctor's office to get it.

While we do need to develop diagnostic techniques and vaccines, Koba Associates observes, "the technology for controlling syphilis and gonorrhea is at our disposal today." All that is needed is an effective delivery system for that technology.

The delivery system Koba proposes is sensible. Physicians will probably resist it just as they resisted free immunization programs. They will oppose it because:

1. The strategy reduces the physician's status from that of an indispensable god-healer to that of a technician.

2. This preventive health program will threaten the fee-for-service system. Each person must be compelled to wait until illness strikes and then go to the doctor's office and pay his or her money.

So this is how physicians have handled the VD health menace: In earlier centuries, they inspected lower-class women and imprisoned the diseased ones. Later, they half-heartedly tried to trace and treat infected people.

In neither control program did physicians attempt to teach women VD prophylaxis. During both programs, they have shown indifference to the effects of these diseases on women.

Insisting that sex and procreation be linked, physicians helped create a situation in which people who made love for pleasure risked punitive treatments or even death.

Perhaps that moral view explains:

—The physician's failure to discuss VD prevention at medical meetings and failure to insist that medical schools teach venereology well.

—Why doctors, who see the excruciating suffering gonorrhea causes women through Pelvic Inflammatory Disease have not been clamoring for the development of a vaccine or a cheap, accurate diagnostic test for women.

—Why physicians have not told patients that foams and jellies may protect them from VD as well as from pregnancy.

—Why doctors have remained indifferent to studies showing a striking association between exposure to gonorrhea and death due to cervical cancer.

—Why doctors have not passed out VD handbooks to their patients, along with their pamphlets on the dangers of socialized medicine.

—Why a doctor who treats a lot of VD becomes known to his colleagues as The King of Whores.

Of course male physicians are merely holding the values of the male-dominated society in which they live. That is why it is important that they not be the *only* physicians. If women had fully shared the power in medicine (rather than taking the few token posts offered them and becoming "honorary white males" in the medical fraternity), it seems unlikely that they would have blamed females for VD and ignored the suffering it inflicted on them. The passionate denouncements of antifemale VD control programs delivered at the 1919 International Conference of Women Physicians support that belief.

Chapter / SEVEN

HISTORY OF
THE BIRTH-CONTROL MOVEMENT

JACK SACKS RETURNED FROM HIS JOB HUNT TO FIND HIS WIFE Sadie lying hemorrhaging on the floor. She had stuck a sharp instrument inside herself to prevent the birth of yet another child they could not feed.

Jack called a doctor. The nurse who also came, Margaret Sanger, stayed three weeks. Though death was likely, twenty-eight-year-old Sadie did recover. But she was still despondent.

"Another baby will finish me, I suppose," she told Margaret, begging her for The Secret. But Sanger knew nothing of contraception.

When the doctor appeared for the final checkup, Sanger told him Mrs. Sacks was worried about having another baby.

"She might well be," the doctor responded. "Any more such capers, young woman, and there will be no need to call me."

"Yes, yes—I know, Doctor," Sadie said. "But *what* can I do to prevent getting that way again?"

"Oh, ho!" the doctor laughed. "You want your cake while you eat it too, do you? Well, it can't be done." Slapping her on the back, he added, "I'll tell you the only sure thing to do. Tell Jack to sleep on the roof!"

He left.

Three months later, Sanger was called back to Mrs. Sacks's house. It was too late. She had died of another abortion.

The year was 1912. It marked the beginning of Margaret Sanger's campaign for birth control. Women needed an activist like Sanger to bring contraception to them because physicians were making no effort to do it. To physicians, the prevention of pregnancy was as unacceptable as the prevention of VD.

But Sanger could not be so indifferent to the suffering uncontrolled childbearing caused. As a nurse, tenement misery distressed her: She saw unwanted children beaten. She saw fathers frantic as child after child was conceived and mothers thankful when a baby was born dead. Women could prevent births only through abortions and if they could not find a quack doctor to do it, they tried to abort themselves.

"I saw these women taken off to hospitals, many of them never to come back," Sanger recalled.

In 1912, the year Mrs. Sacks died, 250,000 other women also died, all from causes related to pregnancy. An estimated two million illegal abortions were performed that year.

Before abortions became prevalent, women whose fertility had driven them to despair used the earliest birth-control method: infanticide. Kinder early techniques were douching, withdrawal, intravaginal sponges, and late marriages. In the 1800s, rubber condoms and the diaphragm made their debuts.

The first half of the 19th century witnessed the publication of several essays advocating contraception—not for relief of individual misery or woman's rule of her body—but largely for population control.

Until 1873, the United States had allowed birth control. Then Anthony Comstock, president of the New York Society for the Suppression of Vice, engineered passage of a law forbidding the transport of contraceptive information and techniques through the U. S. mails. Margaret Sanger told her followers that Comstock frightened the congressmen in Washington, "sort of intimated that they were all immoral and they wouldn't dare oppose him."

Sanger's effort to thwart the Comstock Laws began after she

witnessed the death of Sadie Sacks. Deciding that she would no longer soothe wounds but would, instead, eradicate the cause of them, she studied "birth control"—a term she coined—in Europe.

Back home in 1914, Sanger published a magazine, *The Woman Rebel*. Because of their articles on contraception, several issues were declared unmailable. Sanger was indicted. When the judge denied her request for a month's trial delay so she could prepare her defense, she decided to take a year. Dramatically, she left for Europe. While she gathered more information on birth control, her case was dismissed.

During Sanger's exile in 1915, a group of largely upper-middle-class women formed the National Birth Control League to change laws prohibiting contraception. Sanger later joined the group. In 1921, when it became the American Birth Control League, she was installed as its president, a position she held until 1928. (She resigned then to devote more energy to the Clinical Research Bureau, an organization she founded in 1923 for the study of contraceptives.) During the 1920s, the League boasted 37,000 members.

Sanger gathered public support for birth control and sympathy for herself by delivering frequent and forceful speeches around the country (organizing as she toured), and by occasionally being locked out of meeting halls and being sent to jail.

One of her eight arrests came in 1916 when, after her return from Europe, she and her sister Ethel Byrne opened the first American birth-control clinic in Brooklyn. In the first few days, five hundred mothers with babies in their arms attended it.

Nine days after its opening, the police raided the clinic and closed it as "a public nuisance."

They arrested Margaret Sanger. As she sat in the patrol wagon, she heard a scream and then saw a woman who had just rounded the corner with her baby carriage, preparing to enter the clinic. When the woman saw what had happened, she left the carriage on the sidewalk and, wild-eyed, rushed through the crowd to the wagon crying to Sanger, "Come back! Come back and save me!" As the wagon moved, the woman ran after it until other women stopped her, catching her weeping body in their arms.

Sanger knew why women wept. She received 1,200 letters a week from them, pleading for her help.

In letter after letter, young women said they felt old and would rather die than go through another pregnancy and care for yet another child. Many described their trapped feeling: "I am a mother of six children all under eight years old," one wrote. "I am almost a nervous wreck being confined so close. I am almost a prisoner."

Women described the childbed fevers they had endured, the lacerations, the paralyzed arms, kidney trouble, the afterbirths grown to the uterus, the abortions, the repeated stillbirths, the sickly children. Yet, after all that, they would write that they were pregnant again.

Some women described what Sanger called "slave maternity." A young woman with ten children wrote that doctors had told her

> that I was good for five or six more babies if I could live through it . . . My husband always told me it was a sin to do anything to keep from having children but I know better . . . I get desperate sometimes and feel like killing myself to get out of my troubles, then I am ashamed of my weakness and determined to stay and care for the little helpless things I've brought into the world, but many the times I've got desperate and almost crazy.

A feminist, Sanger believed that women had the right to control their own bodies and live lives that served their own purposes, not just the purposes of men. Childbearing and rearing were *not* the end and aim of woman's existence, she declared in a 1933 speech.

For women, Sanger knew, birth control meant no less than freedom. That was why so many men, whether physicians or laypersons, opposed it so strenuously. Contraception undermined male supremacy because it made female independence possible. Liberating her from constant pregnancy, contraception lets woman work outside the home and so, frees her from economic dependence on man. With birth control, woman was no longer obliged to be an instrument of pleasure, a breeding machine, a nursemaid, Sanger declared. She could be a person.

"Behind the objections to birth control in nearly every country," Sanger wrote after a tour abroad, "is the fact that it is going to give woman more power, greater freedom, and a greater chance to develop her personality; and from this growth her economic dependence on man, and on the male members of her family clan, will be lessened."

Contraception also thwarts state plans for population growth. In power politics, the leader with the larger, stronger population has the better hand. Women are needed to produce settlers, laborers and, quite importantly, soldiers. During World War II, European governments passed laws restricting access to birth control and abortion so that their armies could realize their manpower needs. When the United States entered the war in 1941, it too made contraception available according to the state's needs. In this case, the government did not need more children produced; it needed women working in munitions factories.

As the Industrial Hygiene Division of the U. S. Public Health Service pointed out in 1942, pregnancy interfered with the efficiency of female workers. Their absenteeism increased.

Moreover, if soldiers were continually worried about their pregnant wives, and if female munitions workers were constantly fearing pregnancy, they would never be efficient warriors or weapons-makers, one Planned Parenthood official argued in 1943 in an unsigned paper. He concluded—as did Dr. Richard N. Pierson and D. Kenneth Rose, both past presidents of Planned Parenthood—that birth control "should be an essential part of the war health program."

Most male doctors greeted the birth-control movement with aloofness, indifference or cynicism while others expressed outright opposition.* Contraception would lead to immorality,

---

* When contraception was illegal, no one polled male and female physicians to compare their attitudes toward it. But one is struck, in reading the history of the birth-control movement and the proceedings of medical women's conferences, by the many women who supported contraception.

The very first female doctor in Holland, Aletta Jacobs, immediately learned that women suffered enormously from too many and too frequent pregnancies. So she investigated contraceptives, helped develop the diaphragm and, in 1878, opened the world's first birth-control clinic in Amsterdam.

Her male colleagues actively opposed her. Some physicians, she recalled, charged her with causing pelvic diseases by giving women diaphragms.

The 1919 International Conference of Women Physicians—the first medical conference to consider contraception a fit subject for discussion—expressed concern, as Jacobs had, for "slave maternity." Later, in 1934, the Medical Woman's International Association discussed birth control at its meeting in Stockholm but

they warned. It would physically injure its users, they claimed, growing vague when asked for specifics.

During the century's infancy, doctors had been legally allowed to give contraceptive advice for "disease prevention," a category they interpreted as including only venereal disease. But, on an appeal of the Sanger clinic case, the U. S. Supreme Court in 1918 extended the definition of "disease" to give doctors more latitude in dispensing contraceptives.

Some doctors did give contraceptives to "deserving" women —sickly mothers with large families. But it was the doctors who made the decision; women were not given contraceptives merely because they wanted them. (These doctors may well have agreed with the New York County Medical Society which, in 1916, took the first formal action on birth control of any American medical group. The Society feared, it stated, that birth control, "indiscriminately employed," would undermine personal morality and national strength.)

Despite the fact that 22,000 mothers were dying each year from causes incidental to pregnancy, many other less liberal doctors, who were now legally allowed to prevent those deaths, chose not to do so. Placing "morality and national strength" above female lives, they sent the women back to their homes without any assistance.

Since physicians were not dealing with the need for contraception, two lay groups, the American Birth Control League and Sanger's Clinical Research Bureau, filled the void. They published the *Journal of Contraception* to give information on the latest research. They conducted a number of pioneer studies on various contraceptives. They trained medical students in birth control and drew up proposed syllabi for such instruction in medical schools. (Before 1937, few medical schools mentioned contraception. Shortly afterward, some schools taught it but devoted only six hours' instruction to the subject.)

---

found it so controversial a subject that it dared not pass a declaration stating that it had talked about the matter.

Several female doctors there assumed that they, not their patients, had a right to decide who could use contraceptives. But most of the women supported birth control. Physicians from Denmark, Finland, Holland, Norway and Sweden recommended the establishment of birth-control clinics and said that, so rich and poor alike could have access to contraception, no laws should prohibit it.

After the court order, which essentially freed doctors to dispense contraceptives, Sanger had to wait almost five years, from 1918 to 1923, before she could find a physician who would help her reestablish a birth-control clinic. Her difficulty is understandable when one realizes that in 1925 an Illinois medical society resolved that "affiliation in practice with (Sanger's American Birth Control League) does constitute an unethical association and is unprofessional conduct."

That same year, the official representative of the New York State Medical Society opposed a law to grant married people contraceptives on demand.

A police raid of Sanger's research bureau and confiscation of its records in 1929 finally brought some support from doctors; they protested the commandeering of records as an invasion of medical privacy. But then in 1931, American Medical Association President William G. Morgan spoke against birth control.

For control over their own bodies, women owe doctors little thanks. The medical profession never fought for birth control (though it had seen the misery its absence caused) and only accepted it when it became legally available and doctors feared that if they did not assert a medical claim over it, lay groups would control it.

In 1932, Dr. George Kamperman, author of an article on the birth-control movement which appeared in the *Journal of the Michigan State Medical Society,* wrote that despite physician indifference to all contraceptive proposals, birth-control propaganda had been spread far and wide by Margaret Sanger and was here to stay.

"There is still room for medical men to exert their influence and assert their leadership," he told his colleagues.

By the next year, Norman Hines, a layman who had supported birth control when physicians opposed it, found himself apologizing to doctors for his intrusion into medicine. He told the Boston Medical History Club, "I come before you with some timidity as a layman. Let me assure you at once that my investigation of the history of contraception has proceeded from no desire to usurp a medical function . . . The lack of interest on the part of medical historians was the first inducement."

His timidity was unwarranted.

(His timidity would still have been unwarranted in 1970 when the AMA finally approved elective abortions and when the American College of Obstetricians and Gynecologists mentioned birth control in its service guidelines for the first time.)

The Comstock Laws against contraceptives came tumbling down in 1936 when an appellate court, in a case involving Sanger's colleague, Dr. Hannah Stone, ruled that such devices could be advertised and transported through the mails. This meant that people could now obtain nonprescription contraceptives. Since doctors knew little about contraceptives, profiteers filled the vacuum by selling devices. Few were effective. Some were injurious. They sold quickly.

Its hand forced, the AMA cautiously recognized birth control as a part of medicine in 1937 and appointed a committee to study contraceptive methods. In the preceding several years, all reports on the subject had died in committee.

Part of physician opposition to birth control may have been economically motivated. Dr. Aletta Jacobs, the Dutch birth-control pioneer who helped develop the diaphragm, observed in the late 19th century that many doctors "are really inspired by the selfish fear that Birth Control may decrease the number of their patients."

One pregnant woman who, due to difficult deliveries, was almost paralyzed from the waist down, wrote Sanger that in denying her contraceptives, her doctor had said if he saved the ladies from such illness, doctors would have nothing to do.

Sanger suspected that another reason doctors denied women birth control information was that they did not have it but were afraid to admit it for fear of puncturing the physician mystique.

"He has feared to destroy the faith placed in him by his patients," Sanger wrote, ". . . in brief, he has been afraid to admit his ignorance."

Physician attitudes toward birth control are amply documented by the letters women sent Sanger. A pregnant woman with heart disease wrote:

> I dragged myself to my doctor's office and asked, and with tears begged him to help me, that if I pulled through with this one now couldn't he help me so it would be my last one. He got so

angry at me, his eyes looked so terrible fierce, I got so scared, I don't know to this day how in the world I got home, but I cried for two days over the many shameful names he called me. He said he would give me a good licking til I was black and blue if I ever dared myself to ask him such questions again. I thought I would go mad. I just cried.

As Sanger declared in a 1930 speech, "It is the stubborn opposition of medical superstitions which hold progress back. It is the opponents of this humane cause who have increased human misery and at whose doors deaths of women in child-bearing and abortions should be laid."

When Margaret Sanger began struggling for birth control, some male doctors did support her. A few did so on the grounds that a woman had a right to control her own person. In Chicago in 1929, for example, eighteen doctors declared: "We, as men, believe that if we had to undergo sickness, disfigurement, limitation of activities, discomfort, pain, danger and sometimes death for the birth of a child, we would insist that it was our absolute right to choose our own time for the process."

But most male support for the birth-control movement rested on a new "science": Eugenics, the improvement of a race through control of breeding. In this science lie some roots of the modern population-control movement. By examining eugenics, we can see that the physician's motive in advocating certain practices may not be the well-being of his individual patient, as many of us have supposed, but social control. (Later, this realization will give us some insight into the tolerant attitude of many physicians toward the dangers of the Pill, and the recent insistence of certain doctors that they sterilize welfare mothers before delivering their babies.)

How does the physician want society controlled? That, of course, is influenced by his own position in the society. In the United States today, his position is high. Ninety-eight percent of doctors are white, 93 percent are male and, since doctors are the nation's best-paid workers, many are rich.

As a physician, this upper-caste man, perhaps unconscious of his own motives, used "science" to control the reproduction of lower-caste people and create a society in which his privileges remained unassailable. To control nonwhites and the poor, he used the bodies of the women of those castes.

The story of the eugenics movement demonstrates why it is so important that representatives of women, nonwhites and the poor who still identify themselves with their own castes, help define and provide health care.

While physicians were by no means the only members of the eugenics movement, they, along with various university professors, gave it its scientific validity.

In 1869 Sir Francis Galton founded eugenics, based on the evolution theory of his cousin, Charles Darwin. Though Darwin theorized that physical traits were inherited, Galton thought character traits must be too. Wasn't it obvious that children of paupers usually became paupers themselves? Well then. They must have dominant sloth genes.

The solution to social problems became clear: Just sterilize the problem people. Don't let the defectives—deaf-mutes, madmen, alcoholics, idiots, drug addicts, venereal disease carriers, bastard spawners, wastrels and hooligans—reproduce their kind. As one doctor wrote, "We would sterilize these people for the same reason we would weed a garden."

That the unworthy often turned out to be the poor, the black and the immigrant, and that the worthy showed up as the rich, the white and the native-born, did not seem to strike the eugenists as more than coincident.

With knowledge of heredity, they proclaimed, race-making was possible. They could spawn Superman. Galton believed they could breed for "civic worth." All they had to do was encourage the "worthy" to produce more children and discourage the unworthy from breeding at all.

Eugenists were not just a few kooks. As those attending the 1921 International Eugenics Conference in New York City would have testified, eugenics was a widespread, respected movement. Its proponents addressed clubs, church societies and youth groups. They wrote many books up until the mid-1920s.

When the eugenics and birth-control movements embraced, the emphasis of the latter changed from individual well-being to a concern with population growth and "racial hygiene."

Eugenists saw birth control as a tool of their own powerful

class—not as a method by which woman might gain control of her own life. The state still claimed jurisdiction over women's bodies. Though, before, woman could only be forbidden contraceptives, now she could be forbidden them or compelled to use them according to the state's needs.

As eugenist Dr. Thurman B. Rice wrote in 1929, to advocate the teaching of birth control to everyone is "dangerous." Birth control is for "unworthy" families; good families must not use it.

"Babies, better babies and more better babies," he wrote in *Racial Hygiene*, "are by all odds the most important need of the times."

Eugenic ideas became embodied in law. The first sterilization bill was introduced in Michigan in 1898 and the first legislation passed in Indiana ten years later. By 1935, twenty-seven states had enacted sterilization laws applicable to at least thirty-four categories of people. Courts ordered nearly 64,000 persons sterilized between 1907 and 1963. As late as May 1972, sixteen states still had eugenic laws.*

Ten other countries followed America's example in passing sterilization laws. As one American eugenist noted approvingly in 1935, "Germany has, during the last year, planned for sterilization on a colossal scale." (Adolf Hitler was holding power then.)

In 1927, Supreme Court Justice Oliver Wendell Holmes issued a memorable decision. An attempt was being made in Virginia to sterilize a "feebleminded" woman, Carrie Buck, whose mother and daughter had also been judged mentally retarded. When the case reached the high court, Holmes said: "The principle that sustains compulsory vaccination is broad enough to cover cutting the fallopian tubes. Three generations of imbeciles are enough."

---

* Since then, at least seven of these states have repealed or somewhat modified those laws. Among the states retaining the sterilization laws are California, South Carolina and Oklahoma. According to the state statutes, Oklahoma's law applies to patients who are about to be discharged from certain state penal and mental institutions "if such patients are likely to be a public or partial public charge or be supported by any manner or form of charity" or patients who "are afflicted with hereditary forms of insanity that are recurrent, idiocy, imbecility, feeblemindedness, or epilepsy, or any person incarcerated in any penal institution in this State who is an habitual criminal . . ." (Title 43A, Section 341, et seq., of the Oklahoma Statutes).

Those who judged a person's worthiness to reproduce often used pseudoscientific jargon to mask their racism and elitism from themselves. Amid talk of "defective germ plasm," "recessive traits," and "Mendelian ratios," the fear of immigrants and blacks and the disdain for lower economic classes are clear.

The immigrants coming from eastern and southern Europe, Dr. Rice declared, do not mix well with "our stock." He added: "If they do cross with us their dominant traits submerge our native recessive traits; they are often radicals and anarchists causing no end of trouble; they have very low standards of living; they disturb the labor problems of the day; they are tremendously prolific."

He suggested that the state "discourage or prevent a high birth rate in the inferior strata of society, and at the same time encourage it in the middle and better classes."

In 1934, Guy Irving Burch, founder of the Population Reference Bureau and a leading educator on population problems, seconded Dr. Rice: "I think there is good reason to be optimistic about the future of the native American stock if birth control is made available to the millions of aliens in our cities and the millions of colored people in this country."

Besides contraception, sterilization was advocated for "race betterment." Dr. William J. Robinson, author of *Practical Eugenics, Four Methods of Improving the Human Race,* thought paupers who refused contraception should be sterilized. So should nymphomaniac prostitutes who, he asserted, were cruel to children and liked to torture animals.

Eugenists also suggested the imprisonment of the "unfit." In 1911, one physician defined this segregation method as "the permanent care, under humane medical supervision, and primarily in their own interests, of the naturally defective." *

A few medical women were involved in this movement too. In a 1928 magazine article, Dr. Mildred Staley of New Zealand cited divorce, crime and illegitimate childbearing as symptoms of mental illness and suggested that prison inmates be used in a preventive mental-hygiene program. When released, the mentally irresponsible prisoners should not be allowed to breed "a fresh generation of feebleminded wastrels and criminals!" She

* Caleb Williams Saleeby, M.D., *The Methods of Race Regeneration,* New York: Moffat, Yar & Co., 1911.

added, "If the feebleminded boy was to be completely sterilized (castrated) * at the age of eleven to thirteen, when he has attained his full mental equipment for life, this problem would be fairly solved."

(It is interesting that this woman emphasized male castration while male doctors—by far the more numerous—concentrated on female sterilization or segregation. Perhaps with equal numbers of male and female doctors, the two sexes could counteract each other's cruelty.)

Margaret Sanger, too, became a eugenics advocate. In 1925, on behalf of the Sixth International Birth Control Conference, Sanger urged President Calvin Coolidge to appoint a commission to study the need for sterilization of the unfit.

Asked by Yale students in 1934 if there weren't a danger that the more intelligent classes would practice birth control while the lower classes would not and that society would thus degenerate, Sanger replied that that was exactly what the Birth Control Movement aimed to prevent "by more birth control among the illiterate and uneducated classes."

Moreover, Sanger's "Way to Peace," outlined in a 1932 radio talk, called for giving the unfit a choice of segregation or sterilization. Those "morons, mental defectives, epileptics, illiterates, paupers, unemployables, criminals, prostitutes and dope fiends" who chose segregation would be put on farm lands and taught to work "for the period of their entire lives."

The Birth Control Movement's eugenic roots are showing now.

In 1935 the American Birth Control League resolved at its annual meeting to unite with the American Eugenics Society in making plans to provide welfare families with contraceptives. Two years later, Sanger noted that the nation's nine million unemployed had the highest birth rate of any class even though they were the least fit to rear children who would be an asset to the country.

"That must be our answer to attacks against birth control," she wrote. "Inclusion of contraceptive service in public health will do something to help solve the problem and a start is being made in that direction."

* The parenthetical word is Dr. Staley's, not mine.

That same year, 1937, North Carolina became the first state to approve contraception in its public-health service. Six other Southern states followed, raising the suspicion that control of the black population might have been a motive in the approval.

In 1939, the American Birth Control League and Sanger's Clinical Research Bureau merged to form Planned Parenthood Federation of America, an organization with a board dominated by physicians. Again, the first conferences to interpret the Planned Parenthood program of birth control to health and welfare agencies were all held in the South.

Private citizens also organized in the 1940s and 1950s to deal with a great menace it had discovered: The population explosion. Their groups were composed of some of the richest, most powerful persons in this country. The Du Ponts, Fords and Mellons joined others from the world of business and high finance in attacking the population problem of the poor, especially the poor in "underdeveloped" countries. The Rockefellers founded, funded and administered the most influential group, the Population Council.

Perhaps these businessmen formed their groups solely out of a desire to serve the human race. The Rockefeller Fund's *Prospect for America*, however, suggests another possible motive. In this book, study groups headed first by Nelson A. and later, Laurance S. Rockefeller defined the country's future problems and offered suggestions for national policies to solve them. The book observes that in a rapidly expanding population, the young predominate. Hungering for the good things in life, they are apt to be restless and impatient.

"Extreme nationalism has often been the result," *Prospect* stated. "No assessment of the contemporary scene can ignore this mushrooming increase of population and the awakened aspirations of the less developed areas."

Pronounced nationalism, of course, would threaten the access of America's multinational corporations to the oil and other resources of "underdeveloped" countries. Native peoples would want to control the resources of their own lands.*

* See, on pp. 218–219 in *Prospect for America*, a discussion of the essential role of private foreign investment, especially of American companies, in less developed nations. For more information on this whole issue, see Steve Weissman's "The Population Bomb Is a Rockefeller Baby," *Ramparts*, May 1970. Also see Ben Wattenburg's "The Nonsense Explosion," in *The American Population*

In 1957, an "Ad Hoc Committee" of population experts from Planned Parenthood, The Population Council, the Rockefeller Fund and Laurance Rockefeller's Conservation Foundation issued a report, *Population: An International Dilemma*, which further suggested that the goals of some population groups were not entirely humanitarian. The report stated that population growth would threaten political stability. The plan it proposed to solve the problem domestically involved using tax, welfare and education policy to "discourage births among the socially handicapped." It added: "Ultimately government policies may seek to encourage genetic improvement from one generation to another."

The report was issued in the name of Frederick Osborn, then president of the Population Council and now honorary trustee. In 1968, Osborn published a book entitled *The Future of Human Heredity, An Introduction to Eugenics in Modern Society*. While he is careful, in the book, to repudiate the obvious racism of earlier eugenists and to insist that environment, as well as heredity, shapes human beings, he offers proposals with as much potential for control of lower classes as the proposals of his predecessors.

To achieve a eugenic society, he observes, "responsible" parents should be encouraged to have large families and "irresponsible" ones, small families.

"For people on relief or otherwise in contact with social agencies," he wrote, " a discriminating attitude on the part of community social workers together with advice on the availability of birth control should have a substantial effect."

There is much in the current literature of the population-control strategists reminiscent of the eugenists. That literature is written by university professors, physicians, and businessmen who are among the most respected members of our society, just as the eugenists were of theirs. They often blame every imaginable social ill—civil riots, famine, pollution, high taxes, slums, delinquency and poor health—directly on population growth while ignoring the maldistribution of land and mineral

---

Debate, edited by Daniel Callahan, Doubleday & Co., Inc., N.Y., 1971. Wattenburg argues that population growth is a manageable, long-term problem which has been manufactured into a "crisis," thus taking our attention away from the real causes of various social problems.

resources, and racist, sexist discrimination in the labor market.

Some of their proposals for slowing population growth, such as putting as yet nonexistent fertility-control agents in the drinking water, would affect everyone equally but others would mainly afflict the poor:

—Sterilization of unwed mothers.

—Compulsory abortion of all out-of-wedlock pregnancies.

—Elimination of welfare payments for mothers with more than two children.

—Imposition of a "child tax."

—Payments for those who undergo sterilizations and abortions.*

Planned Parenthood, the direct descendant of Sanger's birth-control groups (which had themselves been involved in the eugenics movement) joined the population-control forces in 1962. That year, it merged with the World Population Emergency Fund, a group fostering support for birth control abroad. Until it became Planned Parenthood-World Population, it had stressed the relationship of contraception to maternal and child health. After 1962, it had another concern: Slowing population growth.

The private population groups continue to publicize what they see as the threat of a burgeoning populace. They have lobbied very successfully over the last fifteen years for government financing of birth-control programs in less developed countries and in the United States.

In 1967 Congressional legislation designated family planning for special emphasis in the antipoverty program and required the states to offer contraceptives to all welfare recipients. Though there had been only about 150 public and voluntary health agencies offering birth-control programs in 1960, by 1972 there were three thousand.

Sometimes, as in Louisiana in 1974, danger signs clearly flash. That year, a family-planning foundation attacked for alleged misuse of funds was defended by its founding doctor this way: The nonwhite population, he pointed out, had decreased by 13.4 percent since 1967.

---

* For more details and a complete list of references, see "U.S. Population Growth and Family Planning: A Review of the Literature," by Robin Elliott, Lynn C. Landman, Richard Lincoln and Theodore Tsuoroka, *Family Planning Perspectives*, October 1970.

If welfare and poverty agencies, considering a person's control over his or her own body an inalienable right, offered birth-control services only to those who wanted them, there would be no complaint—only commendation. It must be emphasized that many agencies, anxious to give low-income people the same access to contraception that wealthier people have, probably do just that. But evidence suggests that other programs do coerce women into infertility with an enthusiasm eugenists used to display.

Sometimes the "women" are really children. Such was the case with Minnie and Mary Alice Relf, twelve- and fourteen-year-old black girls from an impoverished Alabama family. They were sterilized in June 1973, after their mother signed an "X" on a form from the family-planning clinic of Montgomery Community Action Agency. Mrs. Relf thought the form authorized "shots" for them. In a suit filed against the agency, the Southern Poverty Law Center said the agency contended the operation was needed because "boys were hanging around the girls," and "they felt the most convenient method for the agency to prevent pregnancy was sterilization." *

In defending the clinic's action, the clinic director said the mother had been thoroughly briefed on the operation before she signed the paper. She denies it but the point is irrelevant anyway. The operation was not done on *her*. Her children's bodies are not hers to sign away. It is still, apparently, a radical idea that children are not their parents' possessions, nor wives their husbands', nor women the state's.

One Relf girl was allegedly "mentally retarded." (In the heyday of the eugenists, the word used was "feebleminded.") An investigation by the Justice Department soon revealed that nine other females—eight of them black, five of them minors

---

* A few weeks after filing suit, the Southern Poverty Law Center asked the U. S. District Court for the Middle District of Alabama to dismiss the case so the plaintiffs could refile seeking broader relief. That request was granted. The case involving the Montgomery Community Action Agency was dismissed with no judgment rendered. The plaintiffs filed a new class action complaint in the U. S. District Court in Washington, D.C. on behalf of all poor persons subjected to involuntary sterilization under regulations of the U. S. Department of Health, Education and Welfare (HEW). Several high HEW officials were named as defendants. On March 15, 1974, the district court in Washington ordered the establishment of HEW regulations to prevent involuntary sterilizations. Aspects of that court ruling are now being appealed both by the plaintiffs and the defendants. A ruling is not expected before the spring of 1977.

and seven of them "retarded"—had also been sterilized. In addition, the Justice Department charged that during the past ten years, fourteen residents of an Alabama school for the retarded had been submitted to the surgeon's knife.

Subsequent federal investigations showed that in the previous fifteen months eighty other minors had been sterilized at government-sponsored clinics serving the poor throughout the nation.

Women on welfare are particularly vulnerable to involuntary sterilizations. Annie Smart, a National Welfare Rights Organization director, says many young women have had hysterectomies in family-planning programs because they have not known medical terms.

"If I give my consent," she explains, "that doesn't mean I understand what's going on. Lots of women consent to not having babies, but the doctor doesn't explain the various birth-control methods and the dangers of each. He just does a hysterectomy."

Often, she says, the women are too intimidated to complain.

Susan Wells (pseudonym) complained eight years after she had been sterilized, when she first learned of her condition. A 1973 lawsuit contends that Wells's mother was coerced into agreeing to her daughter's "temporary" sterilization. A welfare worker, the suit alleges, repeatedly threatened to cut the mother and her ten children off welfare if eighteen-year-old Susan, who had just delivered a baby, did not have her tubes tied. Wells was sterilized under a North Carolina eugenics law which permits sterilization of the "mentally defective," but, the suit notes, her mentality had never been tested by a qualified person before the operation had been ordered.

The same month the Wells and Relf sterilizations were reported, a thirty-year-old mother of four revealed that obstetricians in her town—Aiken, South Carolina—had denied her maternity care because she refused to be sterilized.

Three Aiken doctors confirmed that they required sterilization before agreeing to deliver babies for welfare patients with three or more children; they stressed the doctor's right to decide whom he will treat. One said he was trying to help reduce the welfare rolls.

Reporters soon revealed that almost half the welfare mothers who had had babies at Medicaid expense in Aiken County that year—eighteen out of thirty-four—had been sterilized. All but two were black.

In ordering the government to redraft sterilization rules, Federal Judge Gerhard A. Gesell stated in 1974 that there was undisputed evidence that poor persons had been coerced into accepting sterilization under threat of losing welfare benefits.

"Over the last few years," he noted, "an estimated 100,000 to 150,000 low-income persons have been sterilized annually under federally funded programs."

Urging caution on the federal government, he wrote, "The dividing line between family planning and eugenics is murky."

Chapter EIGHT

MODERN BIRTH CONTROL

ONCE THE COMSTOCK LAWS TOPPLED, THE QUESTION WAS SET-
tled: Doctors would have to make contraception available. New
questions: What kind? With what safeguards? For what purpose? For whom?

Those questions too were quickly resolved. Birth control was
for women. Almost any kind that prevented births was acceptable, the regard given to its safety varying with the color and
economic status of the women who would use it. A primary
purpose of contraception became the control of population
rather than the well-being of individual women.

An examination of the development of modern female contraceptives reveals that too often devices and drugs have been
inadequately researched before being widely sold and that, once
available, many women have used them without their informed
consent.

The physician sometimes decides what method will be offered to what women. Dr. Alan Guttmacher, the late president
of Planned Parenthood-World Population, said as much at the

1970 Senate hearings on the Pill conducted by Wisconsin Senator Gaylord Nelson.

Commenting on the fact that 55 percent of the women at a ghetto clinic in New York City had been given intrauterine devices (IUDs), Dr. Guttmacher explained that the chief of service there was researching a new model. (That model, the Majzlin Spring, had been developed by a physician on the clinic staff. FDA subsequently recalled the Majzlin Spring after this IUD had become associated with an undue number of serious complications.*)

"It has been my experience," Dr. Guttmacher continued, "that the man in charge of the clinic largely dictates the contraceptive used in that clinic."

Medical researchers, as well as practicing physicians, have limited the options available to women. Few women could choose to share contraceptive responsibilities with their partners because there were no new male methods available.

When Sanger's work had finally felled antibirth-control laws, men could use condoms and women, diaphragms. While, for males, new research produced only the vasectomy, for females it came up with the Pill, several intrauterine devices, the laparoscopy sterilization, vaginal spermicides in creams, jellies and foams, and the morning-after pill.

One suspects from this that, initially, almost 100 percent of the research was directed toward female contraceptives. Now, 75 percent of government research funds supplied by the National Institutes of Health (NIH) goes to female contraceptive research and the rest to male.

Experimenters are now investigating these female contraceptives:

—Depo-Provera (Progesterone injections).
—Silastic implantations. (The implantation under the skin of a tiny plastic pillow filled with progesterone which is continuously released.)
—The once-a-month pill.

* See "Hearings before the Subcommittee on Monopoly of the Select Committee on Small Business, U. S. Senate, Second Session on Present Status of Competition in the Pharmaceutical Industry, Parts 15, 16 and 17, Oral Contraceptives," pp. 6203 and 6564. Also see pp. 204, 237 and 276–293 in "Regulations of Medical Devices (Intrauterine Devices), Hearings before a Subcommittee of the Committee on Government Operations, House of Representatives, May and June, 1973."

—Vaccinations against sperm.

In developing contraceptives, male physicians and researchers have devalued women. Especially nonwhite women.

The Pill's development is a prime example.

In 1951, Margaret Sanger gave seed money to Dr. Gregory Pincus to develop a contraceptive pill. G. D. Searle and Co., the drug manufacturers, helped. By 1955, Pincus had isolated a group of chemical steroids which would inhibit ovulation. Five years later the Pill was on the market.

As I noted previously, the Food and Drug Administration (FDA) approved its sale to American women on the basis of studies on only 132 Puerto Rican women who had taken the Pill consecutively for twelve or more months, and 718 other women who took the Pill for less than one year. Five of the women died. No doctors from the study examined the women during their illnesses.

In 1960, *The New York Times* quoted Dr. Pincus as saying that a periodic examination of women taking the experimental Pill revealed no deleterious effects and no significant side effects.

"What was not looked for was not found," Dr. Herbert Ratner, director of Public Health in Oak Park, Illinois, later testified at the Senate Pill hearings. "What was not surveyed was not seen. What perhaps happened was ignored."

In fact, there appears to be no organ system in the body that is not affected by the Pill. During the Pill hearings, Dr. Victor Wynn, professor of human metabolism at the University of London, noted that many metabolic changes could be described in Pill users. These abnormalities, he said, contribute to many untoward symptoms in users "such as weight gain and obesity, salt and water retention, liver dysfunction including jaundice, neuropsychiatric abnormalities such as anxiety, depression and loss of libido, chorea and increased susceptibility to attacks in epileptics, headache, migraine, weariness, changes in skin pigmentation, rheumatic complaints, leg cramps, vaginal moniliasis (thrush), and an increased incidence of cervical erosion."

The drug has been connected with more than fifty side effects. One, as Dr. Wynn mentioned, is the loss of sexual desire (libido) experienced by 10 to 15 percent of users.

At the Pill hearings, Dr. M. James Whitelaw, a private physician in San Jose, California, asked, "How many adult males would be willing to take an oral contraceptive faithfully if they were told that instead of a possible fifty-plus adverse side reactions only one remained, that being the possible loss of sex drive and libido?"

After that question, the hearing transcript merely records: "(Laughter)."

The Pill, of course, has graver consequences.

A cause and effect relationship between the Pill and thromboembolic (or clotting) disorders has been firmly established. Risk of developing such disorders is five to ten times greater for users than nonusers, according to *Population Reports: Oral Contraceptives*, a 1975 publication of the George Washington University Medical Center. British studies found that one in every 2,000 women taking the Pill get blood clots serious enough to require hospitalization.

Pill-takers also have a risk of stroke three to nine times greater than nontakers, according to *Population Reports*.

Moreover, as a collaborative study coordinated by Dr. Albert Herman at Duke University Medical Center found, arteries burst in the brains of Pill-users twice as often as nonusers.

Studies suggest, but have not proved, that the Pill can cause, among many other ailments, liver tumors, diabetes, and gall bladder disease.

Heart attack is another side effect Pill-takers hazard. In August 1975, the FDA told doctors in a drug bulletin that, as two British studies strongly suggested, Pill-takers face a risk of coronary thrombosis 2.7 to 5.7 times greater than that of nonusers. (The higher risk is for women over forty.)

From the Pill's inception, various physicians have worried about its cancer-producing or -nurturing potential.

At the 1970 Senate hearings, Dr. Roy Hertz, former chief of the Reproductive Branch of the National Institute of Child Health and Human Development, noted that the female hormone estrogen, which is contained in the Pill, causes cancer in five species of laboratory animals. It seems reasonable, he said, that women may share with animals a carcinogenic response to estrogen.

Dr. Max Cutler, director of the Beverly Hills Cancer Research Foundation, sounded an equally ominous note at the hearings. The Pill's risk of increasing the incidence of breast cancer "is a potential time bomb with a fuse at least fifteen to twenty years in length," he said. "I share the hope that the concern about this danger may be unfounded, and that the considerable experimental evidence may be inapplicable to women, but this is a gamble which is difficult to justify because of the large numbers of women at risk."

The gamble was taken.

Five years later, Dr. Ralph S. Paffenbarger of the University of California reported a study suggesting a link between the Pill and breast cancer. His study indicated that women who use the Pill before having their first child and women with a history of benign breast tumors, may face an increased risk of cancer. (More studies are needed to establish a cause and effect relationship.)

That same year, 1975, researchers at the University of Colorado School of Medicine in Denver reported thirteen cases of endometrial cancer—a very rare disease among the young—in Pill-users still in their twenties and thirties.* Eleven of the thirteen women had taken the sequential Pill. (It is called sequential because women ingest pills containing estrogen during the first two weeks of the month's supply and pills containing estrogen and a related female hormone, progestagen, during the third week. In the combination pill, which most Pill-users buy, estrogen and progestagen are taken for twenty-one consecutive days.)

After publication of this study, the FDA asked three major drug companies to stop marketing the sequentials and the companies agreed in February 1976.

Until that date, between 60,000 and 80,000 American women —10 percent of the U. S. oral contraceptive market—had been using the sequentials. Now we wait to see what happens to them.

It is frequently asserted that despite all its adverse effects,

---

* Steven G. Silverberg, M.D. and Edgar L. Makowski, M.D., "Endometrial Carcinoma in Young Women Taking Oral Contraceptive Agents," *Obstetrics and Gynecology*, November 1975, pp. 503–506. This paper reports the first twenty-one cases recorded in the Registry for Endometrial Carcinoma in Young Women Taking Oral Contraceptive Agents, a registry established in November 1973. In eight of the twenty-one women, a close relationship between the Pill and the cancer did not seem to exist.

both potential and proven, the Pill is safer than pregnancy. This is a fallacious argument because:

1. We cannot compare the known risk of pregnancy with the unknown risk of the oral contraceptive. Many necessary studies on the Pill's safety have not been performed, as the FDA has acknowledged, and most Pill complications are never reported, as Dr. Charles Edwards, then FDA Commissioner, and Dr. Louis Hellman, chairman of the FDA's Advisory Committee on Obstetrics and Gynecology, both testified at the Senate hearings. Dr. Hellman explained that since the physician incurs a legal liability in reporting an adverse reaction, he is often "very hesitant" to do so.*

2. This argument incorrectly assumes that women who do not take the Pill become pregnant. But other, safer, contraceptives exist. So we must compare the acknowledged risks of the Pill to the risks of pregnancy—not in all women—but only in the few women who might get pregnant because of another contraceptive's failure.

3. Most deaths related to pregnancy are due to incompetent or nonexistent obstetrical care and to the prior poor health of a woman. So the risk of pregnancy is not the same for all women. A healthy young, middle-class woman runs almost no risk while an older woman with a heart disease may take a considerable one. For a valid comparison, the death rate of healthy women on the Pill should be contrasted with the death rate of healthy pregnant women. Then we will see if the Pill is "safer" than pregnancy.

The prescribing of the Pill over the past ten years, Dr. Philip Ball, an Indiana internist, testified at the Senate hearings, had been "a massive, double blind, uncontrolled experiment." Now, fifty million women around the world are participating in that experiment.

Did the experimental subjects know, when their doctors prescribed the Pill, that they were running any risks? A *Newsweek*

* For the FDA's admission of incomplete Pill studies, see p. 6821 in the Senate hearings. For testimony on the failure to report Pill complications, see pp. 6190; 6790; 6798; 5936; 6137; 6501; 6729; 6734. Also see, "Our Readers Talk Back About the Birth Control Pills," *Ladies' Home Journal*, November 1967.

poll taken during the Congressional hearings revealed that two thirds of the women questioned had been told nothing about the serious long-term Pill effects.

"In many clinics, the Pill has been served up as if it were no more hazardous than chewing gum," Dr. Hugh J. Davis, assistant professor of obstetrics and gynecology at Johns Hopkins University School of Medicine testified during the hearings. "The colorful brochures, movies and pamphlets which are used to instruct women about the Pill say next to nothing about the possible serious complications."

Private patients were not necessarily better informed. During the hearings, Dr. Robert Kistner, a researcher for several drug companies and a Harvard Medical School professor, was asked if he regularly informed a woman of the Pill's potential side effects. He replied that he did inform her about side effects, but not about possible complications. He added: "If you ask if I sit down and I take this out and I say, 'Now I want you to know you may die of blood clotting or you may get hepatitis or you may get this, that or the other thing . . .' then I would say 'no.' I don't believe it is good medical practice with any medication to go through the list of complications."

Earlier, testifying at a suit brought against Searle by a young man whose wife had died from a blood clot, Kistner was asked why he did not tell his patients there was a risk with the Pill. "Well," he answered, "they might get, if you tell them they might have headaches, they will get headaches."

Though the hearings provided ample evidence that women were not consenting, in an informed way, to taking the Pill, the American Medical Association and the American College of Obstetrics and Gynecology subsequently opposed package inserts explaining side effects and risks of the Pill directly to Pill-users. The AMA house of delegates objected that the insert "intrudes on the patient-physician relationship" and "would confuse and alarm many patients." A *New York Times* story of March 24, 1970 suggested another motivation. According to the *Times,* the AMA had complained to Health, Education and Welfare Secretary Robert H. Finch that the leaflet might lead to malpractice suits.

After protests from organized medicine, from population-control groups and from drug companies, the FDA cut the proposed package insert from 600 to about 130 words. The resulting insert can hardly be said to inform Pill-consumers.

The watered-down version mentions only one complication—blood-clotting. While the original version had noted that the risk of blood-clotting is six times greater for Pill-users than nonusers, the present form omits that fact. The insert, moreover, gives no hint of a possible cancer danger. (The original pamphlet had noted that the hormones in the Pill have caused cancer in animals.)

Unlike the earlier version, the insert describes no symptoms that should prompt a woman to visit her doctor.

How could all this have happened? How could physicians and the government have allowed this potential time bomb to be placed in the bodies of millions of women?

Several factors made this possible and one was certainly drug-company greed. With fifty million women taking the Pill almost daily, the companies made enormous profits. Ignoring the health of Pill-users, they have operated to protect their profits.

The FDA, through its laxity, aided the companies. Rather than requiring that studies be performed to prove the Pill safe, the FDA has merely responded to studies (often conducted in Britain) on adverse Pill effects. At the Senate hearings, FDA admitted that it had approved the Pill on the basis of "rather superficial" data, some of which was "little more than testimonial or opinionative in character."

M. J. Ryan, acting director of FDA's Office of Legislative Services, further explained: "Many areas of investigation that would now be required were either not carried out or were not evaluated to an acceptable extent. The studies conducted were certainly not of as high a quality as we now demand . . ."

He then listed the many deficiencies in the data. Almost all were in the realm of safety.

A 1976 General Accounting Office (GAO) report suggests a partial explanation for FDA's tolerant attitude toward incomplete studies on pharmaceuticals. In a review of the 1974 financial disclosure statements of FDA employees, most of whom were in regulatory positions, GAO found that 159 employees owned interests which were prohibited by FDA regulations.

Another 203 regulatory employees had failed to file statements.*

Another factor in the Pill scandal: Drug companies fund the research or the birth-control clinics of certain physicians. These doctors often become forceful Pill advocates. As Dr. Herbert Ratner, the public health director, has noted, a major reason for the failure to assess the Pill objectively was that some of the experts chosen for advisory committees "are deeply obligated to drug firms for subsidization for their research and other activities."

The ordinary physician's ignorance about the drug also made the massive Pill experiment possible. Most doctors do not read foreign medical journals and the native *Journal of the American Medical Association* has been very slow to print articles on the Pill offensive to its major advertisers, the Pill manufacturers.

Doctors are ignorant, too, because, rather than setting up a system for the objective appraisal of drugs, they have allowed themselves to be educated by the pharmaceutical industry, an obviously biased teacher.

Dr. Hugh J. Davis, assistant professor of obstetrics and gynecology at Johns Hopkins University School of Medicine in Baltimore, was one of several witnesses at the Senate hearings who testified that the average practicing physician depends on drug-company advertising for much of his information on the oral contraceptive. Asked if physicians could be relied upon to give information about the Pill to women, Dr. Davis said that physicians were not fully informed themselves.

"These people are busy," he said. "They read the brochures and information that the drug house tends to pump into them, I am sorry to say, but that is the reality of the situation."

The greatest of all factors in the Pill fiasco may have been the desire to limit population growth. For example, consider the 1969 Report on the Oral Contraceptives by the FDA's Advisory Committee on Obstetrics and Gynecology. That grim report detailed endless adverse effects associated, by various studies, with the Pill yet Committee Chairman Dr. Louis Hellman declared the Pill "safe" in his report summary.

* *Financial Disclosure System for Employees of the Food and Drug Administration Needs Tightening*, A Report to the Congress by the Comptroller General of the United States, January 19, 1976. FPCD-76-21. Copies available for one dollar from: U. S. General Accounting Office, Distribution Section, P. O. Box 1020, Washington, D. C. 20013.

Asked at the 1970 Senate hearings how he had arrived at that designation, Dr. Hellman said that his conclusion had "implied" that there were problems with the Pill, but that he had considered the Pill safe "within the intent of the legislation." That legislation, the Kefauver-Harris amendments regulating the FDA, says "safety" pertains to human health. But Dr. Hellman pointed out that in determining a drug's safety, one should balance its risks against its benefits. He then weighed the benefits of the Pill *in curtailing population growth* against the risks of the Pill to individual women.

"The introduction of modern contraceptive methods has made the problem of population control immeasurably easier," he told Senator Nelson. "With the traditional methods of contraception, it is very difficult, as you must have seen in India, to get any response out of the impoverished people. They have neither the time nor the privacy nor the *motivation* (italics mine) to use diaphragms, condoms, or whatever you will."

Dr. Hellman then said he had also weighed the Pill's benefits to the individual, but he discussed that benefit as though the only alternative to the Pill were pregnancy, rather than a different contraceptive.

Senator Gaylord Nelson, hearing chairman, pointed out the obvious to Dr. Hellman: A drug's risks and benefits *to the individual patient,* not to society, should be weighed.

(Dr. Hellman is now Deputy Assistant Secretary for Population Affairs in the U. S. Department of Health, Education and Welfare.)

It is clear from the Senate testimony that many population controllers view certain castes as those which most need the Pill—castes to which the population experts themselves do not belong. They refer to these castes as "the economically deprived individuals," "low-income groups," or women "in the developing countries." Many of these women would be nonwhite.

Throughout the hearing testimony, one keeps seeing the phrase "well-motivated" associated with middle- and upper-class contraceptive users while doctors imply or assert that the indigent are not "well-motivated," i.e., that they have no desire to practice birth control. If physicians presume to give poor women a certain contraceptive method (the Pill) to solve the problem of the women wanting no method at all, then these upper-class doctors are controlling lower-class people. This is social engineering. This is what the eugenists were up to.

"The sacred birth-control pill has had the halo of being the drug that would control the massive social problems of a burgeoning population," Dr. Philip Ball, an internist, told the Senate subcommittee. "It could be used on the poor, ignorant, illiterate woman who scarcely knew what birth control was all about."

Dr. Herbert Ratner, the public health director, agreed. The Pill acquired an immunity from criticism, he said, "because it was promoted as the solution to the population problem in the undeveloped countries, and to the growing welfare problem in the U. S."

Clearly, there are modern day eugenists—doctors who would sacrifice the individual patient for a broader social goal. That, Dr. John R. McCain told the Senators, was exactly the position of many doctors with whom he had talked. McCain, an obstetrician-gynecologist in Atlanta, said the doctors opposed revealing the facts about the Pill on the grounds that women might then reject it and thus threaten population control.*

National Observer reporter Barbara J. Katz investigated intrauterine devices in 1973 and found that as a result of lack of government regulation, many have been inserted on the basis of inadequate studies that were "short-term, involving small numbers of patients, statistically and methodologically suspect, and often based on the experience of only one investigator."

FDA has declined to oversee these contraceptives. It has had the authority since 1968 to classify IUDs as "drugs" and thus subject them to animal studies and controlled clinical studies. Instead it has bowed to the manufacturers' wishes and classified them as "devices," thus exempting them from all but minimal regulation. So companies have been free to rush potentially profitable IUDs onto the market and use the world's women as experimental subjects. †

Many women assume that their doctors are authorities on

* See Dr. McCain's testimony on p. 6485 of the Senate hearings.
† In the spring of 1976 a bill to protect the public from unsafe medical devices passed both Houses of Congress. The bill requires pre-market testing of any device to be implanted in the body.

IUDs and would never prescribe unsafe ones, but doctors often know little more than IUD manufacturers choose to tell them.

"Advertisements and detailmen (drug salespersons) are major sources of information for physicians," Dr. Harold Aaron, editorial board chairman of the prestigious *Medical Letter* on drugs and therapeutics, told me. "The doctor hasn't got the time to read the medical literature."

Doctors trust that manufacturers would not sell insufficiently tested models and that, at any rate, FDA would not let them, but these assumptions are as unwarranted as the one women make about a doctor's knowledge.

The idea for the IUD is an ancient one: A foreign body placed in the uterus prevents the growth of an egg. (Exactly how it does this is unknown but a widely accepted theory is that the IUD causes a low-grade inflammation which is hostile to the fertilized egg or, possibly, to the sperm.)

The predecessor of the modern IUD was developed in 1909. Modifications of that device were associated with such a high rate of infection and complication that the medical community overwhelmingly condemned them as dangerous in the 1930s and 1940s. Almost all histories of the IUD state that in the late 1950s and early 1960s, "technological progress" and "new data" convinced doctors of the IUD's safety and efficacy so that private physicians and, especially, birth-control clinics began inserting IUDs on a wide scale.

Testimony before and reports submitted to a 1973 House subcommittee hearing, however, suggest that what changed the evaluation of the IUD was—not any convincing new evidence that it was safe—but a perception on the part of population-control advocates and groups that longer-lasting contraceptives were needed for the "unmotivated" and "underprivileged," contraceptives which, unlike the Pill, did not daily give women the freedom to stop controlling their fertility.* It was, in fact,

* *Regulation of Medical Devices (Intrauterine Devices)*, op. cit. For one example, in its 1968 report on the IUD, FDA's Advisory Committee on Obstetrics and Gynecology attributed the rebirth in interest in the IUD to two factors, one of which was "the suggestion that the underprivileged woman is more effectively served when the need for recurrent motivation, required in most other forms of contraception, is removed."

The other factor cited was the development of inert plastics. Straightened for insertion, plastic IUDs return, in the uterus, to a previously-molded shape. Although the sudden availability of inert plastics may have made it easier for

largely one group, the Population Council, which, only ten years after its founding by the Rockefellers in 1952, made the discredited IUD a respectable contraceptive. Today, the Council is widely accepted as the authoritative source of information on the IUD.

IUD advocates claim that a paper by an Israeli physician and another by a Japanese, both published in 1959, indicated that the IUD was safe and effective. However, in a study of all the research ever done on human subjects wearing intrauterine devices, Dr. Thomas W. Hilgers, a fellow in Obstetrics and Gynecology at Mayo Graduate School of Medicine, wrote in 1972, "Unfortunately, the advocates were careless in their reading, for nothing new or revolutionary had been added to the already existent knowledge."

The Israeli researcher's statement that he considered the IUD "absolutely harmless," Dr. Hilgers added, is an assertion that "has never been substantiated in the countless number of similar studies done both before and after his report.

"Nonetheless, it was on the basis of two reports, one of which was solicited [by the *American Journal of Obstetrics and Gynecology*], that the Population Council began to make its decisions and to influence the world's use of this device," he wrote.

In 1962, the Population Council sponsored the First International Conference on IUDs, a conference which marks the beginning of physician acceptance of the device. Two years later, it sponsored a second conference attended by participants from forty-four countries.

The Population Council then initiated, financed and later completely administered a Cooperative Statistical Program (CSP) to evaluate the safety and efficacy of available IUD models. The Council's Dr. Christopher Tietze and his staff pooled information from about thirty public and private IUD programs in the United States and analyzed the data by a

physicians to invent and insert various IUDs, it did not necessarily make the new IUDs any safer than earlier models. In fact, there are many papers in the medical literature reporting cases in which plastic IUDs disintegrated in the uterus and passed out of the woman in fragments, necessitating, as one physician wrote, "a most dangerous office fishing excursion or ultimately hospitalization and a D & C." For more information on problems with plastic IUDs, see, in the above cited hearings, pp. 37, 239–241, 268 and 415–416.

method Dr. Tietze and a colleague had adapted especially for evaluating IUDs.

In 1970, the Ninth Progress Report on the CSP, citing statistics from this "life table" method, reported that, on the whole, the IUD was a safe and effective means of contraception and one fit for use in national family planning programs.

But the life-table method was roundly criticized at the 1973 House hearings as a technique which, in leaving out important data like the rates of certain complications, and the number of patients lost to follow-up, and in combining the data from different studies that may not have been conducted in exactly the same manner, gave a false impression of the IUD's safety.

Dr. Charles Anello, a top FDA statistician, testified that figures produced by the life table would not in themselves prove the efficacy or safety of a device.

Yet most assessments of the IUD, including that of FDA's Advisory Committee on Obstetrics and Gynecology, heavily rely on the Population Council's life-table statistics.

By January 1975, an estimated fifteen million women around the world were carrying IUDs in their uteri, according to the Population Information Program of George Washington University Medical Center.

Today, just one decade after IUDs began to be widely inserted, problems have emerged and they are essentially the same ones which occurred in the 1930s and 1940s before the IUD was suddenly discovered to be "safe." The 1973 House hearings aired some of those problems.

One witness, Dr. Russel J. Thomsen, a Washington physician, testified that IUDs then in use had been proven to cause "death, sterility, hemorrhage leading to anemia, disabling pain, unwanted pregnancy, miscarriage, ruptured tubal pregnancies, thousands of major surgical procedures, massive infection, blood transfusion, and untold numbers of x-rays to the ovaries of young women."

Most IUD researchers, Dr. Thomsen believed, dismissed women's complaints about pain or bleeding as inconsequential.

Dr. John C. Madry, Jr., a private obstetrician-gynecologist in Melbourne, Florida, also testified. Becoming concerned about the number of IUD complications he saw in his practice, he said, he had attempted, in 1970, to learn the mortality rate associated with the device. He wrote to the World Health Organization, American Medical Association, the Population Council, Planned Parenthood-World Population, American Association for Maternal and Child Health, six pharmaceutical companies and the curator of a medical library, asking for data.

On the basis of their replies and his own survey of the medical literature, he concluded that, among many other vital facts, the mortality and morbidity rates associated with the IUD are unknown. (Morbidity is the incidence of disease.)

"If the adverse reporting on oral contraceptives is somewhat inadequate," the medical director of Planned Parenthood-World Population wrote Madry, "I can assure you that that for the IUD is even more so."

There is such a paucity of information on IUDs, Dr. Madry told the House subcommittee, that patients could not be giving informed consent to their use of the device.

Because population planners were bombarding physicians with reports while the press published articles supportive of that cause, he said, "American physicians in private practice appear to have unwittingly become participants in a great experiment in population control."

Some data on the IUD finally did become available a year after the House hearings. The U. S. Center for Disease Control in Atlanta estimated from a physician survey that in the United States, 7,900 IUD-associated hospitalizations had occurred in the first six months of 1973. With approximately 3.2 million IUD wearers at that time here, the risk of hospitalization would have been five out of every two thousand.

But at FDA hearings, epidemiologists later blasted this study for its "major deficiencies." Less than half the 34,000 physicians in the mail survey responded, they pointed out. When researchers called one percent of the doctors who had not answered, they found a much higher rate of hospitalization than the rest of the sample. This suggests that the doctors who did not answer, perhaps conscious of malpractice suits, may have been afraid to report the high rate of complications in their patients.

A special problem turned up with the Dalkon Shield, an

IUD promoted on the basis of one study in which less than half the women used the device for a full year.

Conceding that the Shield was not as effective as its ads first proclaimed, and admitting that his company marketed the device without waiting long enough to collect important data on it, one A. H. Robins Co. official told Barbara Katz, the *National Observer* investigator, "But, after all, we are in business to sell the thing, to make a profit. I don't mean we're trying to go out and sell products that are going to be dangerous, fatal, or what have you. But you don't put all the bad things in big headlines."

About a year after he spoke, the headlines were very bad indeed. FDA reported that the Dalkon Shield had been associated with eleven deaths and 209 cases of septic abortions in women who had been wearing the device. (Septic abortions are miscarriages caused by infections in the uterus.) Planned Parenthood instructed its clinics to stop prescribing the Shield. A. H. Robins, which had voluntarily reported the first septic abortions and deaths in letters it sent to doctors, agreed to halt the Shield's sale.

"We are trying to determine if this problem is peculiar to the Dalkon Shield or to all IUDs," an FDA spokesman said in May 1974. That may have upset the millions of women carrying IUDs who falsely assumed that such things were checked into earlier.

In December, FDA ended its six-month moratorium on Shield sales despite a recommendation of its advisory committee that it be continued. The committee had said serious safety questions could not be resolved without more data.

In announcing the ban lift, FDA Commissioner Dr. Alexander M. Schmidt acknowledged the need for more data. To collect that data, he said, FDA had arranged with A. H. Robins to limit the device's distribution to doctors who would register Shield-wearing patients and keep records of the women's experience with the IUD.

In other words, FDA's solution to the data-deficiency problem was to continue allowing American women to be used as guinea pigs. It meant that unsuspecting women who asked doctors for a contraceptive could well find themselves being experimented upon.

At his press conference, Schmidt said, "I would repeat that on the basis of all the evidence we can get, the IUD is a safe, reliable and perfectly acceptable alternative to the oral contraceptive and other forms of contraception."

But he had already admitted that in the case of the Dalkon Shield, "all the evidence we can get" was insufficient.

In August 1975, while FDA slept on, A. H. Robins announced it would not return the Shield to the market.

Anna Burgess, aged twenty, had a two-month-old child. One day her welfare caseworker in Monterey, Tennessee summoned her.

"We'd rather feed one young one than two," the worker told her as she arranged for Burgess to take a Depo-Provera shot at a family-planning clinic. The drug prevents conception for three months.

Testifying in 1973 at Senate hearings into human medical experimentation, Burgess said she had not been counseled as to the risks and effects of Depo-Provera. She was not told that the drug was experimental, that it had caused breast cancer in dogs, that it could increase her chances of developing cervical cancer-in-situ (localized cancer or a precancerous condition) by up to 9.1 times the national rate, or that it might make her permanently infertile.

Burgess told the Senators she feared she would be cut off welfare if she refused the drug: "From the impression I got, if I did not take the birth control, they would take the check."

After suffering extreme nervousness and unusual bleeding, she testified, she went to a private doctor who told her to stop taking the shots.

Dr. Nathan Kase, chairman of the Ob-Gyn Department at Yale University School of Medicine, had interviewed Burgess and four other Depo-Provera users in Cumberland County, Tennessee. He testified that the women had not given their informed consent to the injections and had not received adequate health care before, during or after the drug's administration.

Such experimental use of Depo-Provera was not confined to Cumberland County, Dr. Kase pointed out. Basing his statement on direct observation and on conversations with colleagues throughout the country, he said that Depo-Provera is widely used as a contraceptive and as a menstrual regulator. As of July 1976, the FDA had approved neither use.

The unfilled demand for a "perfect" contraceptive applicable to the poor and the uneducated has led to the use of non-approved techniques "where the appeal of effectiveness takes precedence over insured safety," Dr. Kase told the Senators.

FDA's Advisory Committee on Obstetrics and Gynecology has tried to change the status of Depo-Provera so that physicians can give the drug with the government's sanction.

The Committee recommended the approval of Depo-Provera as a contraceptive at a meeting in February 1973. Upjohn Co., the drug's manufacturer, presented its studies to the Committee but FDA offered no counterpresentation even though its analysis of the studies differed in important respects from Upjohn's. FDA did not mention to the Committee that at least two of its medical officers who had examined the Upjohn data in detail had recommended that physicians stop administering the drug to humans, as a contraceptive, until certain safety questions had been resolved.

A verbatim transcript of the Advisory Committee meeting shows that the only individuals making presentations, besides the Upjohn personnel, were representatives of several population-control groups. They all favored approval of Depo-Provera.

During the discussion, which should have concerned an evaluation of the scientific data, one physician on the Committee commented, "We all have a gut feeling that injectables (Depo-Provera) could be very important in a certain population and that could be justification for using a compound that happens to cause beagle tumors."

The transcript further reveals that even though from nine to sixteen women in the Depo-Provera studies (depending on whether Upjohn or FDA figures are used) developed cervical carcinoma-in-situ, *these figures were not discussed at any time during the Committee consideration of the safety of the drug.* The Advisory Committee made no attempt to compare the incidence of this cancer in the general female population (it turns out to be 36 per 100,000) and in the Depo-Provera subjects. The latter incidence is 235 per 100,000 according to

Upjohn's figures and 410 according to FDA's. In either case, the rate is extraordinarily high.*

The cancer-in-situ figures reported by Upjohn may have been underestimated because more than 50 percent of the participants dropped out of one study in its first year, many more were lost to follow-up, and test results suggestive of, but not conclusive for, cancer, were not included in the figures.*

Ignoring the cancer problem, the Committee recommended Depo-Provera's approval while leaving yet another safety problem unresolved: Once the drug is injected, it stays in the body for ninety days and cannot be removed if women experience a life-threatening adverse reaction. The Committee did not demand, and did not receive, any assurance that a treatment for such a condition exists.

While FDA has not, as of this writing, approved Depo-Provera, physicians may well believe that it has because FDA keeps giving them that impression. Again and again the drug agency trumpets its decision to approve Depo-Provera for contraceptive purposes and then reverses that decision at the last minute when questions about the drug's health risks are raised.

In September 1973, the FDA *Drug Bulletin,* which goes out to almost every U. S. physician, announced that FDA was approving the drug as a contraceptive for certain women. That bulletin was in error. The federal agency did not approve Depo-Provera.

Two months later, the *Journal of the American Medical Association,* misled by FDA, incorrectly reported that the drug had been approved for selected women.

And two months after that, in January 1974, the *Family Planning Digest,* an official publication of the U. S. Department of Health, Education and Welfare, ran an article headlined: "FDA Okays Limited Depo-Provera Use." At House hearings in 1974, FDA Bureau of Drugs Director J. Richard Crout termed the article "technically inaccurate and premature" and

---

* See *Use of Advisory Committees by the Food and Drug Administration,* Hearings before a Subcommittee of the Committee on Government Operations, House of Representatives, March, April, and May 1974, pp. 323–385 and 445–457. The Subcommittee staff computed the incidence of cancer-in-situ among the 3,857 Depo-Provera subjects and compared it with the incidence among the general female population, using figures from the Third National Cancer Survey, 1971.

* *Use of Advisory Committees by the FDA,* Eleventh Report by the Committee on Government Operations, House Report No. 94–787, Jan. 26, 1976, p. 33.

"probably misleading." The *Digest* containing that "misleading" article was widely distributed among family-planning clinics.*

In the erroneous announcement, FDA Commissioner Dr. Schmidt noted the risk of infertility the drug presented when discontinued. But, he said, "there is a demonstrable need for this long-acting drug among a small but definable group of women." These women, the FDA announced, are those willing to accept the risk of permanent infertility and those who are unable or unwilling to use birth-control pills.

Annie Smart, a Welfare Rights Organization director, fears that doctors and welfare departments will decide that it is poor, black women who belong in the "small but definable" group. They are the ones on whom the drug has been used during its nonapproved status. Doctors have not bothered informing women of the infertility or cancer risk in the past, Smart says, so what makes FDA think they will bother in the future? The women's "willingness" will be based on ignorance and on the fear of being cut off welfare.

"We're the guinea pigs," she says. "When states start using Depo-Provera in family-planning clinics, poor black women will have to take what they're given. They won't be able to ask questions."

Recall the case in which two twelve- and fourteen-year-old black sisters were sterilized by the family-planning clinic in Montgomery, Alabama. The clinic had been giving the children Depo-Provera shots for some time. When the clinic came under the jurisdiction of the Department of Health, Education and Welfare, it had been told to stop using the uncertified drug. (That's when the children were sterilized.)

Asked if the girls were aware that Depo-Provera was experimental and might cause sterility, their lawyer, Joseph J. Levin, Jr., of the Southern Poverty Law Center, said, "No, they weren't told any of that."

Girls like these, as well as older women, had been exposed to a possible carcinogen to prevent them from reproducing themselves. In December 1975, aware of the cancer studies, FDA's

* See Chapter 13 for another instance in which FDA issued a drug bulletin declaring, erroneously, that it had approved a controversial population-control drug—in this case, the morning-after pill. That error has never been corrected so physicians are still prescribing on the assumption that the drug is FDA-approved.

Advisory Committee on Obstetrics and Gynecology again urged approval of Depo-Provera for a certain group of women.

"Most of the members of that committee," FDA Bureau of Drugs Chief J. Richard Crout told a House subcommittee in 1974, "are in the population control business." *

As serious problems show up with individual contraceptives like the sequential Pill, the Majzlin Spring and Dalkon Shield, they are taken off the market. The Pill, the IUD and Depo-Provera may eventually be banned altogether if many women fall ill or die conspicuously enough from them. But researchers will simply replace these contraceptives with new "miracle" drugs which, again, will not be tested adequately before marketing. Cowed by medical terminology, reporters will, as in the past, accept the claims of researchers without scrutiny and in doing so will again aid the population controllers. Once more, doctors will fail to report adverse effects and the new contraceptives will be withdrawn only when the maiming of women reaches scandalous proportions.

This must happen because the same factors that made the Pill, IUD and Depo-Provera experiments possible will still be in operation: The population-control motive of contraceptive promoters and FDA advisors; the profit motive of drug and device manufacturers; the ignorance of physicians about the remedies they prescribe; and the gullibility of the press when presented with "scientific" information.

There is a fifth factor that can change: The assumption by women that doctors and the government know what is best for us.

We had only the diaphragm and the condom when the Comstock Laws were overturned. They do not suit the purposes of population controllers who want contraceptives for "unmotivated" people which do not give them daily fertility choices. But they are still the only contraceptives proven safe. Before we women accept any others, we must form health groups to evaluate the safety evidence ourselves and to lobby against the use of dangerous methods in this country and in international family-planning programs where women of "underdeveloped" countries are the special targets.

---

* Dr. Crout's statement appears on p. 436 of *Use of Advisory Committees by the Food and Drug Administration, op. cit.*

Chapter / NINE

MALE CONTRACEPTION

WHILE FEMALE CONTRACEPTIVES SEEM TO LAND ON THE MARKET shortly after the ideas for them are conceived, research on male contraception proceeds cautiously. That research includes work on a sperm-suppressing pill, bionyx controls (valves in the sperm duct that can be turned on and off), and self-immunization against sperm.

Originally many women wanted a contraceptive they could use themselves so that they did not have to depend for protection on the goodwill of their partners. But woman's expectations have risen; she thinks her regular sexual partner should share the birth-control responsibility.

Dr. Philip Corfman, director of the Center for Population Research at the National Institutes of Health, explains the current research emphasis on female contraceptives this way: The female reproductive system is so much more complicated than the male's that it offers many ways to prevent conception. There are four points in males but twelve in females at which one can halt reproduction.

That explains nothing. Researchers could simply have concentrated on those four points. If they had come up with a safe method at just one of those points, that would have solved the contraceptive problem for millions. Besides, as many researchers in male contraception point out, the external organs of males are easier to work on than those of females and it could be simpler to interrupt sperm than egg production.

"Most physicians are male and some males are afraid of tampering with themselves," Dr. Corfman himself told *Redbook* reporter Marion Child.*

In his 1854 sex manual, Dr. George Drysdale provides some background on male views of birth control. He discusses the three known methods—withdrawal, condom, and vaginal sponge —and dismisses the first two as "physically injurious." The last one is best, he writes, adding, "Any preventative means, to be satisfactory, must be used by women, as it spoils the passion and impulsiveness of the venereal (sexual) act if the man has to think of them."

Dr. Robert Kistner, a Pill defender, could have been speaking in Drysdale's century when he explained why a male birth-control pill had not been tried first. He said, as *The Boston Globe* reported in 1971, "that the male is more sensitive to the psychological factors of the sex act than the female."

How, one wonders, does Kistner know that?

The attitude of Drysdale and Kistner may help explain the pessimism doctors like John MacLeod feel about *ever* developing a male contraceptive. Despite newspaper stories announcing the probable emergence of a male pill, Dr. MacLeod, a specialist in male fertility at the New York Hospital, finds it unlikely.

"It can be done if you use enough testosterone (male hormone) and if men are willing to use the pill for the time they don't want to reproduce," he told me. "But it would be very difficult to totally suppress spermatogenesis. There would have to be regular checks of sperm, so I'm pessimistic about it."

MacLeod added, "There would be risks involved. Testosterone is a powerful hormone. You can't get sex hormones with impunity. We don't know what the long-term effects would be but they might be considerable."

Yet sex hormones are exactly what women take in their Pill.

* *Redbook,* February 1973.

Dr. Andrew V. Schalley, a contraceptive researcher at the Veterans Administration Hospital in New Orleans, said in an interview that some sperm-suppressing drugs have been available for fifteen years. One, an amebicide, had a completely reversible effect but it was abandoned, he reported, because of a "distressing" side effect: The prisoners on whom it was tried got violently sick when they drank alcohol.

Dr. Don W. Fawcett, chairman of Harvard Medical School's Anatomy Department and an expert in male reproductive physiology, told me that the manufacture of a male pill is feasible right now using the same principle on which the female Pill is based. But, in his research, he is trying to find a drug that would affect only the epididymis of the man, not his entire body. (The epididymis is a structure in the testes into which the sperm passes and matures after it has been formed in the seminiferous tubules.) By affecting the epididymis, the drug would prevent maturation of the sperm while causing no adverse side effects in the rest of the body.

It is clear, then, that the pill experiment of the 1960s and 1970s will not be repeated on male subjects. Instead, after years of careful research, a male pill may emerge that acts only on the target organ.

Has contraceptive research focused on the woman because male researchers are reluctant to tamper with the male reproductive organs? I asked Dr. Fawcett.

"That has been true in the past," he replied. "This is changing."

Attitudes probably are shifting. But right now, as we will see in the story of thermatic male-sterilization research, the male bias is still with us.

The idea for the thermatic method of temporary male sterilization (TMS) is not new. Heat's effect on sperm has been known since Hippocrates' time. In 1921, Martha Voegeli, a Swiss doctor practicing in India, put that knowledge to use.

This is her method: A man sits in a bath of 116 degrees Fahrenheit for forty-five minutes daily for three weeks. Six months of sterility results, after which, normal fertility returns. For longer sterility, the treatment is repeated.

Dr. Voegeli arrived at her method, she writes, "after ten years of experimentation with the free and intelligent cooperation of nine male patients." The volunteers, she emphasized, "were motivated by truly humanitarian considerations. Their distress at the sight of the misery around them was as great as my own."

She used the method during famines between 1930 and 1950.

Whether the systematic use of TMS for longer than twenty years would have had any undesirable side effect is not known, she reported, but within that period no such effects, local or general, physical or psychic, could be observed.

After fertility returned to her subjects, Voegeli stated, children subsequently born to them were completely normal.

In 1949, Dr. Voegeli began an unsuccessful twenty-year campaign to spread word of TMS. From her native Switzerland, she wrote to the heads of many states offering the details of her method. (The Japanese government did respond in 1954 and she sent it the information.)

Voegeli also wrote to health professionals and officials asking them to study TMS further so that, if the tests were favorable, the method could be made available on a wide scale. Among those officials were Dr. Clarence Gamble of Harvard, Dr. Warren O. Nelson of the Population Council, Dr. John Mac-Leod, a specialist in male fertility at Cornell University Medical College, a Dr. Krause of the University of Vienna, Dorothy H. Brush, editor of a Planned Parenthood news publication, Dr. Harrison Brown of the California Institute of Technology in Los Angeles, Prof. George H. L. Zeegers, secretary of the Catholic Institute for Social-Ecclesiastical Research, located at The Hague, Julia Brown, executive director of the Maternity Health Association in Cleveland, Dr. Mary Calderone, medical director of Planned Parenthood Association of America, and a director of the Laboratories for Family Planning in London. She also communicated with Dr. Sheldon Segal, then assistant medical director of the Population Council.

One question Dr. Voegeli wanted researchers to explore was this: Did the hot baths kill the sperm or merely slow their movement? She had found that treatment with a saline solution restored sperm motility to normal. This suggested, she thought, that sterility from heat was due to the impaired motility of the sperm rather than its destruction.

TMS seemed to be effective, safe, simple and cheap. The

only cost, Voegeli pointed out, was a bucket of hot water.

To a friend in Ohio, she wrote in 1953: "I have the 'goods,' if I may speak plainly. Can you think of a way to put them *over?*"

Her friend talked to Brown of the Maternity Health Association and Brush of Planned Parenthood. They sent her method to Dr. Gamble of Harvard that year. In August 1954, Gamble reported that he had only been able to find two subjects. In both cases, he confirmed Voegeli's findings. The two cases suggested that sperm count can be decreased by the hot baths, he concluded, adding that he hoped to learn, through further research, how long it takes for the average person and how long the effect lasts.

But Gamble became involved in researching a female method of contraception—a certain tea used by the Shoshoni Indians. He dropped TMS entirely.

As Voegeli later explained to Dr. Nelson of the Population Council: "He said the principle of sterilization through the application of heat worked, but was unable to get sufficient volunteers though he canvassed in two medical colleges."

Next, Voegeli asked Dr. Mary Calderone, medical director of Planned Parenthood, to test TMS. Planned Parenthood had no laboratories, Calderone replied. She referred the method to Dr. John MacLeod of Cornell. Dr. MacLeod, she reported back to Voegeli, thought the technique had real merit but that he would have the same difficulty Dr. Gamble had had in getting a test group together.

Calderone passed the method on to another researcher. There is no correspondence from him in Voegeli's papers.

Voegeli then wrote to Dr. Harrison Brown of California Institute of Technology. The method was interesting, he replied, and passed it on to another doctor at CIT. No correspondence from him is filed.

She wrote to the Catholic Institute for Social-Ecclesiastical Research at The Hague, but this time signing herself "M. Voegeli." The director addressed her as "Mr." and, in succeeding letters, she left that uncorrected.

The Institute's Dr. Zeegers sent the method to a Dr. Krause of the University of Vienna who also confirmed her findings. But, after expressing some interest in a method of which the

Pope might approve, the Institute let the matter drop.*

In 1956, Voegeli tried to get an article on TMS, along with a plea for further research on it, published in London's *Family Planning* magazine. An editor, who was also a physician, turned it down.

"I would prefer," he wrote her, "to publish a report of some work which has been done here on the general effects of temperature on male fertility and include a short letter from you raising the question. Would that be agreeable to you?"

In a revealing comment two weeks later, he wrote her, "I think that much of the work here on temperature fertility has been the reverse of yours—i.e., the effect of cooling in promoting fertility in infertile males."

Writing later about the rejection of her article, Voegeli recalled: "That was, however, at a time when a Dr. Anderson of one of those laboratories was about to publish an article on Fertility, which according to the editor, should not be preceded by mine." However, the editor offered to see that her method was mentioned at the Fertility Congress in Naples in 1956.

It was indeed mentioned—in two sentences. The conference report noted that "a Swiss doctor had worked out a method of male sterilization through the application of heat." Completing the discussion, the report added a comment by the fertility expert, Dr. Anderson, that the method would never be of practical value.

Then in 1960, a friend sent Voegeli a newspaper story on male contraceptive research. Dr. Warren O. Nelson of the Population Council in New York was quoted as saying that Japanese studies had shown hot baths to be effective in reducing the number of sperm below levels of fertility.

Voegeli wrote Nelson urging him to test this method which she had described to the Japanese in 1954. He replied on De-

* My efforts to locate Dr. Krause have been unavailing. Dr. Voegeli does not remember his first name and she fears he might be dead since, in 1931, when he tested the method, he was already a good deal older than she. I corresponded with a physician at the University of Vienna who, in an effort to help, asked me: "Are you sure that he was an M.D.? He could as well have been a zoologist or a veterinarian. In any case, I think he would not have made his tests on human beings. So it might be that the man you are looking for is Curt Krause, a professor of veterinary pathology." I find it interesting that he assumes the method would not have been tried on human males.

An inquiry I sent to Dr. Curt Krause went unanswered.

cember 7, 1960, that the Population Council believed additional research should be done on this form of contraception and that, in all likelihood, the Council would sponsor such research.

It never did.

In 1967, an employee of Dr. John Rock, the co-developer of the Pill, wrote Voegeli asking for information on her work.* During the early 1960s, Rock and his colleague, Dr. Derek Robinson, had begun investigating an alternate method of increasing testicular temperature, the use of insulated underwear.

If the method could be shown to be a cheap, easily available, harmless, effective and reversible contraceptive, it should prove acceptable to many men, Rock and Robinson wrote in 1965. That is what Voegeli had been saying since 1947.

Some of Rock's subjects wore insulated underwear; others soaked in hot water. In both cases, the increased scrotal temperature resulted in suppressed spermatogenesis. Researchers saw no change in the volume of semen. In nine men, the drop in sperm count was followed by a rise to levels higher than those before treatment.

After the period of sterility, the wives of six of the men conceived. All their pregnancies were normal.

Rock and Robinson conclude that the heat method may have applicability not only as a contraceptive technique but, as Dr. Anderson had anticipated, as a means of increasing fertility. Their study supports the contention that close-fitting apparel may sometimes be responsible for male infertility.

In another study, Rock and Robinson had ten men wear, during waking hours, an athletic supporter with some added oilcloth and paper tissue. In 1967 they reported that their studies had led them to suspect that fertility might be affected by a slight but sustained increase in scrotal temperature.

"The importance of such an effect is not to be gainsaid,"

---

* In a paper published in 1965, Dr. Rock stated that, as far as he knew, the first attempt to determine the effect on human spermatogenesis of heat applied to the scrotum alone was made in 1955 by Dr. Clarence Gamble of Harvard. Then, in 1959, he wrote, a Japanese researcher had devised an apparatus for immersing only the scrotum in hot water. Somewhere along the line, the fact that Voegeli's method was sent to Gamble in 1953 and to the Japanese government in 1954 had been forgotten.

they noted. "A simple modification in modern clothing may provide a burgeoning population with an easy method of fertility control."

Voegeli was vindicated.

But the research was dropped.

Interviews conducted in July 1974 with Dr. Sheldon Segal of the Population Council and with Drs. Calderone, MacLeod and Rock reveal that TMS seems to have been rejected without further research because it is not perfect now.*

Along with Segal and MacLeod, Calderone considers TMS an unpromising method. She explains that there is no way of checking when sperm disappears, that test results have been equivocal, that the jock strap might make men itchy, and that most men do not want to sit in a sitz bath for forty-five minutes every night for three weeks.

MacLeod's belief that the method is not feasible rests on his assertion that it is extremely difficult to stop spermatogenesis by applying external heat. He doubts the validity of Dr. Rock's promising test results.

Segal explains the lack of further research on TMS this way: Heat produces abnormal forms of sperm and so, if ever contraception fails, abnormal fetuses might be created. (He acknowledged that no animal studies had been undertaken to determine if that fear were a realistic one.)

Commenting on Dr. Nelson's statement to Voegeli about TMS, Segal says, "I agree that more research should be done on it."

The Population Council—the biomedical division of which Segal directs—has had thousands to spend on contraceptive research, but it has undertaken no controlled experiments of Voegeli's method.

Dr. Rock, now in retirement, says he considers his test findings very promising.

"It does work," he says. "Only one of the total of seventy-five volunteers showed no effect of the heat and his results were so completely at variance with the others that I always suspected he was devious about it. Strange fellow."

* Dr. Nelson died in 1964.

Only one volunteer experienced any bad side effects, he claims. That subject quit the experiment because he kept sweating. No harmful effects have shown up since 1967 and no malformed fetuses have been produced by any of the volunteers, Rock says.

But results varied considerably with time and method. Because the method was not foolproof, he said, no more research was being done on it. Moreover, individual differences in anatomy, like fat thighs or long scrotums, would have required that the garment be individually fitted, Rock explained.

So TMS seems to have been ignored because it would not be a completely efficacious method for everyone. When pressed, doctors acknowledge that it could be an acceptable method for certain couples—those willing to risk an occasional contraceptive failure and either have the baby or undergo an abortion in the first few days of pregnancy. But doctors did not come to that obvious conclusion themselves.

Certainly the notion that a method must be perfect for almost everyone before it can be offered to anyone is a strange notion.

Researchers' criterion for a successful contraceptive seems to be that of population controllers: That it work almost 100 percent of the time. Safety seems a secondary consideration. By this criterion, the Pill, even though it endangers female health, is a successful contraceptive because it does prevent births.

Perhaps researchers ought first to be concerned that their remedies do not jeopardize the health of the normal men and women who will use them. If, in order to ensure safety, the method chosen only enormously decreases the chances of a person's conceiving rather than completely obviates it, perhaps that method ought to be judged successful.

However safe or effective TMS really proves to be, one thing is clear: The reasons for ignoring it are weak.

—The fear of monstrous fetuses can not be given credence when researchers did not even bother to see, through animal research, if that fear were well-founded. According to one reproductive pharmacologist, drugs and alcohol, as well as heat, produce abnormal sperm and these sperm are incapable of fertilizing eggs.

—There is indeed a way to check sperm count. The ejaculate can easily be examined.

—A suspicion that wearing insulated jock straps would cause itching was not borne out by Rock's experiments and, of course, any man who experienced discomfort would simply not be one of those who used the method. (An itch, it must be noted, is nothing compared to the discomforts and risks women on the Pill or with IUDs experience.) Also, other methods of raising temperature could be explored.

—That men would have to be individually fitted for the garment is hardly reason for rejecting TMS. Have women complained that they must be individually fitted for diaphragms?

When I talked with Dr. Rock in July 1974, he knew of no further research being conducted on TMS. But eighteen months later I learned that Dr. Mostafa Fahim of the University of Missouri Medical School in Columbia had picked up the work.

In 1970, Dr. Fahim, chief of the Reproductive Biology Section of the Department of Obstetrics and Gynecology, studied past research on the thermatic method and then performed his own experiments on rats. He used four heat sources: Hot water, infrared, microwave, and ultrasound.

Ultrasound, a mechanical radiant energy, seemed to be the best, Dr. Fahim concluded. It worked more quickly and at lower temperatures than other heat approaches. It impaired fertility for 150 to 210 days after treatment, leaving libido and hormone levels undisturbed. When fertility was restored, all resulting offspring appeared normal.

Dr. Fahim then conducted very successful experiments with three other animal species.

It came time to begin human trials. Dr. Fahim encountered a problem. The male physicians on the committee that approves clinical experiments stipulated that Dr. Fahim first try the ultrasound on men with cancerous prostates. (These were men who would probably have to have their testicles surgically removed.) In three years, Dr. Fahim has only been able to find one patient. He must perform the experiment on ten such patients before he can apply for permission to experiment with healthy subjects.

"But I'm using ultrasound right now to treat herpes simplex in women," he told me in a December 1975 interview. "No one sees any problem with that."

He was not required to first use the ultrasound on women with vaginal cancer. Dr. Fahim attributes this difference in treatment to male chauvinism.

"When it comes to this holy land (the male sexual organs), you can not change the minds of the people," he told me. "Sperm are the holy seeds of life. People get icky about it.

"We inject hundreds of chemicals into the woman's uterus but we never touch the testes," he said.

While researchers remained indifferent or hostile to TMS for decades, Dr. Horace Thompson of the University of Colorado Medical Center managed to get grants to experiment with a method of female sterilization calling for the injection of paraformaldehyde—a tissue-destroying agent—into the uterus. The purpose was to block the fallopian tubes by inflaming them. From 1969 to 1974, the Population Council, which had failed to sponsor TMS research even after Dr. Voegeli had reminded them of its promise, gave Dr. Thompson four grants totaling $76,868 for research on various methods of nonsurgical female sterilization—one of which involved the paraformaldehyde. After some animal experimentation, the success of which was debatable, the paraformaldehyde method was tried on twelve women in Denver General Hospital. (The women, Dr. Thompson told me, "were having hysterectomies done anyway.") The Population Council subsequently ended its funding of the research because, as Dr. S. Bruce Schearer, assistant director of the biomedical office, explained to me, the method lacked promise and the trade-off between potential risks and benefits did not seem good.

I asked Dr. Thompson if his procedure could be applied to men by injecting paraformaldehyde into the testes and causing inflammation of the vas deferens, the tube through which sperm travels during ejaculation.

He replied that it was not necessary because men already had the vasectomy available to them.

Dr. Mostafa Fahim seems to be right in his assertion that

sexual bias affects contraceptive research. But he himself is patient with sexist researchers.

"You can't blame them," he told me. "They have beliefs stuck in the brain. We're swimming in what we were raised, in what we were taught. We have to wash our brains of the idea that woman is an inferior sex."

People will not change overnight, he said, but in the next generation, men and women will be kinder to each other.

Chapter / TEN

ABORTION AND STERILIZATION

JANICE R. WAS RAPED AT KNIFEPOINT IN 1970, THREE YEARS before the Supreme Court overturned restrictive abortion laws. She reported the rape to the police and when she found she had been impregnated, she called a Boston hospital to arrange for an abortion.

The hospital gave her an appointment for three weeks later. Janice explained that she was already seven weeks pregnant and she wanted a D & C (Dilation and Curettage) operation which can only be done safely in the first three months of pregnancy. She insisted on the D & C because it is much safer and less painful than the saline injection method used in later stages of pregnancy.

The hospital told Janice not to worry.

At her appointment, social workers inquired into her emotional problems and asked why she did not want the baby.

"I mean, this is a case of rape," she recalled, "and they're wondering why I don't want the baby."

They kept asking how she knew that her pregnancy was the

170

result of the rape and implied that her sexual experiences might well have been extensive.

Next, doctors examined her and told her she was fourteen weeks pregnant and so, could not have a D & C. She would have to have a saline injection and go through labor. She knew the exact date she had become pregnant—the day of the rape—and knew it had been ten weeks ago, not fourteen. No one listened to her protests.

Janice tried to find a private doctor who would perform the D & C but each one she called said she would have to pay three hundred dollars before entering the hospital. She did not have the money.

Finally, Janice telephoned Legal Aid. Lawyers there called hospital officials. Janice was invited back to the hospital and reexamined by three doctors. The chief physician agreed with her that she was then eleven weeks pregnant, not fifteen. That made the D & C possible.

To have the legal abortion, Janice next had to see a psychiatrist and have her case approved by the hospital's all-male abortion committee. But she had cancelled her psychiatrist's appointment when she thought the hospital would not perform a D & C. The hospital told her she could have another appointment in two weeks. She explained that that would make her too late for the safer abortion. An earlier appointment was impossible, they said.

With the help of Legal Aid, a prompt appointment became possible. The psychiatrist asked her questions like, "Did you have a happy home?" and "Is your sex life satisfactory?"

"He was asking all these questions to find out if I was insane," she told me. "I mean, I'd been raped and I just didn't want the rapist's baby."

When the hospital learned that Legal Aid would sue if the D & C were not performed, doctors operated on the final day of the twelfth week of her pregnancy—the very last day on which the operation was possible.

"By the time it was over," Janice recalls, "I was practically a raving maniac because they kept treating me like an imbecile and alternately reassuring me that everything would be all right and then telling me that the operation was off."

Why have abortions been such a nightmare for women?

These operations have been restricted because some lawmakers felt they were immoral while others thought the availability of abortion should depend on whether the state needed more or fewer citizens.*

Many doctors objected to the operation on religious grounds. Others argued that if a woman were allowed an abortion, she would not learn her lesson but would just become pregnant again. Pregnancy, then, should be a woman's punishment for sexual behavior which is unacceptable to the physician.

Dr. John Marshall, Chief of Obstetrics and Gynecology at Harbor General Hospital in Torrance, California, displayed a much more permissive attitude in an interview with *Newsweek* a month after the Supreme Court's 1973 abortion decision. In noting that his hospital's clinic would provide birth-control services as well as abortion, he said, "If a woman comes into the office and all you do is empty her womb, all you've treated is the symptom. You have to treat the disease—irresponsible sexuality—as well."

Holding only women accountable for sex, Dr. Marshall's "disease" theory ignores imperfect contraceptives, inadequate or nonexistent sex education, rapists, drunken husbands who refuse to use condoms, and doctors who deny contraceptives to certain (usually young) women.

Dr. Robert E. Hall, associate professor in the Obstetrics and Gynecology Department of Columbia University College of Physicians and Surgeons, and Dr. George S. Walter, Maternal and Child Health Consultant to the Indian Health Service in Fort Defiance, Arizona, argue that there is another factor in the physician's reluctance to perform abortions: The desire to control women.

Male doctors feel threatened if women can dispose of the proof of male potency—the fetus—at will, Dr. Walter wrote in the September 1970 issue of *Obstetrics and Gynecology*. Physicians want to make such decisions. For that reason, Dr. Walter

* For more information on the promotion or prohibition of birth control according to the needs of the state, see: Jonathan Kandell, "Argentina, Hoping to Double Her Population This Century, Is Taking Action to Restrict Birth Control," *The New York Times*, March 17, 1974; Kate Millett, *Sexual Politics*, Doubleday & Co., Inc., Garden City, New York, 1970; Roger Morris, "The Triumph of Money and Power," *The New York Times*, March 3, 1974; Kathleen Teltsch, "Women Angered by U.N. Speakers," *The New York Times*, March 2, 1974.

wrote, "One of the largest deterrents to a liberalized abortion policy, in spite of the public clamor, is the health profession itself."

(The AMA did not even approve elective abortions until 1970. And that approval was conditional.)

Agreeing with Dr. Walter's view, Dr. Hall wrote that hospitals adopted arbitrary, inconsistent and largely restrictive hospital abortion policies in New York when a liberalized abortion law went into effect in 1970.

"Some hospitals," he noted the next year in the *American Journal of Public Health*, "make it as difficult as they can for a woman to get an abortion. They make the entire process so expensive that women cannot afford it, so time-consuming that the pregnancy becomes too far advanced, or so restricted that women cannot qualify at all. And none of these stipulations are in conformity with the spirit or the substance of the law."

The time-consuming regulations Dr. Hall writes of are dangerous to the health of women for they result in women having abortions in the second trimester of pregnancy when the risk of death is nine times greater, and the rate of complications three to four times higher, than for early abortion.

Perhaps the physician's opposition to abortion accounts for his failure to make the best and least expensive abortion techniques available to women. The aspirator method, which employs a tiny plastic tube and suction, has long been widely used in other countries. It is safer, quicker and less painful than the D & C. In scraping out the uterus, the D & C involves the dangers of punctured uteri, hemorrhaging, infections and anesthesia deaths.

But the American doctor neglected the aspirator method for years.

Such legal abortions as were performed were generally awarded to rich, influential women or to knowledgeable ones like Janice R. In a review of therapeutic abortions in New York City from 1951 to 1962, Dr. Edwin M. Gold, obstetric consultant for the NYC Department of Health, found a substantial disparity in incidence of abortion at privately owned, voluntary, and municipal hospitals. The greatest number of operations were performed on women in the more exclusive hospital services. Dr. Gold also found that well over 90 percent of all therapeutic abortions had been performed on white women.

The estimated one million women having illegal abortions throughout the nation each year were among the less privileged and, often, the nonwhite. Of these women, five hundred to a thousand died from the operation yearly. In Dr. Gold's study, 79 percent of abortion deaths from 1960 to 1962 occurred among Puerto Rican and nonwhite women.

Hospital abortion committees, composed almost exclusively of men, judged whether individual women deserved abortions. The law never required these boards. Dr. Alan Guttmacher, the late president of Planned Parenthood, began the system thinking he could get more abortions done if he had a committee to protect doctors, Jimmye Kimmey, executive director of the Association for the Study of Abortion, Inc., believes.

"In other hospitals," she told me, "the committee system quickly degenerated into a way of keeping women from having abortions. A quota system—formal or informal—evolved."

The fear of legal prosecution may have been a realistic consideration for some physicians who were reluctant to perform legal abortions, Ms. Kimmey said.

"But more often than not, it was an excuse for avoiding a difficult situation," she added. "Doctors kept saying they were afraid of being prosecuted but doctors never were prosecuted for this. It was not at all a common thing."

In 1970, Dr. Robert E. Hall of Columbia suggested another reason for the doctor's failure to make abortion more readily available. The physician, he wrote, "plays God and often revels in this role. To some extent, legalized abortion will relegate the doctor to the role of technician, a role he resents playing. If abortion were made legal tomorrow, the demand would be enormous. Many physicians would balk."

A January 1973 Supreme Court ruling did legalize abortion and Dr. Hall was right: Doctors balked.

A month after the ruling, *The New York Times* reported that the medical profession was moving with "extreme caution" in implementing it. They needed "clarification," they said. They referred the matter to their legal staffs for study. Even where state abortion laws had been unequivocally declared void, doctors did not act.

"In some cases," the *Times* reported, "medical leaders have said the profession would continue to exercise restraint in agreeing to perform abortions."

Iowa's Attorney General declared the state antiabortion law void but Iowa Medical Society president Dr. Kenneth Lister said the society was awaiting clarification by courts or legislature. He added, "Even if the law is relaxed, they (Iowa doctors) will not be nearly as permissive as the doctors have been on abortion in New York."

Permissive?

By May 1973 many women were still having trouble getting abortions and back-alley operations had not stopped, the *Times* reported.

The Pennsylvania medical society's position on abortion had not been changed by the Supreme Court decision. That position, official John Rienman explained, is "that the society does not condone abortion on demand," but advises doctors to perform abortion only when the mother's health might be impaired, in cases of incest or rape, and only with the agreement of two other doctors.

In June, a New Jersey judge had to order two public hospitals to perform elective abortions on two women. By July, six months after the Supreme Court ruling, lawsuits were underway in nine states to force public hospitals to perform abortions. Other suits were being planned.

The Alan Guttmacher Institute of Planned Parenthood investigated the availability of abortions, nationwide, in 1974. Researchers Dr. Christopher Tietze and Dr. Frederick S. Jaffe found that between 30 and 50 percent of the women believed to need an abortion that year were unable to get one. In other words, between 400,000 and 900,000 women could not obtain the operations they needed.

Only 15 percent of public hospitals had performed any abortions at all by the end of the first quarter of 1974, Drs. Tietze and Jaffe found. Since these hospitals serve the poor, that means that it is still women without money or influence who are denied safe abortions.

Few or no abortions were performed in five states—Louisiana, Mississippi, North Dakota, Utah and West Virginia—and 103 metropolitan areas, the study discovered.

"The Court's decision had little impact on U.S. hospitals, which reported slightly fewer abortions in each succeeding quarter of 1973," Tietze and Jaffe concluded.

They added: "The default of hospitals and other existing health agencies, if it continues, will perpetuate sharp inequities in the availability and accessibility of legal abortion to women in different communities . . . and will perpetuate inequities based on socioeconomic status. Unless these inequities are corrected, women who are poor or very young, and those who live in smaller cities and metropolitan areas, will continue to obtain illegal or self-induced abortions . . ."

Such arguments leave many physicians unmoved.

"The Supreme Court decision said abortion is not illegal," one Massachusetts doctor told me. "It didn't say hospitals *have* to do them. My hospital won't allow elective abortions. That can be challenged legally but it will be a long drawn-out process."

His hospital has eased up though. Instead of having a committee rule on abortions as it did before, it requires only that a staff doctor agree with the woman's doctor on the advisability of a therapeutic abortion.

"It would probably be sticky for a thirty-two-year-old girl (sic) with two kids who decides it would be inconvenient to have another child," he explained. "They'd probably send her out. But they'd probably let a twenty-two-year-old single girl (sic) have an abortion. In both cases, women don't want babies, but in the second case, they'll phrase it so it sounds acceptable as a therapeutic abortion."

Doctors and hospitals have instituted certain rules to restrict access to sterilizations, as well as abortions. None are required by law.

Some hospitals agree to perform only therapeutic, not contraceptive, sterilizations. Many compel the woman to consult with a psychiatrist first and to obtain her husband's written permission for the operation. Then she needs the approval of doctors on a hospital board. The sterilization may be granted her if she is old enough and has borne enough children to satisfy the board.

Many hospitals used the Rule of 120 which held that a woman could be allowed a sterilization only if her age times the number of children she had borne equaled 120. So a twenty-year-old with five children would not qualify, nor would a thirty-year-old with three children.

In 1969, the American College of Obstetricians and Gynecologists deleted this age-parity formula for sterilizations from its manual of standards for hospital services but some physicians seem to be still using it informally.

"Most doctors have some criterion in their heads," Evelyn Bryant, social services director at the Association for Voluntary Sterilization (AVS) comments. "Many feel that motherhood is all-important and that women will never be fulfilled without children. The doctor is saving the woman from herself."

Here is how Judy M., twenty-six, was saved: Anxious to begin a teaching career, she told her doctor during her second pregnancy that she wanted to be sterilized right after delivery. He laughed.

"We'll talk about sterilization when you're thirty-five," he said.

Judy had been participating in the birth-control Pill experiment for two years and the doctor planned to keep her in it for nine more years. Two years after her doctor denied her the sterilization, she read the Senate hearings on the Pill, became alarmed and told her doctor she no longer wanted to take it. He inserted an IUD and made a magnanimous announcement: He would let her be sterilized when she became thirty.

Judy regards this doctor highly. She is not angry with him.

"I think a lot of women have been afraid to stand up to the medical profession," Bryant, of the Association for Voluntary Sterilization, says. "When women call here, I say, 'The only reason you're being denied this operation that means so much to you is because of your doctor.' I tell them to stand up to their doctors and demand their rights."

Hospital and physician policies on sterilization vary widely so a woman's access to the operation depends on the whim of doctors and hospital officials in the area in which she happens to live.

In Holyoke, Massachusetts, according to a prominent local surgeon who requested anonymity, tubal ligations are "frowned upon."

"Most doctors here are very religious people and they won't do these operations unless the health of the patient is endangered," he said. "I've never done one myself."

The surgeon, who is a former official of the county medical society, says that sterilizations are "quasi-illegal operations. This is one of the gray areas legally."

It is not at all gray. No state has any laws forbidding sterilization.

Besides telling women the operation is illegal, some physicians, according to AVS spokesperson Betty Gonzales, have said things like: "Oh no, you'll never get that done in an accredited hospital. You'll have to go to Puerto Rico."

The Joint Commission for Accreditation does not forbid hospitals to perform sterilizations but, Gonzales said, "Doctors have told patients all kinds of things and really, how do patients know the doctors are wrong?"

According to the Association for Voluntary Sterilization, "Misinformation and bias among medical men on this matter causes hospital policies on voluntary sterilization, particularly for women, to be unnecessarily restrictive."

There is no more reason to have a special committee pass on sterilization than there is for a committee to pass on appendectomy or plastic surgery, AVS observes.

Nor is there reason for psychiatric consultations, a requirement which, besides adding another hurdle to be jumped, implies that the woman does not know her own mind. By throwing around jargon like "diagnosis: depression," and "treatment: sterilization," the psychiatrist implies that the woman who does not want to bear more children is sick.

With the American Civil Liberties Union, AVS has filed several successful suits against hospitals that refused to perform sterilizations and Bryant urges women to sue if necessary.

Robbie Mae Hathaway, a thirty-five-year-old mother of eight, did. Doctors had told her another child would endanger her health but Worcester (Mass.) City Hospital refused to allow her sterilization there. In 1972, an appeals judge, ruling in Hathaway's favor, declared that the hospital's unique ban on sterilization operations violated the Equal Protection clause of the Fourteenth Amendment.

Fashions in medicine change. Fifteen years ago, it was not acceptable in medical circles to perform sterilizations on, say, a thirty-five-year-old woman with three children, Dr. C., chief of surgery in a northeastern hospital, explained to me. A doctor who wanted to, would sometimes get around this by saying he was doing a hysterectomy because of fibroids when, in fact, he was doing it for sterilization.

One problem: A hysterectomy is major surgery. It carries a 500 percent greater risk of complication than tubal ligation, the simpler sterilization technique, Dr. C. said. There is also some increased risk of death. But because sterilizations were "unacceptable" to the medical profession, women were obliged to take that added risk.

Dr. C. suspects sterilizations are much more available to people now than they were three or four years ago.

Before the Pill, he explained, lots of babies were being born. Now the average number of babies per couple is down by half while there are half again as many gynecologists.

"This has an effect on the doctor's income," he noted. "Because there aren't as many babies being born, he's probably more apt to do sterilizations now on anyone who wants one."

The acceptability of sterilizations to the medical profession, then, is often what determines whether women will have access to them. That acceptability is governed, not by the needs of women, but by the psychological, financial or educational needs of physicians.

Many ob-gyns in his area, Dr. C. said, have begun drumming up business by cajoling women into submitting to laparoscopy, "Band-Aid surgery." This is what happens during the laparoscopy: The abdomen is blown up like a balloon with carbon dioxide gas to separate the bowel from the abdominal wall. An incision is made in the abdomen. Through the incision, the laparoscope—a tube with a lens on one end and a light on the other—is inserted. Looking through the lens, the surgeon picks up the fallopian tubes with forceps and burns them with electric current. The instrument is removed, sutures taken and a Band-Aid applied.

Dr. C. believes this is a fine sterilization method but quarrels with the way it is presented by many fee-hungry gynecologists.

"The trend recently," he observed, "has been to present this new 'Band-Aid surgery' as a simplified alternative to vasectomy. Laparoscopy is frequently presented to the public as a simple, out-patient procedure."

"It is not," he asserted. "It is major surgery with major complications."

Women should be informed of the dangers involved so they can consider alternatives—including vasectomy for their partners—but many gynecologists actively oppose such consideration.

"One of these gynecologists told me that he presented his patients with an alternative: If they allowed their husbands to undergo vasectomy, they could not return to him as their gynecologist," Dr. C. reported. "Another suggested to his patients that it was they, the women, who had the most to lose from a pregnancy, and therefore, it was they who should be operated on—not their husbands. Frequently, he approached his patients with the query (without the husband present, of course), 'Who wants the pregnancy least of all—you or your husband, ma'am?' and with this he is able to convince his patients that surgery is preferable for them."

The surgery these gynecologists urge has a serious complication rate. Complications, Dr. C noted, include pneumonia, a major blood pressure drop (which could cause a stroke or heart attack), and peritonitis and abscess formation, "a life-threatening situation."

Middle-class women are cajoled into this surgery. But lower-class women sometimes have more dangerous procedures forced on them when they do not even want to be sterilized.

"Sterilization as part of a package deal with abortion is not unheard of in city hospitals when you're dealing with indigent patients," Dr. C. said. "It doesn't happen in private practice though."

Why does it happen at all?

"The doctor feels that a girl (sic) with lots of kids, on welfare, and not intelligent enough to use birth control, is better off being sterilized," he explained.

("Not intelligent enough to use birth control" is often a code phrase for "black" or "poor.")

Here is the population-control motive again. Dr. H. Curtis Wood, an ob-gyn and former medical consultant to the Association for Voluntary Sterilization, spelled it out in a 1973 *Contemporary Ob/Gyn* article. After minimizing the adverse effects of sterilization on women, Dr. Wood noted that an excess population causes many social and economic problems.

"As physicians we have obligations to our individual patients, but we also have obligations to the society of which we are a part," he wrote. "The welfare mess . . . cries out for solutions, one of which is fertility control."

Dr. C. told me that another reason for the insistence on sterilization along with abortion is the resident's desire to get many surgical cases under his belt before going out into private practice.

Before Medicaid, doctors had lots of teaching material (indigent patients) to work on but now poor people on Medicaid can get private doctors and they do, he said.

"This reduces patients at city hospitals," the surgeon noted. "So it's hard for residents to get surgical experience."

At a public hearing Boston women held in 1972 to relate their experiences with abortion, birth control and sterilization, Diana, thirty, told of her narrow escape from the knife when she was admitted for an abortion:

"I was in there for the operation and they were talking about tubal ligation. I'm just glad I know—I mean, what if I had not heard the words before? They were just slipping it right by. And I said, 'Do you think I'm an idiot?' My blood pressure just shot up. And I said, 'No.' I would have done anything to get out of there. They said, 'You're in now.' I got kind of scared. I couldn't believe it. I worked at the university. I had never been on welfare. It (the abortion) had been recommended by the psychiatrist. I looked up the statistics later and out of 600 legal abortions, half of them were sterilized. I said, 'Why?' and they said, 'You've had your chance,' and I said, 'Who gets by then?' and they said, 'Seventeen-year-olds, first time, maybe.' I got out, and they said they'd let me out for one reason. Can you imagine? They'll *let* me out for one reason . . ."

(She did not state the reason.)

In 1972, medical students questioned whether physicians in Boston City Hospital's (BCH) obstetrics and gynecology department were sometimes performing procedures on women without their knowledge and without recording these procedures in the women's medical records. The Boston University Medical School students, who had all served in the hospital's obstetrics ward, raised the issue in a report alleging unnecessary gynecological surgery at BCH. One student stated that she had been present during a Caesarian section when physicians also performed a tubal ligation and listed it as an appendectomy.

"To my knowledge, neither the patient nor her husband were ever informed that the patient had been sterilized," the medical student wrote.*

A hospital spokesperson, as well as residents and interns then serving at Boston City Hospital, denied all the allegations of the students.

The next year, a report by the Health Research Group, a Ralph Nader–affiliated consumer organization in Washington, D.C., charged that coerced sterilizations had occurred not only in Boston but throughout the nation.

The report stated that in many cases, sterilizations were being "sold" to women—many of whom were black—deceptively. One noted ob-gyn, for example, said, "Women seem to accept the procedure (sterilization) more readily if the word 'operation' is not used." He referred to it as a "stitch in the vagina" to prevent pregnancy.

Such "hard-sells" had occurred in hospitals in Los Angeles, Baltimore, Boston, New Orleans, Nashville, Chicago and Louisville, the report charged. More than half of twenty-five interns and residents informally surveyed at Los Angeles County Hospital (LACH) admitted that female sterilization had been sold hard at the hospitals where they had just trained.

Almost every major American teaching hospital had at least doubled the number of elective tubal ligations in the previous two years, the consumer report added. At one institution— Women's Hospital, Los Angeles County-University of Southern California Medical Center—there was a 470 percent increase

* See, Carl M. Cobb, "Students Charge BCH's Obstetrics Unit With 'Excessive Surgery,'" *The Boston Globe*, April 29, 1972.

in the number of elective tubal ligations and a 742 percent increase in elective hysterectomies in the two-year period from 1968 to 1970.*

At a Massachusetts hospital, according to the report, a staff member said that while prolapse of the uterus used to provide many opportunities for residents to learn vaginal hysterectomies, "now the residents have to get their vaginal experience by doing vaginal hysterectomies for sterilization."

A medical student further reported that "on many occasions, patients requesting sterilizations . . . usually by tubal ligation, were talked to for several days until they agreed to hysterectomies."

Hysterectomies have an extremely high rate of operative complications (50 percent), the HRG report noted. So, in order to let hospital staffs get experience, women have not only lost their uteri, but been unnecessarily subjected to the risk of, among other complications, bladder trauma, excessive blood loss and pelvic hematomas.

The report cites twelve cases at a Maryland hospital in which women—most of them eighteen to twenty-one years old—were given sterilization permits to sign "literally minutes before a Caesarian section (and sterilization) was to be carried out." Most of the women were in labor when asked to sign the permit. Most had only one child. There was no evidence that any of the women had expressed any interest in sterilization previously though the hospital routinely inquires into that when a woman registers weeks before delivery.

Nader's Health Research Group doubts that women under such circumstances can give their "informed consent" to an operation.

In April 1974, the U.S. Department of Health, Education and Welfare issued interim federal regulations protecting an adult's right of informed consent to sterilization. A year later, the American Civil Liberties Union (ACLU) found many leading hospitals in "gross noncompliance" with these regulations. ACLU surveyed 154 teaching hospitals. Of the fifty-one responding, 23 percent were ignoring the regulations substantially and 70 percent, totally.

* Lester T. Hibbard, M.D., "Sexual sterilization by elective hysterectomy," *American Journal of Obstetrics and Gynecology*, 112, 1076, 1972.

Chapter / ELEVEN

CHILDBIRTH

THE WOMAN WHO IS ABOUT TO GIVE BIRTH IS REMOVED FROM her loved ones, taken to a cold and sterile delivery room, strapped to a table, her legs spread apart and elevated, her knees in stirrups, her arm attached to an intravenous bottle, her belly to an oscilloscope. She looks up into a spotlight. Gleaming instruments and masked strangers surround her.

No longer is the American mother an active childbearer nor has she been since the days of the midwives. Now, strapped down and drugged, she is the object on which the doctor works and her unborn baby is "the intrauterine patient."

The physician, who regulates woman's access to abortions and sterilizations, also controls childbirth and he has transformed it from a natural event into a physician-centered operation.

In the late 19th and early 20th centuries, doctors did develop aseptic techniques, x-ray technology, anesthesia and blood transfusion—advances which reduced deaths in the small proportion of seriously abnormal deliveries. But even though more than

90 percent of births are normal, doctors use scientific advances not just for difficult deliveries but for routine cases as well and in doing so, turn nativities into technological nightmares.

Besides seizing the childbearing experience from women, the obstetrician's interference in normal births may well play a role in the staggering incidence of brain damage among American babies.

Yet doctors often make a woman feel that any reluctance on her part to accept any of the interventions—the labor inductions and stimulants, the fetal monitor and Caesarian section, the episiotomy and stirrups—directly threatens the infant's life and reveals that the woman is a bad mother. The doctor's shocked, "Do you want your baby to die?" is enough to stop most women from questioning medical intervention in birth.

Two American women—one born in the 19th century and the other in the 20th—discovered the results of intervention and documented them, each in her own time. Both women, Dorothy Mendenhall and Doris Haire, tried to end physician meddling in normal childbirth.

When Dr. Dorothy Mendenhall became pregnant in 1907, she went to the best doctor in Madison, Wisconsin. During her labor, he examined her without washing his hands or changing his dirty clothes. Mendenhall had had intermittent pains for several days, she recalled, and the doctor evidently did not know what to do. He finally sent her to the operating room and performed a version, changing the baby's position within the uterus.

"All I remember of it was turning my head into the pillow and thinking, 'This will be the end. I shall die; he doesn't know what to do.'"

That night, Mendenhall later wrote, "Margaret, my first born and only girl, died of cerebral hemorrhage from bad obstetrics. The little time I had her on my knees was a comfort to me. She was a beautiful, tiny child, dark hair growing in a widow's peak. She weighed little over five pounds. Her birth should not have been difficult."

After Margaret's death, Mendenhall ran a high fever from puerperal sepsis (childbed fever) and was semiconscious for weeks. Before leaving the hospital, she asked the doctor if she had any lacerations to be repaired. He told her there were none.

She knew she was not well and later, when another doctor examined her, he found large tears in the perineum (the skin between the vagina and anus) and in the rectum.

"It was a miracle you survived such obstetrics," he told her.

After that miracle, Mendenhall had three more children and returned to her medical career. As she worked, she realized that her horrible experience with childbirth had not been unique. In fact the development of obstetrics, or lack of it, was shown in her own family.

Her grandmother had died in childbirth. Her mother and she herself had suffered permanent injuries from deliveries. In four generations of her family, a number of babies had died during birth or as a result of birth injuries.

"What crimes have been perpetrated on helpless women all these thousands of years," she wrote.

Mendenhall was able to help reduce the deaths of mothers and infants at childbirth through her work with the U.S. Children's Bureau, an agency which is now a part of the Department of Health, Education and Welfare. In 1925, she studied the maternal mortality rates in the District of Columbia and found the death rate in hospital cases (11.4 per 1,000 births) to far exceed nonhospital cases (3.4), suggesting that women in childbirth were better off at home.

Other Bureau researchers found that the United States had a higher maternal death rate than any other industrial country with the exception of Spain and Switzerland. Nearly half the American deaths could have been prevented, they reported.

In 1926, under Bureau auspices, Dr. Mendenhall went to Denmark to find out why it had one of the lowest maternal mortality rates in the developed world while the United States had one of the highest. (The rates, respectively, were 2.0 and 6.5 per 1,000 births.)

At that time in the United States, childbirth caused more deaths among women fifteen to forty-four years old than any other conditions except tuberculosis. Every year 16,000 mothers lost their lives from conditions caused by childbirth, conditions which were almost entirely preventable.

Besides a high incidence of maternal mortality, the United

States had a neonatal (newborn) death rate six to nine points higher, per 1,000 live births, than Denmark's. The percentage of deaths from birth injuries was also increasing here.

What was Denmark doing that it did not have these problems?

Dr. Mendenhall found that midwives handled 85 percent of all deliveries. They used drugs infrequently and did nothing to hurry the delivery.

When she told Dr. S. A. Gammeltoft, a leading Danish obstetrician, that she was trying to discover the cause of the high maternal mortality rate in the United States, he replied that the answer was easy.

"You interfere—operate too much," he said. "We give nature a chance."

Danish childbed fever mortality rates since 1920, Mendenhall discovered, were less than half similar rates for the United States. While cases of childbed fever declined during this time, the percentage of Danish women delivered by midwives increased.

Midwives took time with mothers. They stayed two days and then sent nurses to replace them.

After witnessing one Danish birth, Mendenhall wrote: "It was a marvel to an American doctor to see a long difficult delivery of a primipara (woman having her first baby) by a pupil midwife, without the use of any anesthetic, the woman making absolutely no outcry until the actual expulsion of the head. The child was skillfully brought into the world vigorous and uninjured. No exhaustion apparently followed the delivery, for a few seconds after the birth of the baby, the mother inquired in a loud voice, 'Is it a boy?' I wondered if the Scandinavian woman had more fortitude or less sensibility than her American descendant—or have we developed a fear complex in our mothers?"

Operative interference in deliveries was much less frequent in Denmark than in the United States and Mendenhall thought that that was partly because midwives rarely used anesthesia. Mothers were awake to participate in the delivery. Forceps were seldom used. Deliveries were not operations, Dr. Gammeltoft said.

Any operative interference, Mendenhall pointed out in her

report, means a greater chance of infection, even in the hands of the best surgeons. "Less well-trained physicians, less careful . . . resorting to operative procedures because they have seen it advocated by a great obstetrician or because they like to operate or even because they are in a hurry, cannot be expected to show such good surgical results."

She also observed "how prone imperfectly trained physicians in this country are to shorten a maternity case by some form of operation."

Hurry had become part of the national temperament, Mendenhall noted, and it had infected doctors. "When hurry in the confinement attendant meets fear in the mother, the combination certainly militates against safe and sane obstetrics," she wrote. "Hurry and fear, resulting in too frequent operative interference, is at the basis of our high maternal mortality."

The Children's Bureau issued Mendenhall's report in 1929.

Yet until the publication of a survey of deaths in New York City in 1932, Mendenhall wrote, the medical profession was not willing to assume the responsibility for the high death rate of mothers in the United States. It generally belittled the Bureau's work and questioned its statistics.

"The midwife was their favorite scapegoat," she added, "not just for the loss of mothers but for our high birth mortality and neonatal deaths among infants."

(Midwives, it must be pointed out, then practiced only in the far South, in pioneer communities and in city ghettos.)

Though most physicians disparaged the Bureau's childbirth reports, the three leading obstetricians in the country, along with expectant mothers, supported them so hospitals were compelled—for what turned out to be a short time—to change some delivery practices.

"Most of my work came out of my agony and grief," Mendenhall recalled in her memoirs. "All the writing and teaching on safe maternity, I have thought of as a memorial to Margaret, my first child and only girl."

In 1950, Doris Haire, a Boston housewife who had been raised in Oklahoma, was pregnant with her first child. She read a magazine article by Dr. Herbert Thoms, an advocate of natural childbirth, warning that drugs and obstetrical instruments posed dangers to the baby. Alarmed, Haire decided to deliver her baby without anesthesia.

The Vanderbilts' obstetrician attended Doris bceause her husband, John, was a lawyer for the family. Doris had a private room and John stayed with her during labor.

Natural childbirth, the absence of any physical or chemical conditions which would disrupt the normal birth process, was so unusual then that student nurses came in groups of five to watch it.

Haire received excellent care.

"But I realized it wasn't typical care," she recalled. "We were associated with an influential family so we got things other people didn't get. If I'd been Doris Haire, girl Oakie, I might not have been treated so well. I saw how the other women were treated and the way they looked when they came out of the delivery room. Just by a flick of fate, I could have been the woman screaming in the labor room. I kept comparing the me-that-was with the me-that-might-have-been and I got damn mad at what they'd have done to the me-that-might-have-been."

As it was, the birth was joyous.

"The moment Betsy was born, I could have held the sun in my hand," she said.

So that childbirth could be as joyful to other women as it had been for her, Haire eventually studied childbirth practices around the world. She tried to account for the still high infant and maternal mortality rate in the United States. Her report, published forty-six years after Dr. Mendenhall's, cited the same basic problem: Too much physician interference with childbirth.

Between Betsy's birth and her 1972 report, Haire delivered three more children and happily spent fifteen years at home caring for them.

When her children entered school, she began volunteering in a pediatrics ward. She saw many children there with eczema so bad they were entirely bandaged. All these children had been bottle-fed, she noticed.

Haire had breast-fed her children on a doctor's advice, because both she and John had asthma. Something in the mother's milk, the doctor had explained, seemed to provide protection against allergy.

Haire remembered the doctor's comments and began reading the scientific literature on the subject in the hospital's library. From her research, she wrote a breast-feeding instructions pamphlet that was sponsored by the International Childbirth Education Association (ICEA), a federation of groups and individuals interested in education for childbearing and in family-centered maternity care.

In 1965, she joined the ICEA and began studying childbirth in depth. She started with some questions:

Why, she wondered, was an infant born in the United States four times more likely to die in the first day of life than an infant born in Japan?

Why did the United States lead all developed countries in the rate of infant deaths due to birth injury and respiratory distress?

Why is there such a phenomenal incidence of mental retardation in this country? Could it have anything to do with our obstetrical practices?

To find answers, Haire read exhaustively in the medical literature, took the obstetrics course in a medical school and, later, a nursing school, and visited hundreds of maternity hospitals around the world. In Great Britain, Western Europe, Russia, Asia, Australia, New Zealand, the South Pacific, Africa and South and North America, Haire observed obstetrical techniques and interviewed physicians, midwives and parents. Then she compared the childbirth practices here with those employed in countries boasting low maternal and infant mortality rates.

The United States, she learned, has a number of obstetrical practices which are not beneficial to mother and infant and in which few other countries engage.

To share her information, Haire wrote an extensively referenced report, *The Cultural Warping of Childbirth*. It was issued in 1972 by the International Childbirth Education Association, which Doris and her husband John presided over as co-presidents from 1970 to 1972.

On the following pages, we will examine the American childbirth practices she found so "warped." To her list, we will have to add two others which have become problematic only in the last few years:

—Birthing women are attached to machines to monitor the fetal heart rate in perfectly normal labors.

—Obstetricians are increasingly tending to bypass the birth canal and deliver babies directly by lifting them out of the abdomen through a Caesarian section.

No effort is made to ease a woman's fear of childbirth through education about it and through the emotional support of a husband or friend during labor.

In many American hospitals, women are denied the comforting of their husbands or friends and forced to go through this stressful experience amid strangers. When, in the intimidating hospital environment, women do not know what is happening to them or why, they can become frightened. A number of studies have shown that fear, leading to tension, increases the length of labor and duration of contractions.

In the late 1960s, psychologist Niles Newton performed several experiments at the Medical School of the University of Mississippi which suggested that, by frightening laboring female mice or disturbing their environment, their labor was slowed up to 72 percent and they produced 54 percent more dead pups than mice in the undisturbed group.

Noting that an adverse psychological environment appeared to have raised death rates among the animals, Newton wrote that taking poverty mothers in labor away from their familiar surroundings and placing them in a hospital environment which may be extremely strange to them, may contribute to the higher infant mortality rate among the low-income group.*

Ms. Newton, now of the Northwestern University Medical School, became interested in the effect of environment on laboring women when, with anthropologist Margaret Mead, she reviewed cultural patternings in childbearing. She found that the Cuna Indians of Central America and the Sirione Indians of Bolivia handle childbirth very differently. Cuna women fear

* Niles Newton, "The Effect of Psychological Environment on Childbirth: Combined Cross-Cultural and Experimental Approach," *Journal of Cross-Cultural Psychology*, Spring, 1970, pp. 85–90. In Newton's experiments, the mice were frightened by picking them up and holding them after the births of their second pups, thereby completely changing what they could see, touch and smell.

birth and are kept ignorant of it. Their labors are long and they sometimes pass out during them.

But Sirione women treat childbirth casually. In contrast to the Cunas, who accompany labor with frightening rituals, the Sirione women chat and keep a mother company while she labors. Sirione labors are very quick—often only one to three hours long.

Like the Cunas, American doctors surround labor with frightening rituals such as shaving the pubic area and attaching women to monitoring machines.

Nurses often do not reassure the woman during the disconcerting rituals. Instead, they increase her feeling of vulnerability by playing "I've Got a Secret" with the doctor and refusing to answer her questions. Gretchen Walker, an R. N., and a speaker at a 1973 childbirth conference feminists held in Stamford, Connecticut, explained: "The knowing winks and nods, the use of medical jargon, the nursing response, 'I can't tell you that. You'll have to ask your doctor,' only serves to deepen the patient's conviction that she is merely an ignorant observer, a nonparticipant, a person totally dependent upon the ministerings of the doctor-father and the nurse-mother."

Having a husband or friend in the delivery room with the woman to calm her fears would help, Doris Haire thinks, but many doctors vehemently oppose this suggestion.

Obstetricians at St. Vincent's Hospital in Billings, Montana are among them. One physician, however, Dr. Bob E. Hulit, wanted to use the Lamaze technique in which the husband coaches his unanesthetized wife in breathing exercises. So Dr. Hulit spent five years going through hospital channels trying to change the rule forbidding husbands in the delivery room. When his colleagues ruled against husbands, he went to court.

The judge decided in his favor but the hospital won an appeal before the Montana Supreme Court in 1974. (Because of a court injunction, St. Vincent's was obliged to admit fathers into the delivery room from 1971 until March 1974. However, even after the Supreme Court ruling, the hospital continued to admit Lamaze-trained fathers. They are an unknown percentage of all fathers whose babies are born there.)

Paul Baier, a lawyer who filed a brief for the International Childbirth Education Association (ICEA) supporting Dr. Hulit, noted that the obstetricians' group at St. Vincent's had based its opposition to husband access on "imaginary horribles." Something might go wrong if husbands are admitted, the doctors reasoned. A husband might faint, bring a malpractice suit against the hospital, cause confusion in the delivery room or increase infections.

"In 45,000 documented cases of Lamaze deliveries with the husband present, not once did a husband faint," Baier reported, citing a five-year study in eight states. "There were no lawsuits filed. There was no confusion. There was no infection."

An eleven-year study in Seattle, Washington came up with similar findings.

St. Vincent's had not even attempted to show that its fears were based on any facts, Baier pointed out in his brief. Since doctors' fears were unfounded, maybe they had clung to the exclusionary rule for reasons unrelated to patient welfare.

Some obstetricians oppose husband access, Baier added, because they feel that their professional prerogative is being seized and they do not want to give it up. Strangers—the husbands—suddenly invade their delivery rooms and upstage the physicians.

Baier, whose interest in this issue developed after he attended his own child's birth, cites another reason: "The trained parent realizes that it's the woman who delivers the baby; the obstetrician is just there to catch it. The father knows how little the doctor actually does."

He also knows when the doctor does not make it to the delivery at all. This fact, as Doris Haire points out, may lie behind physician opposition to the presence of husbands.

Hospitals do not keep statistics on how frequently obstetricians miss deliveries but widely traveled childbirth observers like Haire say it is very common.

In an article in the February 1974 *American Journal of Nursing*, nurse-midwife Ruth W. Lubic, general director of the Maternity Center Association in New York City, also referred to this situation: "One only has to talk with labor and delivery room nurses away from teaching centers . . . to know that often, due to pressures in the delivery suite, nurses must conduct deliveries."

Since many physicians, planning to arrive at the hospital just before delivery, handle labor through telephone conversations with the obstetrical nurses, it seems reasonable that they would often misjudge the split-second timing and miss the birth. When this happens, Haire told me, there is a common trick the obstetrician uses to cover up:

"He dashes up the back stairs, puts on a scrub suit, washes his hands and walks out to the waiting room wiping his hands. 'You have a fine baby girl,' he tells the husband, letting him assume that the doctor delivered her."

When husbands attend childbirth, Haire notes, physician attendance at deliveries improves.

Doctors at university medical centers, Haire points out, have been slow to accept husband presence "due to the concern that the husband may object to his wife's being used as a teaching subject."

In the last few years, some maternity services, especially those near large cities, have begun responding to parents' demands and allowing husbands in delivery rooms. In cities, hospitals tend to locate near each other so women who do not like the regulations of a particular obstetrics service can take their business to a more obliging one.

But with increasing frequency, hospitals are agreeing among themselves to let only one of their number handle *all* maternity cases. This regionalization of medical care eliminates competition for obstetrical patients and makes hospitals immune to consumer pressure. According to Peg Beals, a childbirth educator and current president of the ICEA, hospitals in these locations and in rural areas still tend to bar husbands from the delivery room.

Women are unnecessarily submitted to a shaving of the birth area.

Alone in the unfamiliar hospital environment, the woman may well feel uneasy. The pubic hair-shaving procedure heightens her apprehension. Doctors have justified the practice by saying it reduces infection but they have no evidence to support that contention. In fact, a study conducted at the Research and Educational Hospitals in Chicago in the early 1960s showed that the practice failed to reduce infections. The 7,600 patients who were not shaved had slightly fewer postpartum complications than women who were shaved.*

Gretchen Walker, the R.N. who spoke at the 1973 childbirth conference, thinks nurses have gone along with the shaving practice partly because women, absorbing society's disdain for females, have not liked women. The nurses' own sexuality, as well as that of other women, arouses fear and shame in them.

"We shave the pubic hair, continually trying to 'keep things clean,' implying that there's something dirty about the entire process," she said.

Birthing women are attached to machines during normal labor.

After the woman has been shaved, the nurse will often wheel a box-like machine, the fetal monitor, into the woman's cubical to audit her labor. This can be done internally by rupturing the woman's membranes and clipping electrodes to the fetal scalp in a procedure doctors claim—without benefit of testimony from the principal subject—is painless to the unborn baby. This method produces highly accurate records of the fetus' heart rate.

But most hospitals monitor labor externally. For this procedure, the nurse encircles the woman's abdomen with two straps which are attached to the machine. Placing jelly on the electronic devices on the straps, she fastens those devices firmly onto the woman's abdomen. When she turns the machine on, a strip of paper containing tracings of the fetal heart rate and the uterine contractions begins rolling out.

Dr. Edward Hon, then of Yale and now chief of prenatal research at the University of Southern California Medical School, developed the monitor in the late 1950s.

Two studies have suggested that it is very useful in detecting complications in high-risk pregnancies. (The risk might be caused by, among other conditions, maternal diabetes, heart or kidney disease, Rh incompatibility, fetal malposition, or the relatively advanced age of a woman bearing her first child.)

Originally, the machine was used only for potentially abnormal births but now many hospitals are using it in about 75

* Clay R. Burchell, "Predelivery Removal of Pubic Hair," *Obstetrics and Gynecology*, August 1964, p. 272.

percent of all deliveries, even though the vast majority of births are normal.

Though largely unnecessary, monitoring has proven to be safe except for one problem which it invites. The woman often lies on her back, almost immobile, for hours because any movement affects the tracings. One of her arms is attached to a continuous blood pressure gauge and the other is often connected to an intravenous bottle from which she is receiving glucose. Her immobility can cause "supine hypotension," a condition in which her blood pressure is lowered and, along with it, the amount of oxygen available to the fetus. (Since brain cells die without oxygen, any reduction in the baby's supply is cause for concern. The brain of the fetus and the newborn is particularly vulnerable to damage from oxygen deprivation because it is still developing.)

Dr. Hon found that compression of the umbilical cord most frequently caused the fetal distress pattern detected by the monitor. That distress could usually be relieved by having the mother sit up instead of lying on her back. Another common cause of distress could be eradicated by stopping the administration of oxytocics, a drug many obstetricians give to speed up labor. In other words, the monitor is often used to detect mischief caused by physician interference in birth. The "treatment" largely consists of returning labor to normal.

Madeleine H. Shearer, editor of *Birth and the Family Journal*, is disturbed by the common use of the monitor in American maternity wards. A San Francisco physical therapist who has taught childbirth education classes to parents for ten years, she read the studies of fetal monitoring and spoke with several obstetricians who had helped develop the machine. Besides the increased risk of hypotension, she found other aspects of the practice unsettling.

Fetal monitoring "gives an entirely false suggestion of precision," she observes. The commonly used external monitors, which tend to pick up interferences from the mother's intestines and circulation, are variously estimated to be from 43 percent to 66 percent inaccurate.

Even if the tracings were entirely accurate, Shearer notes, various physicans still interpret the same data in very different ways.

Dr. Hon, the developer of the monitor, confirms this. He thinks some doctors are performing unnecessary Caesarian sections because they misread the monitor tracings. It takes time to learn exactly what "those squiggly lines" mean, he points out. All physicians have not learned yet.

Shearer has another concern. The monitor requires frequent surveillance but some hospitals do not provide it. When personnel do watch the machine, the decrease in infant mortality, observed in the two studies of high-risk mothers, may be due as much to the more attentive care as to the monitoring itself, she believes.

"Many of us in parent education and a few people in medicine are dismayed at the sudden pre-empting of birth by machines and technicians," Shearer wrote. "We worry about the direct side effects of the monitors and about the less tangible costs of fetal monitoring."

One of those less tangible costs is the machine's replacement of the husband at the bedside in hospitals where he is allowed in the labor room. When the monitor is wheeled in, the husband must move. He can no longer reach his wife to rub her back. He can no longer hold her hands, both of which are hooked up to different devices.

"We're all for gadgetry in this country," Peg Beals, the president of International Childbirth Education Association, commented, "and if it plugs into electricity, we're thrilled."

She wonders whether, if women were given a choice, they would prefer a $6,000 monitor in their labor room or a rocking chair. The chair, she observes, keeps the woman in a healthy position for the baby and is very comfortable for a woman in labor. But when maternity ward budgets are devised, she said, women are not consulted.

Elective induction of labor is practiced for the doctor's convenience in spite of dangers to mother and child.

As Doris Haire learned, elective induction is an American idiosyncrasy. Most other developed countries (with the notable exception of Britain) frown upon it.

Doctors perform this procedure by either breaking the mother's sac of waters with a sterile, blunt instrument (amniotomy) or by administering the labor-stimulating drug oxytocin to her. (Some combine both methods.)

At least 10 percent of all births in this country are induced through oxytocin, according to statistics compiled by the National Institutes of Health. No comparable figures are available for amniotomies. Rates of elective induction vary greatly among hospitals. Statistics from the New Jersey State Department of Health, for example, show that in 1974, one hospital induced .1 percent of its deliveries while another induced a full 25 percent.

Though provoking labor allows doctors to plan schedules efficiently (all deliveries on Tuesdays), it creates certain hazards for the mother and, especially, the infant.

The artificially stimulated contractions come faster and stronger than normal ones so induced women tend to experience a much greater incidence of pain than the noninduced. The greater pain leads to a greater use of pain-relieving drugs, most of which can cross the placenta and affect the fetus. A 1975 study prepared for Britain's Department of Health and Security by the prestigious National Childbirth Trust, an organization of childbirth educators, compared 614 drug-induced mothers with a control group of women who had begun labor naturally. It found that 50 percent of noninduced mothers, but only 8 percent of induced women, managed to endure labor without drugs.

One of the induced women recalled: "The contractions were fierce. There was no buildup to them. They seemed to come on full force. Quite soon the contractions were one on top of the other. Life suddenly became too much." *

Researcher Dr. Harry H. Fields, who reviewed 3,324 elective inductions at the Hospital of the University of Pennsylvania, has reported that among the other hazards of the procedure are: malpositioning of the fetus (which often leads to a complicated delivery); infection; the descent of the umbilical cord before the delivery of the baby (which can cut off his or her oxygen supply); uterine spasm with possible tearing of the cervix and

* Sheila Kitzinger, "Some Mothers' Experiences of Induced Labor," October 1975. This is a devastating report not only on induced labor but on women's general experience of modern childbirth practices. Women's health groups can send for this valuable source at the following address: The National Childbirth Trust, 9 Queensborough Terrace, London W2 3TB, England.

birth canal, rupture of the uterus and the separation of the placenta, another condition under which the fetus can be denied oxygen; fetal distress brought on by anoxia (the absence of oxygen) and bleeding within the head; fetal trauma from the tumultuous uterine contractions; and maternal hemorrhaging after delivery.

Prematurity is another hazard of the elective induction and it is a disturbing one because premature babies, whose organs are less developed than term infants, are particularly vulnerable to brain damage. They have a high incidence of mental retardation and cerebral palsy.* Dr. Ralph Gause, former head of obstetrics at Roosevelt Hospital in New York City and former director of research at the National Foundation-March of Dimes, estimates that 10 percent of premature births result from planned deliveries following elective induction of labor and elective Caesarian section.

Dr. Robert Caldeyro-Barcia, president of the International Federation of Gynecologists and director of the Latin American Center for Perinatology and Human Development of the World Health Organization, worries about elective inductions performed by either of the two methods. They result in the compression of the umbilical cord which can cause infant asphyxia, he observes. (That is a condition in which there is a lack of oxygen and an increase of carbon dioxide in the blood and tissues.)

Dr. Caldeyro-Barcia also points out that when birth progresses without interference, the mother's membranes and her "bag of waters" remain intact until late in labor, cushioning the fetus' head against the impact of contractions. But to induce birth by the amniotomy procedure, the doctor ruptures the membranes prematurely, thus subjecting the baby to a battering he or she would not normally have to endure. The contractions may squeeze the baby's suddenly unprotected head, pushing the bones at the top out of alignment. In studies Dr. Caldeyro-Barcia supervised in twelve Latin American medical centers, he found that the parietal bones of the induced baby's skull were shoved out of alignment with twice the frequency of infants who had not been induced. Oxytocin inductions in-

---

* Abraham Towbin, "Latent Spinal Cord and Brain Stem Injury in Newborn Infants," *Developmental Medicine and Child Neurology*, 1969.

tensify contractions so markedly that they can also cause disalignment of these bones, he found.

Furthermore, in these inductions, fetal heart monitor tracings show that almost 75 percent of the mother's contractions result in a reduction of oxygen to the baby's brain.

Dr. Caldeyro-Barcia thinks, on the basis of his studies, that doctors subject most babies to these risks for no reason. At the March 1974 conference of the American Foundation for Maternal and Child Health, he stated that it was "unnecessary" to use oxytocics in as many as 90 percent of births where they are administered today.

Advocates of elective induction say that the benefits of convenience must be weighed against the risks to health. One benefit frequently cited is that the mother, knowing in advance the date of her hospitalization, has time to make babysitting arrangements for her other children. When this slim advantage is weighed against the possible lifelong blighting of her child through brain damage, what woman would choose induction?

The 1975 British study by the National Childbirth Trust found that, in fact, most induced women were given no choice at all. They were simply told that their labors would be provoked.

No study of this kind has been performed in the United States so we do not know whether women here are presented with all the facts—the hazards as well as the benefits of induction—and allowed to make informed decisions.

Even women who are not induced are frequently given oxytocics, after labor has begun naturally, to strengthen or speed up the contractions. One in every five women in this country has her labor artificially stimulated, NIH statistics reveal.

Again, there can be a wide discrepancy in rates between regions of the country and even between hospitals in the same state. In New Jersey in 1974, almost a third of women had their labors stimulated. One hospital in the state sped up 3 percent of its births and another hospital, 71 percent.

Sometimes physicians stimulate labor for medical indications, but often they undertake it "to satisfy the American propensity for efficiency and speed," Doris Haire, now president of the

American Foundation for Maternal and Child Health, wrote. In doing so, they expose mother and child to the same hazards involved in elective induction.

During a contraction, the unborn baby usually receives less oxygen. What happens to the baby during artificially stimulated labor when contractions come faster and harder than they normally would? We have no information on that. But Haire wonders if the gradual buildup of contraction intensity in normal labor is a natural means of protecting the baby. No one knows the long-term effects of tampering with that process.

A birth is occasionally delayed until the obstetrician arrives.

While some doctors induce labor for their convenience, others infrequently slow the birth process. To prolong labor so they can get to the hospital on time or sleep through the night, these doctors order nurses, by telephone, to give a labor-slowing drug, or to hold the mother's legs together. (Of course that latter procedure presents the danger of infant brain damage due to oxygen deficiency.)

It is impossible to get figures on the incidence of such practices. Drugs given to slow labor are the same ones given to ease pain. As one obstetrics nurse said after telling me about a doctor in her hospital who engages in the practice, "You'll never see in the records, 'Sedation given so doctor could finish his dinner.'"

Letters women wrote to the *Ladies' Home Journal* suggest that the practice was fairly common in the 1950s. A registered nurse sent a note to the *Journal* in 1958 reporting abuses she had witnessed in delivery rooms and demanding an investigation of "the tortures" that were going on there. That brief note brought a greater response from readers than almost any full-length feature article the *Journal* had ever printed. Many hundreds of women from all over the country wrote letters and most of them confirmed the nurse's charges. Fully half the correspondents wrote that their babies had been artificially held back from birth because the doctor was not on hand.

Some health professionals wrote angrily denying other charges the mothers made, which prompted the *Journal* to comment:

"Strangely, this charge that babies are held back from being born in order to suit the doctor's convenience drew few denials from nurses and doctors." *

Obstetrical medicine is routinely used despite the fact that it tends to reach the fetus as well as the mother.

While Dutch women usually give birth with the emotional support of their husbands and midwives as their only (and very effective) form of pain relief, American women are often frightened into believing that they could not possibly endure childbirth without some drug or anesthesia. Yet anesthesia can harm mother and child. As Doris Haire points out, its routine use by American obstetricians leads to other interventions in childbirth including the following common ones:

—Stimulating the mother's contractions with drugs.

—Moving the mother to an emergency room because the need for resuscitating the infant will be increased.

—Placing the woman in the more dangerous lithotomy position (on her back) because she will be unable to control her legs.

—Delivering by forceps and performing an episiotomy (an incision to enlarge the vaginal opening) because the numbed mother has lost her bearing-down reflex and become incapable of participating in the delivery.

—Clamping the umbilical cord early so the infant can be resuscitated immediately and his or her accumulation of obstetrical medication shortened. (Dr. William F. Windle, former director of research at the Institute of Rehabilitation Medicine at New York University Medical Center, points out that clamping the cord immediately is like subjecting the infant to a massive hemorrhage because almost a fourth of its blood is in the placental cord at birth. Such a blood deprivation can contribute to the danger of brain damage through asphyxia.)

—Manipulating the uterus, pulling the cord or removing the placenta by hand to deliver the afterbirth promptly and thus prevent maternal bleeding. The drugged woman is often not able to do this quickly enough herself through normal contractions of her uterus.

* Gladys Denny Shultz, "Cruelty in Maternity Wards," *Ladies' Home Journal*, May 1958 and December 1958. Shattering.

Despite these hazards, the doctor sometimes prefers a drugged mother because it is easier to work on an inanimate object than on a responsive person.

"He can cut, pull, and tug and no one says, 'Ouch!' " nurse-midwife Naomi Mayer of East Orange, New Jersey, explained to me.

Also, when anesthesia renders the star of childbirth, the mother, incapable of performing, the obstetrician takes the leading, rather than the supporting, role. He does not "catch" the baby. He "operates."

It was the indignity to which women were subjected in American hospitals that spurred Brenda Doyle's interest in a midwifery career. Doyle, now of New York City, nursed in Central America for five years and saw women there taking almost no medication. They would get up on the table by themselves and often, with minimum assistance from midwives, have the babies by themselves. And they would be perfectly fine.

"Back in the states at that time," she told *New York Times* reporter Judy Klemesrud, "there was a heavy drugging of pregnant women. One woman I know of jumped out a labor room window and others would claw and bite. It was all supposed to be in the name of painless labor but the doctors used forceps and dragged the babies out. Sometimes the mothers didn't come to for three days and the babies were often in poor condition for several days too."

In large cities, doctors are tending now to use much milder doses of anesthesia and obstetrical drugs but as Peg Beals, the ICEA president points out, heavy medication is still used in many parts of this country today. One Detroit hospital, Beals told me, now commonly uses general anesthesia for births.

No current national figures on use of anesthesia exist because hospitals are not required to report such figures to any federal agency. However, New Jersey Department of Health statistics show that in 1974, more than 95 percent of mothers delivered in that state were given some form of anesthesia.

While anesthesia robs women of the childbirth experience, it can take from babies part of their potential for learning. Here is how:

Regional anesthesia can lower maternal blood pressure, thereby reducing the oxygen supply to the fetus. In *The Cul-*

tural Warping of Childbirth, Doris Haire cites a study on the effect of paracervical block, a regional anesthesia given to mothers through the vagina around the cervix. The incidence of infant depression and of Apgar scores of six or less (ratings which indicate infant distress) was almost three times greater among those mothers who had received the anesthesia than among the control group. As one neurologist has pointed out, the Apgar score essentially measures the condition of the central nervous system (the brain and spinal cord).

With nerves deadened by drugs, women also have difficulty pushing the baby down the birth canal so the obstetrician must often use forceps, metal instruments which can grasp and pull the baby's head. Doctors employ forceps in about one third of all American births. In countries where mothers are routinely unmedicated and, therefore, capable of using their voluntary muscles to deliver the child, the combined rate of forceps and vacuum extractor deliveries is only about 5 percent. (A vacuum extractor, which is not commonly used in the United States, involves the application of a suction cup to grasp the baby's head so he or she can be pulled down the birth canal.)

Research in Europe, Haire writes, shows that forceps-delivered babies are more likely to sustain brain hemorrhage. As we will see in the discussion of obstetrics and mental retardation, the ordinary traction used in forceps deliveries can injure the infant's brain stem and spinal cord.

In view of this, a situation Doris Haire encountered when she took the core obstetrics course in a medical school recently is particularly upsetting. She was horrified, she told me, by the custom of intervening in normal birth for teaching purposes.

"Time after time," she said, "I saw women doing fine in their labor. They were pushing down and seemed to be fully in control. Then the doctors would lay the women down, let some guys practice their spinals on them, and then extract the babies with forceps.

"I finally asked the senior resident why they kept doing that and he said, 'The thing you don't understand, Mrs. Haire, is that if every woman had natural childbirth, we wouldn't be able to practice techniques.' "

While anesthesia can lead to the dangers of forceps deliveries, obstetrical medication may directly affect the fetus. Shortly after administration to the mother, almost all these drugs reach the fetus through the placenta, a sieve which for years doctors considered a barrier. Barbiturates and tranquilizers given for pain relief during labor have been found circulating in the newborn's blood a week after delivery.

At birth, sleepy from the drugs, the baby may have difficulty in taking his or her first breath. It is not comforting to know that 35 to 67 percent of infants delivered of sedated mothers delayed their first breath. (Less than 2 percent of the infants of unsedated mothers experienced the delay.)

Women can not assume that the Food and Drug Administration protects their babies from unsafe obstetrical medication. The FDA has no regulations whatever regarding drugs and the childbearing woman. It does not require that obstetrical drugs be proved safe for the fetus.

Doctors often prescribe more than one drug for the laboring woman, yet the effect of the interaction of these drugs in the fetus is an almost completely unexplored field.

There is evidence, however, that obstetrical drugs generally affect the baby's behavior and learning ability.

Studies conducted in Denver hospitals by child psychologists Esther Conway of the University of Denver, and Yvonne Brackbill, now of Georgetown University Medical Center, indicate that the muscular, visual and neural development of the infants of drugged mothers was significantly retarded in the first month of life. The more medication at birth, they found, the poorer the infant's performance on standard behavioral tests.

Animal studies indicate that such drugs can affect an offspring's future learning ability. Research conducted at the Animal Behavior Laboratory at Lafayette Clinic and Wayne State University in Detroit showed that the tranquilizer meprobamate, when given to pregnant rats, decreased the maze learning ability of the offspring.* Meprobamate is known to have a depressing effect on the cerebral cortex of the brain, the researchers observe. The drug, which passes through the placental "barrier," could have directly influenced the central nervous system of the developing fetus, they wrote.

The use of tranquilizers during labor may also affect the

* Werboff, J. and Kesner, R., "Learning Deficits of Offspring After Administration of Tranquilizing Drugs to the Mother," Nature, 197: 106–107, 1963.

relationship between the mother and her new baby. Dr. T. Berry Brazelton, professor of pediatrics at Harvard Medical School, discovered this in studies conducted at Boston Lying-In Hospital and at Mount Auburn Hospital in Cambridge, Massachusetts. He compared babies whose mothers had received tranquilizers prior to delivery with babies whose mothers had received little medication.

Although the medicated babies appeared alert immediately after birth, they became lethargic within a few hours, he found. They would lie quietly in the nursery for long periods, breathing shallowly. The skin on their hands and feet, reacting to the reduced activity of the heart and vascular system, would become mottled.

Most babies experience a temporary depression of the central nervous system after the ordeal of birth, but Dr. Brazelton found that the tranquilizers given to the mother prolonged that depression for one to two days. The medicated baby's ability to breast-feed lagged behind that of the unmedicated baby. So did its weight gain.

The extent of the baby's depression seems positively correlated with the type, amount and timing of the medication given the mother, Dr. Brazelton found.

The worst result of this depression seems to be that the baby does not respond to nursing right away.

"I don't like it (the use of tranquilizers) because it makes it harder for the mother to relate to her baby in the first few days," Dr. Brazelton told me. "It would be nice if the mother and baby started their relationship when both had their wits about them."

Research suggests that the first twenty-four hours after birth may be a critical time for establishing mother-infant bonds, so it is unfortunate that many eager, nervous new mothers first meet their babies when the infants are sleepy, unresponsive, drugged.*

In view of the risks of anesthesia and obstetrical drugs, American women should consider doing without them, as most of their sisters throughout the world manage to do. But the Amer-

* K. Robson, "The Role of Eye to Eye Contact in Maternal-Infant Attachment," *Journal of Child Psychology and Psychiatry*, 8:13–25, 1967, and M. Klaus, et al., "Human Maternal Behavior at the First Contact with Her Young," *Pediatrics*, 46:187–192, 1970.

ican obstetrician has a standard method of discrediting drugless birth. He charges that the natural childbirth educator makes women feel guilty if they can not stand the pain without medication. Women then consider themselves failures and assume they will also fail as mothers, he asserts.

This is the tack the physician always seems to take whenever anyone tries to provide women with information about drugs and medical procedures so that they can make informed decisions about the matters that may so seriously affect their lives. The physician evokes an image of a helpless woman who will only be upset, confused or frightened by knowledge and who will then do or feel something that will be harmful to herself. (Certainly that is what various physicians did at Senator Gaylord Nelson's Pill hearings. They charged that information coming out of the hearings would scare women who, in their silly fright, would stop taking the Pill and—never thinking to use another contraceptive—would begin producing what one witness called "Nelson babies.")

But whether doctors believe it or not, women can survive information. One fact about drugless birth may even delight them: When a laboring woman is given constant support and encouragement from a husband, friend or midwife, childbirth is not only bearable, it can even become enormously pleasurable.

Dr. Elaine C. Pierson of the University of Pennsylvania Student Health Service explained in *Sex Is Never an Emergency*, a guide for college students, that an orgasm is difficult to describe and that women who have had natural childbirth have the same trouble describing their "fantastic experience." She continued: "I think it is for the same reasons; they are trying to describe the same thing. Natural childbirth, without complications, is an expansion of the orgasmic experience. This is quite logical because the same physiological mechanisms are operating, namely vaginal distention and total genital stimulation."

That must be one of the world's best kept secrets.

During delivery, the woman is laid on her back, solely for the obstetrician's convenience, in a position which creates a need for an episiotomy. Since the birth canal is curved upward, she is thus forced to give birth uphill.

Before men took over midwifery in the United States, a woman used to sit upright, sometimes on a birthing stool, and deliver a child while the female midwife coaxed and encouraged her. When male doctors became the birth attendants, they adopted the lithotomy position (back flat, knees drawn up and spread apart by stirrups) for their own convenience and not for any medically valid reason.

The squatting, sitting or sideway positions seem to be more comfortable for women, Dr. William J. Sweeney, author of the popular book, *Woman's Doctor,* wrote, but "it doesn't fit in with U.S. hospital routine. Of course it's easier to work on a patient when her legs are up."

Doris Haire advances another explanation: "When the mother is lying down, it's the doctor who is having the baby. When the mother is sitting up, it is she who's having it. Many doctors don't like that."

The lithotomy position may be beneficial to the obstetrician but it can be hazardous for the baby. When the mother lies on her back with her legs elevated, the pregnant uterus tilts back against the pelvis and can compress the blood vessels supplying the placenta. That compression can sharply reduce the oxygen available to the fetus.

By reading the medical literature, Haire found that the lithotomy position also tends to:

—Adversely affect the mother's blood pressure and ventilation.

—Decrease the normal intensity of contractions.

—Inhibit the mother's voluntary attempts to push her baby out.

—Augment the need for forceps and the traction necessary for a forceps extraction.

—Inhibit the spontaneous expulsion of the placenta which increases the need for its removal by hand—a procedure which raises the incidence of bleeding.

—Increase the need for an episiotomy because of the heightened tension on the pelvic floor and the stretching of area tissue.

"Australian, Russian and American research bears out the clinical experience of European physicians and midwives," Haire wrote, "that when mothers are supported to a semisitting position for birth . . . [they] tend to push more effectively, appear to need less pain relief, are more likely to want to be conscious for birth and are less likely to need an episiotomy."

Obstetricians justify routine episiotomy in the United States by stating that, theoretically, it reduces damage to the muscles in the pelvis and reduces brain impairment of the child.

As Haire points out, there is no evidence at all to support this theory.

Another rationale is that episiotomies prevent the perineum from tearing. The straight incision they make, doctors argue, is easier to sew up than a ragged tear.

But it is the lithotomy childbirth position that puts the big strain on the perineum, Dr. William J. Sweeney, the obstetrician, points out. When women give birth in bed, before they can be strapped onto the delivery table, Sweeney notes, "everything's relaxed and usually she doesn't tear."

After citing the tear prevention theory, doctors explain that episiotomies prevent unsatisfactory love-making due to an enlarged vagina, and, in later life, prevent the woman's uterus from falling down and her rectum and bladder from protruding into, her vagina. Haire notes that, once again, no evidence exists to support these theories.

It is true that the use of anesthesia may sometimes necessitate an episiotomy. When a woman can not feel the childbirth sensations, she does not know when to hold back to allow for a less stressful delivery. She may simply push, not feeling the perineum tear. By performing episiotomies in these cases, obstetricians are correcting an adverse situation which they themselves created.

Today, while in many American hospitals doctors perform episiotomies on 70 percent of mothers, there is only a 6 percent episiotomy rate in Sweden, the country which also has the lowest infant mortality rate. Mothers and babies there appear to be doing just fine without this operation.

Why do our doctors do it then?

Prof. G. J. Kloosterman, chief of obstetrics and gynecology at University of Amsterdam hospital in Holland, offered this explanation to Doris Haire: "Since all the physician can really do to affect the course of childbirth for the 95 percent of mothers who are capable of giving birth without complication is to offer the mother pharmacological relief from discomfort or pain and to perform an episiotomy, there is probably an unconscious tendency for many professionals to see these practices as indispensable."

Obstetricians are increasingly bypassing the birth canal.

Caesarian section, the manual removal of the baby through an incision in the woman's abdomen, totally takes the childbirth experience away from the mother. Its incidence has been skyrocketing in this country in the past few years.

There are certainly medically valid indications for the operation. When the placenta develops in the lower portion of the uterus and covers the opening to the birth canal, or when the mother suffers from a condition like diabetes, or when the baby's head is too large for the woman's pelvis, then C-sections are valuable procedures.

But from 1968 to 1974—the only years for which figures on Caesarians are available—their rate has almost doubled. It zoomed from 5 to 9.2 percent. According to the Commission on Professional and Hospital Activities in Ann Arbor, Michigan, doctors in the United States performed 171,000 Caesarians in 1968, but 281,000 in 1974. In many hospitals, the Caesarian rate is up to 30 percent and going higher, Peg Beals, president of ICEA, told me.

"Doctors justify C-sections by saying they will prevent brain damage," she said. "I've seen no studies to support this."

In Holland, only 2 to 4 percent of deliveries are Caesarian. (Holland, by the way, has a much lower infant mortality rate than the United States: 11.1 deaths per 1,000 deliveries compared to 19.2 in the U.S. in 1971.)

As previously discussed, the increased use of the fetal monitor, and the tendency of some doctors to misread the complicated tracings, account for some of the alarming increase in these operations.

Sometimes Caesarians are performed because they are interesting to the doctor, not because they are medically necessary, nurse-midwife Naomi Mayer of New Jersey told me.

"Doctors want to use their skills," she said. "They're bored by normal births. They want the spectacular stuff."

The mother is immediately separated from her baby even

though bonding between mother and infant seems to occur shortly after delivery.

After the birth, babies are taken from their mothers and then brought to them again only briefly for identification and for feedings. At one New Jersey hospital until November 1972, anesthetized mothers first saw their infants when they left the hospital, three days after delivery. Today many hospitals allow the mother a quick glimpse of the baby on the delivery table and then take the child away for sixteen hours, Peg Beals of the ICEA told me.

"The father may be in some birth rooms now, but you still have to really pound and scream to get to see your baby," she said.

The first twenty-four hours after birth seem to be a crucial time for the mother to develop a maternal feeling toward her baby. But research has indicated that when the contact between mother and infant has been restricted by the usual hospital schedule, maternal response and nurturing are adversely affected a full month after birth.*

Hospital personnel often discourage breast-feeding despite evidence that, among breast-fed children, there is significantly less illness.

Colostrum, a thin, milky fluid secreted by the breasts around delivery time, and breast milk contain antibodies which enhance the baby's resistance to infection. Repeated studies in England have shown that breast-feeding is related to a lower incidence of infant mortality and sickness, Doris Haire points out.

But as one woman wrote to the *Ladies' Home Journal* in 1958, "Most hospitals consider breast-feeding an unusual quirk on the part of the mother which should be squelched at once."

Apparently that is still true. In the United States today, only 38 percent of mothers even attempt to breast-feed their babies and that rate represents a great improvement. A 1966 study in

* Marshal H. Klaus, et al., "Maternal Attachment; Importance of the First Post-Partum Days," *New England Journal of Medicine*, March 2, 1972. Before discussing their study among humans, the authors note that in certain animals like the goat and sheep, a mother who is separated from her offspring immediately after birth for even a few hours, later treats her young in an unmotherly manner—butting it away, feeding it and the young of other animals indiscriminately, or refusing to care for it at all.

two thousand hospitals found that just eighteen percent of mothers were breast-feeding. The hospital's attitude toward the practice definitely seems to affect the number of mothers who try it. In the hospitals which had a program providing women with information on breast-feeding, twice as many mothers nursed their babies as in hospitals with no program.

Haire contends that the low incidence of breast-feeding is largely the fault of the hospital regimen forced upon the mother and child. That regimen, which has not been demonstrated to benefit the infant, includes:

—Delaying the first feeding.

—Offering the baby water before that feeding, and after subsequent ones.

—Insisting the mother follow a rigid, four-hour nursing schedule, with no feedings at all during the night, a routine which, by spacing the feedings so widely apart, restricts the suckling stimulation necessary to bring about adequate production of the mother's milk.

—Giving the baby formula in the nursery rather than letting it feed on demand.

Engorgement of the breast with milk—a painful condition which causes many women to abandon breast-feeding—is basically a condition created by the hospital's nursing regimen, Haire contends.

Women who quit, or never attempt, breast-feeding, are often administered the estrogen Diethylstilbestrol (DES) to suppress their milk production. This drug has caused cancer and abnormal glandular structures in the daughters of women who were given it during pregnancy for the prevention of miscarriage. (Chapter 13 contains a detailed discussion of Diethylstilbestrol.) Over the past twenty years, an estimated forty million American women have been given DES as a lactation suppressant, most often without their knowledge, Haire reports. Many of these women must be among those who, later in life, are given more estrogen to relieve the symptoms of menopause. Haire is concerned that no follow-up studies have been performed to see if these women are especially susceptible to the cancer-producing effects of DES.

Some obstetrical observers believe that physician intervention in childbirth plays a role in the staggering incidence of cerebral palsy, mental retardation and minimal brain damage in the United States. The extent of that role is debatable because there is a great deal of information we simply do not have, but what we do know is disquieting.

First, how high is the incidence of mental deficiency?

The United Cerebral Palsy Association, the National Association for Retarded Children and the President's Committee on Mental Retardation supply these facts:

—Of every one thousand babies born in the United States, four to five have cerebral palsy. Today, 750,000 Americans suffer from that affliction.

—Mental retardation causes more disability among children than any other physical or mental abnormality. One in every thirty-five children born in this country will eventually be diagnosed as retarded. Six million of our citizens are retarded and almost 100,000 more are born each year. They come from every socioeconomic group.

—One out of every ten Americans has a mentally retarded person in his or her family.

—One in every ten to seventeen children has been found to have some form of brain dysfunction or learning disability requiring special treatment and in seventy-five percent of these cases, there were no genetic predisposing factors.

In a review of the studies on obstetrical medication and outcome of infants, Dr. Watson A. Bowes, Jr., an obstetrician at the University of Colorado Medical Center in Denver, observed that "almost certainly" abnormalities of pregnancy, labor and delivery have important consequences for the fetus and newborn. He referred to a 1955 study of 1,107 children with IQs below 80. The study revealed that various complications of pregnancy such as premature separation of the placenta and descent of the umbilical cord before the baby, occurred significantly more often than in a comparable group of children with normal IQs.*

Dr. Abraham Towbin, while a member of Harvard Medical School's Department of Neuropathology, came up with equally

* B. Pasamanick and A. M. Lilienfeld, "Association of Maternal and Fetal Factors with Development of Mental Deficiency," *Journal of the American Medical Association*, 1955, 159, 155–160.

sobering findings in his study of spinal cord and brain stem injuries at birth. The most important cause of these injuries, he reported, is excessive traction on the spinal column during delivery. Forceps applied to the head, or pulling on the baby's trunk during breech (bottom or feet first) deliveries, provide that traction.

"During the final extraction of the fetus," Dr. Towbin wrote, in *Developmental Medicine and Child Neurology*, "mechanical stress imposed by obstetrical manipulation—even the application of standard orthodox procedures—may prove intolerable to the fetus."

Over 50,000 newborn deaths occur yearly in the United States, Dr. Towbin observed. In many cases, the cause of death goes unexplained and nothing of significance is found at the standard postmortem examination. But the spinal cord is not routinely removed at these exams. If the cord and brain stem were carefully examined, he wrote, "a significant percentage of neonatal deaths, otherwise unexplained, will yield evidence of spinal and brain stem injury."

In one study in which the spinal cords of infants were inspected, researchers were startled to repeatedly encounter bleeding in the space between the vertebral canal and the sheath surrounding the cord. Often, that was the *only* abnormality found.

Several studies in which the spinal structures were examined at autopsy found spinal damage in 10 to 33 percent or more of newborn deaths, Dr. Towbin reported.

He states that there must be many children with mild injuries who, because they are not severely paralyzed, do not attract attention. It is likely, he wrote, that trauma and spinal cord injury incurred at birth accounts for the moderate degree of spasticity from which the children suffer.

Spinal and brain stem injuries lead to respiratory depression and "hypoxia," a state in which there is a comparative lack of oxygen in the body. Hypoxia can, in varying degrees, cause damage to the cerebral cortex, the portion of the brain which, among other functions, controls voluntary muscular movements, and is concerned with hearing, vision, other sensory stimuli and intellect. Even a short period of hypoxia, Dr. Towbin wrote in *Archives of Pathology*, "may lay the foundation for ultimate blighting of mentation, for the appearance of motor defects which characterize cerebral palsy, and for the development of epilepsy."

In his examination of over six hundred human fetal and newborn brain specimens, Dr. Towbin found that in some instances hypoxia causes a minimal form of brain damage. In fact, he reported, although researchers like to study the rare but interesting cases caused by genetic or metabolic disorders, *most* cerebral damage that occurs before or soon after birth is caused by, or occurs as a result of, hypoxia.

Dr. Towbin found a basic similarity between the brain lesions incurred by the fetus and newborn as a result of hypoxic damage, and the chronic brain lesions of those suffering from mental retardation and cerebral palsy. His research demonstrated how, as the person grows out of infancy, these injuries change from acute to chronic ones.

Earlier research had indicated the relation between injuries deep in the brain and exposure to hypoxia during fetal life, he reported. In the cases described by the studies, pregnant women who had tried to commit suicide by asphyxia delivered babies with hypoxic brain damage.* The suicide attempt of the mother some months before delivery deprived the fetus of oxygen. The infant subsequently born showed evidence of severe mental retardation and motor disturbance. Postmortem exams revealed extensive brain damage.

Dr. Towbin observes that while a relatively long period of oxygen deprivation can severely injure the brain, shorter periods can cause lesser brain damage. Infants, children and adolescents with this minimal brain dysfunction commonly have learning and reading difficulties and are awkward.

Minimal brain damage is a common occurrence in the fetus and newborn—a fact that is not generally realized, Dr. Towbin wrote in a 1971 *Journal of the American Medical Association* article. He estimates that more than three million adults and children suffer from it, while others may have less noticeable damage.

"With the brain marred at birth," he wrote, "the potential of performance may be reduced from that of a genius to that of

* See references 17 and 18 in Dr. Towbin's paper, listed in the source notes and entitled, "Mental Retardation Due to Germinal Matrix Infarction."

a plain child, or less. The damage may be slight, imperceptible clinically, or it may spell the difference between brothers, one a dextrous athlete and the other 'an awkward child.' "

The influence of these brain injuries on the victim's later life has not yet been fully explored, Dr. Towbin continued. However, dropouts, delinquents and youths with behavioral disturbances are frequently found to have been premature or to have had other birth complications, and to have residual brain damage, he observed, referring to several studies.*

So the fetus and newborn infant are highly vulnerable to injury.

"Biologically, the maternal-placental-fetal relationship is delicately balanced," Dr. Towbin wrote. "The placenta has a narrow margin of safety."

The hypoxia which can so devastate the brain may develop before or after birth. Researchers can estimate time of injury by the location of the lesions seen during the autopsy. Towbin found that in the majority of cases he examined, the hypoxia had occurred weeks or months *before* delivery. (Maternal disease or premature separation of the placenta could have caused the oxygen deficiency.) So in those cases, obstetrical practices could not have caused the damage.

If "most" hypoxic incidents occurred before delivery, that could still leave as much as 49 percent of the cases happening *during* birth, so it is necessary to pin down the percentages. Necessary but not possible at this time. All that could be said, Dr. Towbin explained to me, was that it was the conclusion of his research team that most hypoxic cases were caused before delivery, and that there was not enough information available to be any more precise than that. We simply do not know what percentage occurred during birth, he said in a telephone interview.

We do know, however, that most of the physician's interferences in birth can lead to oxygen deficiency in the baby:

—The lithotomy childbirth position.

—The hypotension sometimes resulting from the immobility imposed by the fetal monitor.

* The studies were: E. Dehoff, "Bridges to Burn and Build," *Developmental Medicine and Child Neurology*, 7:3–8, 1965, and E. J. Rosen, "Behavioral and Emotional Disturbances Associated with Cerebral Dysfunction," *Applied Therapeutics*, 11:531–543, 1969.

—Elective labor induction which can lead to cord compression, premature separation of the placenta and narrowly spaced contractions.

—Chemical stimulation of labor.

—Tranquilizers, almost all of which enter the fetus' bloodstream shortly after administration to the mother and tend to depress the fetal respiratory system.

—Analgesics (pain-killers) which tend to inhibit a newborn's efforts to breath.*

—Anesthesia, which can reduce the mother's blood pressure.

—Forceps delivery.

—Early clamping of the umbilical cord which reduces the newborn's blood supply.

Dr. William F. Windle, former research director at the Institute of Rehabilitation Medicine at the New York University Medical Center, does not have any more exact percentages of birth hypoxia or asphyxia than Dr. Towbin does, but he has some disturbing research results.

In experiments on over five hundred monkeys, Dr. Windle found that asphyxiation lasting from eight to twenty-one minutes leads to brain lesions. Birth asphyxia lasting long enough to require resuscitation, he reports, always damages the brain.

"A great many human infants have to be resuscitated at birth," he wrote in a 1969 *Scientific American* article. "We assume that their brains too have been damaged. There is reason to believe that the number of human beings in the U. S. with minimal brain damage due to asphyxia at birth is much larger than has been thought."

A few years after birth, the monkeys in Windle's experiments appeared to be normal but testing found brain damage eight to ten years after birth. These monkeys, Windle speculates, may be comparable to human infants who experienced some asphyxia at birth and had low Apgar scores (an index of the newborn's general health), but later seemed normal. If their brains could be inspected as the monkeys' had been, the same lesions would probably be found, Windle believes. The few postmortem studies of the brains of human infants asphyxi-

* Watson A. Bowes, Jr., et al., *The Effects of Obstetrical Medication on Fetus and Infant,* Monographs of the Society for Research in Child Development, Serial No. 137, 1970. Vol. 35, No. 4.

ated at birth did show damage similar to that sustained by the asphyxiated monkeys. He concludes we can no longer assume that the human infant escapes unharmed from short periods of asphyxia.

Addressing the American Academy of Cerebral Palsy in 1956, Windle said that in his experiments on primates, "cerebral palsy and mental retardation would not have occurred had we not meddled with the natural course of events during birth . . . The role of asphyxia in cerebral palsy and mental retardation is large, indeed so large that, try as we will, we cannot much longer hide it behind a façade of lesser or contributing causes, ones that may be less troublesome to the conscience of those upon whom rests the responsibility for our safe conduct into the world."

It might be time to reexamine current obstetrical practices, he suggested in his 1969 article, "with a view to avoiding conditions that give rise to asphyxia and brain damage."

Infants who annually survive the delivery process in poor condition with part of their potential already wasted exceed "the combined annual number of deaths from all types of cancer, the number of deaths in automobile accidents each year, and the total loss of American life in the war effort in Vietnam," a 1967 report by the National Institute of Child Health and Human Development, *Optimal Health Care for Mothers and Children: A National Priority,* observed. Proclaiming a "right to be well-born," the report noted that in the United States, "the annual production of a quarter of a million inadequate citizens . . . each year is mute evidence that for many this right is abrogated by circumstances surrounding the birth process. "

The report goes on to discuss "social pathology"—that is, inadequate nutrition, housing, sanitation and prenatal care. But as Doris Haire, president of the American Foundation for Maternal and Child Health, points out, " 'Social pathology' is a scapegoat for those who don't want to change their childbirth techniques. Many of the countries with a lower infant mortality rate than ours have diets and prenatal care we'd consider inadequate. And we still have many babies born damaged who are full-term and come from middle-class mothers."

It may be easier on the conscience to blame brain damage

solely on socioeconomic factors and on birth defects, Haire stated, but it is time to stop looking for scapegoats and realize that there is something wrong with American obstetrics.

STATISTICS FROM MATERNITY SERVICE ANNUAL
REPORT FOR NEW JERSEY HOSPITALS, NEW JERSEY
STATE DEPARTMENT OF HEALTH, 1974

Total Number of Mothers Delivered	**91,601**
Total Number of Babies Delivered	**92,554**
(Including twins and triplets)	

I. Percentage of Babies

Forceps Deliveries (Low, mid and high)	33.77
Caesarian Sections	9.95

II. Percentage of Mothers

Induction	8.80
1. Elective induction	6.49
2. Indicated induction	2.31
Stimulation of labor	30.76
Antepartum oxytocics	31.40
Amniotomy (excluding those done within two hours of delivery)	18.27
Inhalation anesthesia	37.69
Conduction anesthesia (Caudal, saddle, etc.)	40.40
Local anesthesia	18.64
Paracervical anesthesia	2.54
No anesthesia	4.71

Chapter / TWELVE

MIDWIVES

Men cannot give birth. nonetheless, they have taken control of childbearing and now they teach women how to do it properly. They started in Europe in the 16th century. Excluded from the birthing room, doctors who had never witnessed a delivery wrote books on the subject.

In the 17th century, men began actually practicing midwifery. A male midwife named Boucher attended the mistress of Louis XIV. Although middle- and lower-class women still considered male midwifery indecent, it soon became fashionable among ladies of the court.

Men gradually drove women from midwifery through the use of version and the forceps, a technique and a device which transformed the male midwife into a savior of dying mothers.

Version—turning a malpositioned baby in the uterus to enable its delivery—was hardly a new technique. Cleopatra had taught it in the 1st century A.D., Soranus of Ephesus in the 2nd, Trotula of Salerno in the 11th. But version had been forgotten. During the Middle Ages, midwives feared to use it because, if

the baby were born dead or deformed, they could be accused
of witchcraft and hanged. In the 13th century, the wife of
Frederick II and the sister of Henry II both died because midwives were afraid to turn the babies in the uterus. How many
obscure women died for the same reason, we can only guess.

The midwife's fear of the witchcraft charge may well explain
why, rather than using version and the obstetrical skills she had
formerly displayed, she began calling on male surgeons for help
in difficult births. Sometimes, as in England during the 14th
century, the law required that she do so. The surgeon would
come, insert a speculum into the mother, and use hooks and
knives to deliver the child piece by piece.

Through disuse, version was gradually forgotten. Ambroise
Paré, a man in little danger of the witchcraft accusation, re-
discovered it in the 16th century. Surgeons then began to consider midwifery a potentially lucrative occupation.

Forceps also helped men take over midwifery. A father and
son, Peter the Older and Peter the Younger Chamberlain, developed the device in 1588. They kept it secret and then announced that they could deliver at a difficult birth when everyone else had failed.

Since midwives did not know the secret, they were forced to
call in the men who miraculously delivered the babies and
collected hefty fees. The Chamberlains could keep the forceps
secret because, as a concession to female modesty, a drape was
placed over the woman and its ends tied around the male midwife's neck. While he delivered by touch, he could hide the
forceps under the drape.

The Chamberlains kept their secret for a hundred years.

In the 17th century, Hugh Chamberlain sold the secret to
Holland's medical licensing board. The board, in turn, sold the
secret to each of its licensees for a stiff sum. Eventually a group
of kindly men bought the device to release it for general knowledge and then they discovered they had bought only half the
forceps. Either Hugh Chamberlain or the board had pulled off
a swindle.

The forceps came into common use when Hugh's son,
another doctor, let the secret out before he died.

After the forceps became public around 1700, historians
Charles Singer and Ashworth Underwood inform us, "men

midwives began to replace the ignorant female midwives with a consequent decrease in mortality." *

Once men entered midwifery, women struggled to maintain their hold in the field. In 1878, three women applied to England's College of Surgeons to be examined for the midwifery license. They were accepted so Dr. Robert Barnes, a midwifery examiner, resigned. Then the College wrote the women promising their admission to the examination. So two more doctors—that is, the whole remaining examining board—resigned.

"Since then, there have been no examiners and no examinations," observer Dr. James R. Chadwick reported the next year in his paper, *The Study and Practice of Medicine by Women*. "There was, however, immediately a meeting of the Obstetrical Society of London, at which a vote of thanks to these gentlemen was carried by 'Universal acclamation.' "

The American medical profession opposed midwives just as strenuously as European doctors though the skill of "obstetricians" here was hardly impressive.

Midwives had handled all births in the colonies at first, rarely interfering with their natural course. But in the 17th century, they too had been liable to the charge of witchcraft. The first "witch" executed in Massachusetts Bay Colony, in fact, was a female physician and midwife, Margaret Jones of Charlestown. Incurring the disfavor of some ministers and "regular" doctors, she was hanged in 1648.

A male midwife was first reported in 1745. More men entered obstetrics after Dr. William Shippen, Jr., opened a midwifery school in Philadelphia in 1762 "to instruct those women who have virtue enough to own their ignorance and apply for instruction, as well as those young gentlemen now engaged in the study of that useful and necessary branch of surgery, who are taking pains to qualify themselves to practice . . . with safety and advantage to their fellow citizens."

Three years later, the first of many American medical schools was established. It then became easier for men to take over midwifery because they barred women from the schools and

---

* A number of historians have helped doctors in their campaign against midwives by accepting the doctors' assertions as truth. Since doctors and historians shared the same class, race and sex, that may have facilitated their sharing the same viewpoint.

claimed that doctors alone possessed a scientific knowledge that could make childbirth safe. After the 1780s, physicians gradually replaced midwives among the more affluent in the cities. Midwives were allowed to continue attending the poor.

While proclaiming their own excellence, doctors kept attacking midwives as dirty hags and old drabs. In lobbying for anti-midwife laws, doctors blamed these women for the prevalence of childbed fever (puerperal sepsis) but the fever's history suggests that the blame lay more with the accusers than the accused.

Childbed fever had occurred relatively infrequently when women gave birth in their own homes with a midwife's help. But when women delivered in hospitals—centers of germs—the disease became epidemic. During the 1840s, every tenth mother died of it. In European hospitals, women were often put four to a bed on the dirty linen used by women who had just died of puerperal sepsis. Dressings from wounds lay on the floor along with the vermin.

In 1847, when the germ theory of disease was unknown and the need for cleanliness unappreciated, Ignaz Semmelweis, a Viennese doctor, discovered the fever's cause.

There were two maternity wards in his hospital. In one, only midwives attended the mothers and in the other, only doctors. The mortality rate from the fever was so much greater in the second ward than the first that women, on seeing they were being taken to the doctors' ward, screamed in terror.

The doctors often dissected corpses in a laboratory across the street from the hospital. Then, wiping their hands on their coats, they would walk to the hospital and deliver babies.

One day Semmelweis performed an autopsy with a fellow doctor. The doctor cut his finger and subsequently died, after exhibiting the same symptoms as women with childbed fever. Remembering that doctors performed dissections and then delivered babies, Semmelweis concluded that it was doctors who were bringing the disease to mothers.

He instructed his students to wash their hands with a solution of chloride of calcium. The mortality rate of the patients they treated dropped greatly.

When Semmelweis announced his discovery, the other doctors were incensed at the clear conclusion that they had been angels of death. They denounced his theory and refused to disinfect their hands.

He wrote a book defending his theory. Most obstetricians attacked it and ridiculed him. During the violent controversy, they declared him mad. He was confined to an insane asylum where he died of infection in 1865.

Victims of physician pride, women continued to perish of the fever.

The year of Semmelweis' death, Dr. James Edmunds enraged English doctors by reporting that fewer women died at the hands of female midwives than at their own. He had gathered statistics on puerperal deaths in London and at the Royal Maternity Charity. Poor patients delivered by midwives at the Charity expired from puerperal causes at the rate of one in every 556 births, he found, while private London patients, delivered mostly by medical men, died at the rate of one in every 204.

And yet, he noted, Charity patients were poor and more apt to be weak and ill fed. What, then, made them less vulnerable to childbed fever? Like Semmelweis, he concluded that doctors, contaminated by wounds and postmortem exams, infected their maternity patients.

To solve the problem, Edmunds suggested that midwives again handle all childbirths.

His report incensed many doctors. Several attacked him in the *Lancet*, a medical journal. Edmunds responded: "The author begs, in reply thereto, to specifically disclaim hostility or disrespect to the medical profession; at the same time, he is unable to alter facts."

Childbed fever raged in America as well as Europe. In New York City's Bellevue Hospital, nurse Linda Richards remarked that no one who saw the dirty wards would have wondered at the high death rate. The expectant mothers were required to sew shrouds from their hospital beds and Richards used to wonder "if they speculated as to whether they were making their own."

Charles Meigs, a leading American obstetrician, attributed such deaths to "justification of Providence; a judgment instituted to remind us of the sin committed by the mother of the race."·

Indifference to puerperal fever deaths continued into the 20th century. The U. S. Children's Bureau reported that from 1900 to 1916 there was no decrease in maternal deaths although most causes of such deaths were preventable. As late as the 1920s, 7,000 women a year were dying from the fever.

"Women who die in childbirth are few beside those who suffer preventable illness or a lifelong impairment of health," the Bureau wrote. Every year, 20,000 women survived the fever but remained invalids.

In the United States in 1929, 6.8 women died in every thousand births compared to Sweden's 2.8. Historian W. H. Haggard noted this striking difference between the two countries: Here, doctors conducted 80 percent of deliveries; in Sweden, midwives did. America's persisting high maternal mortality rate, he concluded, is not fundamental to its economic condition but is merely an expression of indifference.

Besides a greater risk of contracting childbed fever, modern obstetrics brought other dangers to parturient women. Men had originally been called in only at difficult births, to assist surgically. Obstetrics remained a surgical specialty (even as, shockingly, it remains today) and surgeons viewed childbirth as an operation. Anxious to use the techniques they had learned, and impatient with the long labor period, they tended to use instruments routinely and administer drugs to speed up labor. Unlike midwives, many also blood-let habitually, a practice which must have weakened the laboring woman.

Thomsonians and Botanics, both unorthodox 19th-century doctors, vigorously opposed male midwives and condemned them for routinely trying to force births.

"Instead of assisting the efforts of nature," one Thomsonian complained, "they go to work like a galley slave tugging at the oar."

Thomas Hersey, in his 1836 midwifery book, is equally bitter: "Many of the men-midwives resort to instruments on every slight emergency, using the forceps to expedite a lingering labor that would have resulted more favorably if they had been dead or consigned to Botany Bay, before they raised those instruments of cruelty, merely to evince their scientific skill."

The lameness, lacerations, dropped uteri and other disastrous consequences of male skill he had seen, warned Hersey to avoid the numerous tools of the scientific accoucheur.

"The midwife who understands the principles of nature's operation in bringing forth children," he added, "will not resort to pincers, tongs nor crowbars to dig for babies."

The surgeon's inclination to interfere with his knife led him to sometimes perform a new operation he had devised: the symphysiotomy. It enlarged the space in the pelvis for passage of the baby. The operation killed one third of the mothers and two thirds of the babies and it maimed a great many more women for life.

"Irregular" doctors believed a mother could be aided in childbirth, not by surgery, but by encouraging and soothing her so her muscles would relax. Women could render that assistance better than men because their own childbirth experiences qualified them to empathize with the mother.

Such aid sounds so simple. But regular doctors, by using big words and mystifying their practice, had made people believe that "obstetrics" was complicated and difficult. (Their descendants do the same today, wielding scientific terms to obscure every clue to childbirth's simplicity.) Howard Horton, an irregular doctor, explained that physicians "by their marvelous tales of the hairbreadth escapes of numerous women to whom they have been called just in time to save life, strike a terror in the mind of the suffering woman, which confirms her in the determination, no matter how repulsive to her delicacy, to employ none but doctors."

The doctor tells his stories in the presence of the woman's friends and they, in turn, employ the same doctor, feeling themselves safe in the care of no one else.

When the doctor is called to a case, Horton noted, he "makes a great display of affected knowledge; discovers something wrong, which however, by his superior skill and experience, is soon set right; the patients and attendants acquire confidence, and, no matter whether difficulties, real or imaginary, exist or afterward occur, the woman is delivered, for which the doctor is applauded, whilst the unfortunate midwife is silently condemned."

The midwife would probably have delivered the woman

sooner and easier, Horton commented. But who believes in the skill of a midwife—a mere woman, an "old hag"? Conversely, as Hersey noted, the multitudes "believe much . . . from anyone they account a learned man." They do so despite the fact that, in medical school, the learned man learned how to deliver babies by cutting up the reproductive organs of dead women.

Only in 1931, encouraged by Columbia Medical School's Dr. Benjamin P. Watson, a former midwifery professor at Edinburgh, did midwives begin to return. The Maternity Center Association's school for midwives opened in New York City that year. Twenty years later, only 231 nurse-midwives had graduated. That is an average of eleven per year.

In 1948, when Yale School of Medicine was establishing the first prepared or "natural" childbirth program in the United States, it added to its staff a team of two nurse-midwives and a doctor. Dr. N. J. Eastman of Johns Hopkins Hospital gave another boost to midwifery when he used nurse-midwives to train other nurses as Obstetric Assistants. The midwives and their assistants then handled the complete care of parturient women.

Dr. Eastman noted, "I have watched all this with my own eyes and am convinced that the meticulous type of care they give is the answer to the greatest weakness in American Obstetrics, lack of emotional support both in pregnancy and labor."

In 1963 there were only four hundred trained midwives in the United States. In 1973, there were 1,400. Still, midwives delivered less than one percent of our babies while they delivered 80 percent of babies in the rest of the world.

It wasn't until 1961 that New York City's municipal hospitals let nurse-midwives practice on their staffs, and not until 1964 that the first voluntary hospital—Roosevelt—did so. Now, in 1976, one hundred nurse-midwives are working in nineteen New York hospitals.

But midwives were not allowed to deliver babies until 1971. Until that time, they could only *assist* doctors.

Here we come to the crucial difference between early midwives and modern ones: The modern midwife is under the doctor's thumb. In the battle between the midwife and the doctor, the doctor is still winning. Women—both as mothers and midwives—are still losing.

A pamphlet put out by the American College of Nurse-Midwifery emphasizes the midwife's subservience to the doctor. "The American nurse-midwife always functions within the framework of a medically directed health service: she is never an independent practitioner." (That last phrase is in boldface type.) She works "under delegated medical authority," the pamphlet adds later.

"We aren't independent practitioners," Mrs. Ruth Lubic, Maternity Center Association director, says, perhaps to reassure doctors nervous at the prospect of competition. "We aren't hanging out a shingle."

In 1971, the American College of Obstetricians and Gynecologists (ACOG) finally agreed to work with nurse-midwives. But it allows them to work in hospitals only under the obstetrician's supervision. This means midwives who threaten doctors in any way can be disposed of. Midwife Naomi Mayer, for example, resigned, under threat of dismissal, from a New Jersey hospital in 1973.

"The nursing director told me the chief of obstetrics wanted me dismissed for 'overstepping my bounds' and 'being too permissive with fathers,'" Mayer said. "I let fathers into the labor room and that infuriated him."

Why did the ACOG decide, in 1971, to endorse midwives at all?

"I'd like to say doctors feel that midwives develop a rapport with women and give good care," Mayer said, "but there's the suspicion that that isn't the reason they tolerate us. They accept us when they need us—because of the lack of obstetricians or because they're no longer interested in doing it. As doctors get paid more and more and want to work less and less, they let midwives practice."

Almost 15 percent of residency positions for obstetrician-gynecologists have been going unfilled so that has left room for midwives.

Though doctors may have opened the door a crack, women may push that door wide open when they discover that, with a midwife's help, childbirth can be a "mountain top" experience. A number of New York City hospitals have found that if a woman has had a midwife before, she will choose one a second time.

Women say they like them because midwives treat them like whole persons, not like uteri. Midwives, they report, are concerned with their comfort and well-being throughout the labor. They do not regard it as an annoying period before the real business of baby-digging. Mothers ask midwives questions they would not dare bother a doctor with, they say, and it reassures them to have the answers.

"Midwives really take time with mothers," Mayer explains. "They coax them and bring on the same effects as tranquilizers, but they do it through support. The doctor walks in right before delivery and walks out when he's finished his job. But the midwife really attends the birth. She stays from beginning to end, cleaning up with the nurses."

Another reason for the midwife's popularity is her cost. She charges less than the obstetrician. At Roosevelt Hospital in New York City in 1976, the entire cost for a delivery, including prenatal and postnatal care, was $459 if attended by a nurse-midwife, but from $1,200 to $1,800 if handled by an obstetrician. The obstetrician's fee alone ranges from $600 to $1,000, the higher fee being charged those who want a guarantee that their own physician, and not one of his colleagues, will deliver the baby.

Nurse-midwives are not the only midwives practicing. There are also lay midwives or "grannies." They're unschooled, which is not at all synonymous with unskilled. Almost five thousand grannies are practicing in such isolated poverty areas as the borderlands of Appalachia, Mississippi, and Texas. There, because the $10 to $25 fees are rarely paid, midwifery is called Rural Free Delivery.

Midwifery has certainly not hurt the infant and maternal mortality rates of those countries using the system. Every major industrial nation except the United States and Canada uses midwives. Our rates, for which we have doctors to thank, are nothing to brag about. We are fourteenth in infant and tenth in maternal mortality.

It is true, as Dr. W. K. Griffin asserted in the *Thomsonian*

Manual in 1836, that learned doctors "have clad the most simple and delicate art of the nursery in the masculine garb of the far-fetched sciences, which sets harshly upon it."

What makes the "scientizing" of childbirth all the sadder is that the experience that is often turned into a nightmare for women could be one of the most wondrous and joyous of their lives.

Lee Slavin, who gave birth at her home in Staten Island in 1973, certainly found it so. Her family and a friend sat nearby comforting her, timing her contractions, holding her hand, joking gently.

When her water broke, she laughed.

"I heard it pop!" she exclaimed. She looked so happy, her family laughed with her.

When the baby crowned, her six-year-old son, amazed and delighted, stood open-mouthed. When the baby made his breathtaking entrance, the family greeted him with awe, then tenderness.

"We were all so proud," Lee Slavin said.*

So that women and their babies can have deliveries as happy as Slavin's, they must dispel the mystery with which doctors have surrounded childbirth. They must take back control of their bodies. That may not be easy.

I have read exposés of American childbirth practices written in 1836, 1929, 1958, 1972 and 1975. All, like the latest, Suzanne Arms' important *Immaculate Deception,* came to the same conclusion: Physician interference in normal childbirth degraded women and endangered their babies. Each time, the exposé provoked a spurt of outrage from at least some women. Physicians responded by making token concessions—allowing some fathers in delivery rooms or teaching women breathing exercises for a "natural" childbirth that the doctors would discover, in the labor room, was beyond the strength of each particular woman. These concessions, while taking the heat off physicians and giving the appearance of obstetrical reform, obscured the fact that nothing had changed. Physicians were still convincing women that bearing a child was so complicated and so dangerous that men—with their forceps and drugs and

* I witnessed this birth through a film by Eric Reiner presented at a childbirth conference in Stamford, Connecticut, June 2, 1973.

IVs and episiotomies and monitors and Caesarians—had to do it for them.

Peg Beals, president of the International Childbirth Education Association, even sees a backlash from obstetricians today. Referring to the phenomenal increase in Caesarian sections and the growing use of machines in the labor room, she explained, "This development of technology to me is stating: You women say you can handle natural childbirth but we're going to make it so unnatural that you won't be able to."

If women really are to take back control of their bodies this time, then, they do not need any obstetrical "reforms." They need thousands of assertive midwives.

Women can set up and run their own midwifery schools and serve as independent practitioners, working in homes (as midwives safely do in Holland after screening out high-risk mothers) and in centers built exclusively for birth. There is no reason for midwives to be under the control of doctors, subject to dismissal for "permissiveness" toward the mothers, fathers and babies they serve.

Chapter / **THIRTEEN**

TREATMENT OF COMMON FEMALE HEALTH PROBLEMS

ORDINARY AILMENTS, LIKE ORDINARY CHILDBIRTH, FREQUENTLY seem to bore physicians. Therefore, when women suffer from vaginal infections, menstrual or menopausal disorders or other peculiarly female ailments, they often find little relief because doctors do not know much about them. Medical research has largely ignored such disabilities so women get over-generalizations, overkill treatments (some of which may be cancer-causing), and the impression that if they returned with an operable ailment, doctors would find their cases more interesting.

In this chapter, I examine some common health problems women have and the difficulties they experience in getting care. Those difficulties are caused, in part, by:

—An aggressive attitude toward healing.

—A fee-for-service system of medicine that rewards doctors for performing surgery.

—The physician's tendency to prescribe drugs about which he or she knows very little.

—The drug industry's concern with profits and indifference toward drug-caused illness and death.

—FDA's alignment with drug company interests and failure to protect consumers.

Let's consider vaginal infections first. There are two common ones for which women consult doctors—trichomonas and yeast. Both organisms normally reside in many women and apparently do not infect them unless the balance of organisms in the vagina is thrown off. That healthy environment is a somewhat acidic one, nurturing helpful bacilli (Döderlein) which keep harmful bacilli under control.

But if the vaginal tract is traumatized or becomes alkaline, the harmful bacilli can go to work. Antibiotics, the Pill, diabetes and pregnancy can upset the vaginal balance. So can the retention of menstrual secretions or seminal fluid, the irritation of douches or chemicals, increased temperature, and low resistance due to exhaustion, stress, illness, poor nutrition or anemia.

Many gynecologists, however, view vaginal infections, not as imbalances in vaginal environments, but as invaders which must be conquered.

They try to fight the infection by getting a zero bacterial count. Often they do not ask what changes in the woman's constitution caused the normally harmless bacteria to act up. They fail then to help the woman build her strength so she can resist the infection better. (That would be the homeopathic approach.) Instead, doctors shoot their pharmaceutical guns at the "enemy" bacteria, the allopathic way.

In 1959, new ammunition against vaginal trichomonas was introduced: Flagyl, a brand of metronidazole. It became the most popular therapy for trichomonas in the United States.

But distressing side effects like nausea and diarrhea appeared in up to 39 percent of Flagyl-takers, making the side effects of the cure often worse than the symptoms of the ailment.

While Flagyl's cure rate was high, so was the rate of recurrence. Dr. Jane Hodgson, a gynecologist at the University of Minnesota Medical School, sets that recurrence rate at least as high as 30 percent. Other estimates run higher.

Dr. Hodgson was anxious to devise another treatment for trichomonas because, beginning in 1972, studies indicated that Flagyl was carcinogenic in animals.* Since the latent inhabitants of the vagina seem to be activated by changes in vaginal flora, and since the infection can be destroyed by exposure to air, she suggested a regime including baths, powders, loose clothing, the removal of any interference with normal vaginal flora, and a mild alternative medication. She has had much success with that treatment. Nonetheless her proposal has been largely ignored.

By 1975, eight studies had shown that Flagyl caused cancer in animals. Two indicated it caused gene mutations. One revealed that it led to premature delivery, stillbirths and birth defects in animals.

But even though it has been well-informed of the drug's dangers, FDA has done nothing to protect consumers. The agency was alerted to the danger, not only by its own scientist, Dr. M. Adrian Gross, but by the Health Research Group (HRG), one of Ralph Nader's Washington-based consumer organizations. In March 1974, HRG cited the tumor studies and petitioned FDA to ban metronidazole (Flagyl) for trichomonas treatment. FDA denied the petition.

In August 1974, FDA Commissioner Dr. Alexander M. Schmidt, referring to Flagyl, stated that just because a drug caused cancer in animals did not mean it would cause cancer in people.

FDA was, in effect, ignoring animal studies and saying, "Let's sit back and wait until we have female victims," HRG attorney Anita Johnson charged.

The environmental factors are too numerous to ever be able to isolate the Flagyl ingested twenty years earlier as the cause of a particular cervical cancer, she pointed out.

So FDA knows that despite Flagyl's plain risks, we will never be able to pin cancer deaths on it.

In June 1975, *The Medical Letter*, a prestigious newsletter written by physicians who are experts on drugs, recommended that, in view of the sobering studies on the drug, Flagyl be

---

* One of the earliest was: M. Rustia and P. Shubik, *Journal of the National Cancer Institute*, 48:721, 1972.

restricted to cases that cannot be treated by any other means. FDA has still taken no action.

Often, women with menstrual and menopausal health problems receive inadequate care from men whose sexist upbringing clouds their understanding of such ailments. One is struck by the lack of information on these ailments, a situation apparently created by the fact that physicians have not found them interesting enough to research. The result is that physicians often base their treatments on these unfounded generalizations: 1. Much menstrual pain (dysmenorrhea) is caused by the woman's psychological deficiencies. 2. Most women experience disabling menopausal symptoms.

Dr. Katharina Dalton, menstrual specialist, reported that a colleague of hers excused the routine neglect of dysmenorrhea sufferers by observing that since no abnormalities were detected during the examination, it was assumed that the pain came from the mind.

Indeed, Dr. Jean Lennane, a psychiatrist, and Dr. John Lennane, Senior Registrar of the Renal Unit at Prince Henry Hospital in Australia, found in a recent study of the therapeutic literature that menstrual pains are commonly considered to be partly or entirely psychogenic.* In *Principles of Gynecology*, published in 1967, Dr. T. N. A. Jeffcoate attributed dysmenorrhea to "faulty outlook . . . leading to an exaggeration of minor discomfort." Another text, published in 1972, asserted that "the pain is always secondary to an emotional problem." †

Since about half of all women experience menstrual pains, this means that emotional illness is epidemic among females. The Drs. Lennane dispute such medical pronouncements. The cause of menstrual pain is unknown, they write, but it seems dependent on ovulation. When ovulation is suppressed with estrogen, the pain does not occur at the next period.

Dr. Dalton also observes that dysmenorrhea can be induced in any woman by administering the wrong hormone—a fact

* "Alleged Psychogenic Disorders in Women: A Possible Manifestation of Sexual Prejudice," *New England Journal of Medicine*, 288:288–292, 1973.

† R. C. Benson, *Gynaecology and Obstetrics, Current Diagnosis and Treatment*. Edited by M. A. Drupp and M. J. Chatton. Los Altos, California, Lange Medical Publications, 1972, pp. 377–434.

which invalidates any theory that the ailment is purely psychological.

She advises that hospitals run Dysmenorrhea Clinics but wonders, "Would this be regarded as too insignificant?"

While dysmenorrhea sufferers are undertreated, menopausal women are often overmedicated.

Every woman reacts to the change of life differently but doctors tend to assume that all menopausal women will be psychologically and physically at risk. They are expected to have emotional breakdowns, lose their sexual appetites, experience hot flashes and sprout little mustaches. Their breasts and vaginas are supposed to shrivel up.

"Not really a man but no longer a functional woman, these individuals live in the world of intersex," Dr. David Reuben asserts in his widely read book, *Everything You Always Wanted to Know About Sex.*

Nonsense, Dr. William J. Sweeney, author of the popular *Woman's Doctor,* counters. The menopause myths are based on atypical experiences. While some make it sound as though all women experience menopausal symptoms, he notes, in fact, only 20 to 30 percent do. Moreover, any ailment an older woman has is apt to be blamed on menopause. So too are the natural changes of old age and any irregularity in behavior.

As for the "sexlessness" myth, many women find the end of childbearing means the beginning of uninhibited sex. Fear of pregnancy no longer reigns.

Physicians commonly assume that depression is a symptom of menopause but too few have asked these questions: If women were not defined as sex objects and childbearers, would the loss of taut skin and childbearing capacity be so depressing to them? If a woman's children grow up and leave home at the same time she experiences menopause, could the loss of her homemaking job, rather than the menopause itself, account for her sorrow?

The women who do experience real menopausal symptoms undergo substantial suffering and they need to be taken seriously and given help. But many doctors respond with overkill treatments. The enemy is old age and doctors attack it with estrogen, the "youth pill." Some doctors attack wherever old age tries to infiltrate so it is not just the women suffering symptoms who get the ammunition, but any woman who passes a certain age limit.

"I think doctors give an ungodly amount [of estrogen]," Dr. Sweeney noted in *Woman's Doctor*.

The consequences of that overtreatment became apparent in October 1975. Dr. Donald F. Austin, chief of the California Tumor Registry, reported then that from 1969 to 1973, the rate of invasive uterine cancer in California rose 80 percent among white women fifty years and older. He linked the rise in cancer to the stepped-up use of estrogen therapy for menopausal women. (From 1962 to 1973, the estrogen market grew from $17 million to $69 million.) The increasing incidence of cancer, Dr. Austin observed, was most prevalent among affluent white women who are most apt to take the estrogen.

On December 4, 1975, the *New England Journal of Medicine* published two studies which showed that postmenopausal women who take estrogens are five to fourteen times more likely to get cancer of the endometrium (uterine lining) than women who do not use the estrogens.*

FDA's advisory committee on obstetrics and gynecology subsequently recommended that estrogen drugs be labeled to warn users that they may be risking uterine cancer.

That December, Jane E. Brody of *The New York Times* made spot checks around the nation and found that the studies linking estrogen with cancer had hardly affected some physicians' attitude toward estrogen-replacement therapy. Each of the twelve doctors she called said the reports did not *prove* that the estrogens directly cause cancer and that in the absence of that proof, no drastic change in practice was warranted.

American medicine poses another threat to woman's health in the form of "remunerectomies" or "hip pocket hysterecto-

---

* In one investigation, Dr. Donald C. Smith and four colleagues studied 317 patients with endometrial cancer. Patients who had been treated with estrogens were 4.5 percent more susceptible to the cancer than those in the control group.

In the other study, Drs. Harry K. Ziel and William D. Finkle surveyed ninety-four patients with endometrial cancer diagnosed between 1970 and 1974. Patients treated with estrogens were 7.6 to 13.9 percent more likely to contract endometrium cancer than those patients in the control group who were not on estrogen. (See *New England Journal of Medicine*, 293, pp. 1164–1170, 1975.)

mies" which benefit only the surgeon's wallet. In this case it is the physician's greed, as well as his casual attitude toward removal of female reproductive organs, that endangers women.

Hysterectomies are the second most frequently performed operation in the United States. Numerous studies, including one by Dr. Norman F. Miller of the University of Michigan Department of Obstetrics-Gynecology, have concluded that at least one third of them are completely unwarranted. Women are thus unnecessarily exposed to the risks of anesthesia reactions and postoperative complications like pneumonia, blood clots and infection.

One survey of thirty-five hospitals in the Los Angeles area in 1948 found that many women had had their uteri removed solely because they complained of backache, experienced some irregular bleeding or had tilted uteri.* (Tilted or "tipped" uteri are, in most cases, perfectly normal.)

A 1970 comparative study of surgery revealed that the rate of hysterectomies (per 100,000 population) in the United States is more than twice the rate in England and Wales. In *The New England Journal of Medicine,* Dr. John P. Bunker, a Stanford University Medical Center anesthesiologist, cited several reasons for the higher U.S. surgical rate:

—A more aggressive approach to healing.

—Less frequent use of consultation, allowing the doctor to refer patients to himself for surgery, thus creating his own demand.

—A maldistribution of medical personnel resulting in many surgeons lacking enough work to keep busy.

—A fee-for-service method of payment providing an incentive for surgery, which may increase the number of operations in borderline cases.

The financial incentive appears to be strong. When the United Mine Workers Medical Care Program required that gynecological operations be endorsed by specialists in the mid-1950s, Dr. Bunker pointed out, the number of hysterectomies suddenly dropped by as much as 75 percent. Nationally, the number of hysterectomies performed on insured persons is

---

* James C. Doyle, "Unnecessary Hysterectomies," *Journal of the American Medical Association,* Jan. 31, 1953, p. 360. Dr. Doyle is assistant clinical professor of gynecology at the University of Southern California Medical Center.

double that for the uninsured, a fact which also suggests an economic motive in surgery.*

The desire to provide teaching material for young doctors certainly accounts for some unnecessary operations, as we saw in Chapter 10. Diana Scully, a University of Illinois sociologist who observed ob-gyn residency training programs in two medical institutions during 1974 and 1975, found that residents have a regular sales pitch for hysterectomies. They tell women: "Think of the uterus as a cradle. After you've had all your babies, there's no reason to keep the cradle. And removing the uterus will save you from the risk of developing cancer in it later."

The unnecessary removal of ovaries (castration) is another danger women face. In a study of gynecological surgery performed between 1947 and 1951 in five hospitals, the investigator found that only 21 percent of the unilateral oophorectomies (removal of one ovary) were justified.†

Gynecologists are currently debating whether they ought to remove the healthy reproductive organs of *all* women who reach a certain age to prevent development of cancer in the uterus and ovaries. ‡

"Of course it's a good idea for gynecologists," sociologist Scully comments. "They make a lot of money on these operations."

Doctors do not make a lot of money teaching patients how their bodies work and how to preserve their health but such lessons would be more valuable to women than many of the operations and drugs physicians customarily offer them.

Women need to know, for example, how to examine their

* O. W. Anderson and J. J. Feldman, *Family Medical Costs and Voluntary Health Insurance: A Nationwide Survey.* New York: Blakiston Division. Mc-Graw-Hill Book Co., 1956.

† A. W. Diddle, et al., "Gynecologic Surgery in Five Nonteaching Hospitals," *Obstetrics and Gynecology,* February 1953. Dr. Diddle is affiliated with the East Tennessee Baptist Hospital in Knoxville.

‡ Shelton, J. J., et al., "Elective Prophylactic Total Hysterectomy and Oophorectomy," *Audio Digest of Obstetrics-Gynecology,* 1973.

A Health Research Group report points out that while hysterectomy does eliminate the possibility of cancer of the uterus, the death rate from uterine cancer is less than the mortality rate from hysterectomy. See: Bernard Rosenfeld, M.D., et al., "A Health Research Group Study on Surgical Sterilization: Present Abuses and Proposed Regulations," October 29, 1973. Available from the Health Research Group, 2000 P Street, N.W., Washington, D. C. 20036.

breasts. In 1974, 90,000 women learned that they had breast cancer. About 32,000 women died that year from the disease. But even though self-examination can detect breast cancer while it is 80 to 85 percent curable, a 1973 Gallup poll found that most women have not been taught by their doctors how to do the simple exam. Only half the women surveyed even had an annual breast exam by a doctor.

Once a lump is detected (and 80 percent of them are benign), two problems common in woman's health care again crop up: The tendency toward fast, aggressive treatment and an economic motivation for a surgical procedure.

Typical American doctors will do a surgical biopsy, removing tissues from the breast lump to examine them. If the tumor is malignant, they will perform a Halsted radical mastectomy, cutting out the woman's breast, underlying muscles and lymph nodes while she is still under anesthesia.

After Rose Kushner, a Washington reporter, had had breast cancer herself, she thoroughly investigated its treatment here and abroad. Kushner believes that the American practice of combining the biopsy and mastectomy, besides imposing a trauma on women who awaken from a biopsy with only one breast, endangers patients. It leaves no time for staging, the determination of the extent of the malignancy through x-rays, blood tests, and scanning of the brain, bones, liver and lungs. If the disease has already spread, then removal of the breast is unnecessary. While the woman recovers from the surgery, drug therapy vital to her survival is delayed. The combined surgical biopsy and mastectomy is not customary procedure in Europe, where doctors take the time to determine the extent of the disease before beginning the treatment.

Kushner also argues against surgical biopsies which, she suspects, are prevalent in the United States because of an economic incentive to perform them. (The surgeon earns about $200 for each twenty-minute procedure.) In Europe, she found, it is common to diagnose breast lumps by needle biopsy, which can be done on an out-patient basis.

In one procedure, the doctor tries to aspirate the tumor with a fine needle. If the tumor is filled with fluid, that liquid is analyzed to make certain the cyst is benign. If no fluid comes out, a wide-bore needle is used to remove some tissue for analysis. Only if neither of these procedures extracts enough material for a diagnosis is the tumor surgically excised and that is rarely necessary.*

When, after biopsy, American doctors detect a cancerous tumor, 90 percent of them perform a Halsted radical mastectomy. Most do not first inform their patients that breast-cancer treatment has been an unresolved controversy for decades. Neither do they mention that British surgeons perform half as many radical mastectomies (per 100,000 population) as American surgeons with comparable results.

William Stewart Halsted devised his operation for breast cancer in 1882 when, due to late diagnosis, tumors were much more massive by the time they were treated than they are now. Largely on the basis of a sample of fifty women, his radical mastectomy became the standard operation for breast cancer in America.

But later studies at St. Bartholomew's Hospital in London, at the University of Iowa, at the Radiation Center in Copenhagen, at the Cleveland Clinic in Ohio, and in Rockford, Illinois, and Cambridge, England, all indicate no superiority in the survival rate of radical mastectomy over the simple mastectomy in which only the breast—not the lymph nodes and pectoral muscles—is removed.

Even though there has been no proof that the Halsted radical is a superior treatment to more moderate procedures (the partial, modified, simple or subcutaneous mastectomy), no controlled study of the various procedures was undertaken until 1970.

"Right now, nobody really knows what the best treatment for breast cancer is," Dr. Bernard Fisher, chairman of the National Surgical Adjuvant Breast Project and director of the study, told *Newsweek* then.

Fisher's study, sponsored by the National Cancer Institute, took place among 1,700 women at thirty-four medical centers and compared three treatments—radical and simple mastectomies and simple mastectomy followed by radiation therapy. After two years, all three treatments had approximately the

---

* For a complete discussion of the various operations and treatments for breast cancer, see Rose Kushner's excellent book, *Breast Cancer: A Personal History and an Investigative Report*. Harcourt Brace Jovanovich, New York and London, 1975.

same 15 percent recurrence rate of disease. The women will have to be followed for several years before any firm conclusions can be drawn.

Surgeons agree that the study should have been done ten years or more earlier but many have been reluctant to test any modified breast operations. They seem to assume that the more cut out of the body, the greater the chance of cure.

Dr. George Crile, former head of the Department of Surgery at Cleveland Clinic, challenges that assumption. He suspects that removal of nontumerous lymph nodes and the performance of an extensive operation may interfere with the woman's immunologic resistance and promote the spread of cancer.

Until his recent retirement, Dr. Crile often performed a partial mastectomy (removal of the cancer, a wide zone of surrounding breast, the overlying skin and underlying connective tissue).

"Over and over again," he wrote in his book, *What Women Should Know About the Breast Cancer Controversy*, "careful studies performed abroad have shown that the tumor in lymph nodes can be effectively controlled by radiation. Why then, when most European surgeons have abandoned radical surgery, do the majority of American surgeons persist in performing radical mastectomies?"

Whatever the answer—the greater aggression of American doctors, the higher fee commanded by the more extensive operation, or the lack of female surgeons who might show more empathy for breast-cancer patients—women should insist on knowing the alternative treatments and choosing the one with which they will have to live.

Physician ignorance of certain drugs caused what may become one of the saddest episodes in modern woman's health care history.

During the 1940s, 50s and 60s, doctors used diethylstilbestrol (DES) as an antimiscarriage drug despite the fact that there has never been any clear evidence for its effectiveness in preventing miscarriages. Many obstetricians routinely prescribed the drug to women without a history of miscarriage on the unsubstantiated theory that it would ensure a strong pregnancy.

A very small percentage of the daughters subsequently born

developed vaginal or cervical clear-cell adenocarcinoma. Until 1966, that kind of cancer had almost never been reported in young women.

Today, there are an estimated 2.1 million to three and a half million DES daughters. Ninety-one percent of them have adenosis, abnormal glandular structures in the vagina or on the cervix. No one knows how serious adenosis is or what, if anything, will happen to it. Almost all women with the vaginal cancer also had adenosis and cancer often occurred in the same spot as the adenosis.

Dr. Peter Greenwald, director of the Cancer Control Bureau of New York State Department of Health, testified at a Senate hearing in February 1975 that this abnormality in the vagina may be a precursor to cancer, *though that is by no means proven.*

However, in one case not involving a DES daughter, cancer definitely did develop from adenosis, probably over a period of twenty years.*

There is no way to estimate the total number of DES daughters who will eventually become cancerous, Dr. Greenwald told Sen. Edward M. Kennedy, chairperson of the Senate Subcommittee on Health. Agreeing with Kennedy that the 220 known cases are probably "the tip of the iceberg," he added that the incidence of DES-induced cancer continues to rise. †

As Greenwald and colleagues wrote in the August 12, 1971 *New England Journal of Medicine,* it is not known whether a long induction period may be present for those offspring who received a smaller dose.

The cancer seems to be triggered by the hormonal changes at puberty. In the next two decades, hundreds of thousands more DES daughters will reach puberty.

Of the first 220 young women who developed cancer, twenty-four have died. Scores more have had their uteri and vaginas removed.

The enormity of this disaster, though revealed in testimony

* See E. H. Ruffolo, D. Foxworthy, and J. C. Fletcher, "Vaginal Adenocarcinoma Arising in Vaginal Adenosis," *American Journal of Obstetrics and Gynecology,* 11:167–172, 1971.

† The mothers of about 85 percent of these women were known to have been exposed to DES or a related drug during pregnancy.

Since those hearings, the number of reported cases has risen to 280.

at three Congressional hearings, has been greatly soft-played to the public by physicians, the FDA and others responsible for it. "No great problem exists," they have, in effect, argued. The result is that the victims are abandoned, left to wrest whatever information they can from guilty and frightened hospitals, doctors, drug companies and federal agencies.

Physicians often issue reassuring statements to DES daughters but the data on which their reassurances are based is scanty. For example, Dr. Arthur Herbst of Harvard Medical School, the man whose excellent research revealed the DES disaster, believes that the risk of cancer development in stilbestrol-exposed girls is quite small. That belief is grounded on the assumption that most treated cases of the cancer have been voluntarily reported to a clearinghouse he set up to collect information on that disease, the Registry of Clear-Cell Adenocarcinoma in Young Women.

But what about *untreated* cases? They may well exist. Many DES daughters are undoubtedly unaware that they are at risk so they do not request exams. Moreover, few doctors are routinely testing young women for this rare, sometimes asymptomatic, cancer.

"There are probably many undetected cases," Kay Weiss, a cancer epidemiologist at the University of Texas Cancer System, told me. "The Registry is by no means comprehensive."

When detected, the cases still may not be revealed to the Registry. No law compels doctors to report the vaginal cancer and physicians may be hesitant to do so if they are the ones who prescribed the cancer-associated drug in the first place. Even where physicians are legally required to report certain diseases, they report less than one percent the actual incidence to the U.S. Center for Disease Control, Weiss said.

Dr. Herbst also believes that, in general, the prognosis for vaginal cancer is quite good if it is diagnosed early. But that belief is based on the experience of cancer victims, some of whom have been observed for less than two years after treatment.

Physicians, Weiss states, report "success" of surgery or even "cure" with only two months follow-up.

"They know damn well that the five-year survival figures are going to be very low," she charges. "It's easy to say on the basis of one to three year follow-up that most of the victims are surviving. Clear-cell adenocarcinoma has a very high metastasis rate to other parts of the body. The sites that will be affected merely haven't shown up yet."

Dr. Herbst does note that the peak incidence of these tumors may not have been reached yet. He adds, "The possibility also exists that other types of genital cancers or malignant tumors arising elsewhere may be encountered as the stilbestrol-exposed population ages."

The abandonment of DES victims is evident from hundreds of letters women wrote to Kay Weiss, the cancer epidemiologist, after her article on DES appeared in *Ms.* magazine in 1973. At my request, Weiss sent me copies of the letters. They reveal overwhelming suffering, fear, anger and bewilderment. All the women were desperate for medical information they could get nowhere else.

Because of the physicians' reluctance to give information to them, and their own unquestioning faith in their doctors, some women had not known what drugs they were taking during pregnancy. When women did ask, some doctors replied, "The name wouldn't mean anything to you, dear," or "This is a hold-the-baby-in pill." After reading about the stilbestrol problem in the press, women called their doctors who, perhaps fearful of malpractice suits, frequently lied to the women or at first refused to reveal that they had prescribed DES.

One mother with twelve- and fifteen-year-old DES daughters asked her physician about DES effects and was told that a very high amount of the drug would have to be present to have an adverse effect on the fetus and that had not been true in her case.

"I feel that I may have been pacified by this remark," she wrote.

She was right. Both Dr. Greenwald and Dr. Herbst have reported that small as well as large doses may induce cancer.

Another woman who had been prescribed stilbestrol despite her "strong protest" to her obstetrician, learned about the correlation between DES and vaginal cancer while she was pregnant.

"When I confronted my doctor with this news," she wrote, "I was called an hysterical woman who was medically ignorant."

The most positive evaluation of an obstetrician's response came from a DES mother who described her doctor as "concerned but vague."

Neither she nor any other DES mothers who wrote had been called in by their doctors and warned that their daughters needed regular cancer-detection examinations. When many women arranged appointments on their own initiative, the gynecologists took Pap smears and then assured the daughters that they were perfectly healthy.

That assurance could cost the women their lives for this unique cancer is difficult to detect and the Pap smear often misses it. To find cancerous cells in the vagina, it is usually necessary to perform a Schiller test in which the vaginal walls are coated with an iodine stain, revealing any abnormal tissue. Women with suspect tissue must be examined further with a colposcope, a microscope adapted for use during pelvics. The colposcope is an expensive instrument which is not standard equipment in the gynecologist's office.

It is hardly surprising then, that a study of DES daughters conducted at The Medical College of Wisconsin in Milwaukee found that twenty-four of thirty-one girls (77 percent) who had a previous exam had been falsely reassured by their own doctors that they had no adenosis.* In fact, this condition was later detected by colposcopic examination.

When doctors respond to inquiries by DES daughters with admonitions not to be concerned and not to pay attention to the "scare tactics" of the press, Weiss writes in *International Journal of Health Services,* that "too often means that the physicians do not have access to Schiller staining or colposcopic equipment, do not want to admit liability, or would feel an obligation to provide similar testing for all their patients."

One woman, learning that all pregnant women registering at Chicago's Lying-In Hospital between 1950 and 1952 had been automatically entered in a DES-in-pregnancy study, called the hospital and asked for drug information concerning her mother, who had delivered her there during that period. The hospital told her that this data was released only to insurance companies and doctors. Women who had been experimented upon were not entitled to the information.

* Adolf Stafl, R. F. Mattingly, D. V. Foley, and W. C. Fetherson, "Clinical Diagnosis of Vaginal Adenosis," *Obstetrics and Gynecology,* 43:118–128, 1974.

Finding their doctors and hospitals mute, some women turned to the local American Cancer Society but found that it also knew little about this DES-related cancer.

They ran up against blank walls everywhere they turned. Finally they appealed to Weiss, who holds a Master of Public Health degree and is an assistant epidemiologist for a National Cancer Institute Lung Cancer Study at M. D. Anderson Research Hospital and Tumor Institute at the University of Texas Cancer Institute in Houston. Kay Weiss had formed Advocates for Medical Information, a consumer-oriented research organization.

Hungry for answers, DES victims bombarded Weiss with questions like these: Are there any preventive measures to keep DES daughters from developing cancer? Has any research been done on second generation effects of DES? Should DES daughters adopt children rather than risk passing the danger on to their own children? Is any group pooling information for DES parents? What percentage of detected adenosis becomes cancerous? Have there been any studies on the effects of DES on male offspring? What tests and precautions should DES mothers take for themselves since they may have an increased risk of cancer of the uterine lining? Will birth-control pills increase a DES daughter's chances of getting cancer? Where can a doctor knowledgeable about DES-related cancer be found? If DES daughters live to reach menopause, should they take hormones?

There are few firm answers. As Dr. Peter Greenwald, director of the Cancer Control Bureau in New York, emphasizes, "There are many things we just don't know."

We do know that stilbestrol-exposed women must be watched.

Since all the asymptomatic patients with carcinoma have been successfully treated so far, Dr. Herbst stated in 1974, it is very important to search for early cases by screening DES daughters.

No one is making any concerted effort to do that.

"To date," Weiss informed me in July 1976, "no national public health agency has taken it upon itself to even let these victims know that they were exposed to DES."

While these DES daughters face a desperate need for information and for the early examination that might save their lives, the drug companies that profited so from DES sales do nothing.

They have not established free clinics to screen women for the cancer they apparently helped spawn. Instead, they let DES victims pay about forty-five dollars every six months for the rest of their lives for the cancer tests.

They are not even alerting women to their danger. Neither are the prescribing doctors. Nor the AMA. Nor the American Cancer Society. Nor public health organizations. Nor FDA.

Asked, in 1971, why he had not warned DES daughters to have immediate medical examinations, FDA Commissioner Dr. Charles Edwards replied that FDA had to be "careful . . . not to create an emotional crisis on the part of American women."

"I'm sure a woman would rather be in a state of 'emotional crisis' than in a state of death," one DES daughter shot back.

So it is left to the victims—female health consumers—to use their free time and personal money to handle what Weiss calls "the results of mass experimentation with unproven drugs."

They are the only ones heeding a woman who writes that, torn by the fears she imagined her quiet, fifteen-year-old DES daughter experiencing, she took her to the doctor and "listened to her weep while the gynecologist examined her."

They are the only ones who hear when a DES mother says of her twelve-year-old child, "Now for the next decade, every time I look at her, I will be afraid for her life."

Despite the tragic consequences of that massive experiment with DES, another one is now being conducted. This time, most subjects are college students who have often not given their informed consent to participation in the experiment.

After an article in the October 1971 *Journal of the American Medical Association* suggested that DES could abort fertilized ovum within seventy-two hours of intercourse, physicians began giving the drug to hundreds of thousands of college-age women as a "morning-after pill." FDA has never approved DES for this use. Stilbestrol's safety as a postcoital contraceptive has never been demonstrated.

In fact, there is such concern about the drug's carcinogenicity that FDA banned it from animal feeds in 1973. (The District of Columbia Court of Appeals overturned the ban in January 1974 because FDA had failed to hold a hearing on its proposed action.)

The 250-milligram dosage of DES in the morning-after pill series is 55,000 times the amount FDA tried to ban in cattle feed and 168,000 times the amount considered dangerous in the diet.

The exact risk of DES to the woman who swallows it is unknown, but a statement made at the 1971 Congressional hearings on DES by Dr. Roy Hertz, an expert on hormonal cancer and currently research professor in obstetrical pharmacology at the George Washington University Medical School, should make women uneasy. The addition of any estrogen beyond that produced in the body, he said, "disturbs a natural balance which, even under ideal natural conditions is precarious, demonstrated by the fact that one of every sixteen women will develop breast cancer during her lifetime."

(The amount of DES in just *one* morning-after pill is about five hundred times what the body produces daily.)

Many DES daughters are of college age. If they have undiagnosed vaginal cancer, the estrogen in the morning-after pill may further threaten their health. Estrogen has long been known to speed the growth of genital cancers, as Kay Weiss, the cancer epidemiologist, pointed out in *Ms.* in November 1973.

After Weiss' article appeared, one woman wrote her: "I knew that my mother had taken DES during her pregnancy, but I did not know until I read your description of the morning-after pill, that I had taken it on a doctor's prescription without being told what it contained. He (the doctor) did not ask me whether my mother had taken DES and at the time I did not know myself."

The morning-after pill is really a series of pills taken twice a day for five consecutive days. These massive doses of stilbestrol make most women nauseous. Many vomit. Perhaps that is why a 1974 survey of more than two hundred women who had taken the pills in Ann Arbor, Michigan revealed that 24 percent did not take all ten pills in the series.* If pregnant women

* See "Regulation of Diethylstilbestrol (DES), 1975," Joint Hearing before the Subcommittee on Health of the Committee on Labor and Public Welfare and the Subcommittee on Administrative Practice and Procedure of the Committee on the Judiciary, First Session on S. 963, February 27, 1975, U.S. Government Printing Office, Washington: 1975, pp. 94–99. The survey was conducted by Belita Cowan, a health-care instructor at Washtenaw Community College in Ann Arbor, Michigan.

failed to take every pill, and so did not abort the ovum, any offspring would have been subjected to enormous doses of stilbestrol and have a high risk of developing cancer.

If they had been fully informed about DES, 65 percent of the respondents stated, they would not have taken it.

A survey of sixty-nine women given the morning-after pill at the University of Michigan Health Service in 1972 revealed that most of the women had not been told of its potential cancer hazards, observed for side effects or contraceptive failures, or screened for medical conditions that might make them more susceptible to the drug's adverse effects. Only seven of the sixty-nine women were told that the morning-after pill was a non-approved use of DES.*

Dr. Greenwald of the New York State Cancer Registry surveyed 45 large hospitals, college health services and Planned Parenthood facilities in New York in 1973 and again in 1974 and found that use of the morning-after pill was "fairly widespread, especially at the colleges and universities."

FDA bears responsibility for this large-scale misuse of dangerous drugs on healthy women. In May 1973, it sent out its drug bulletin to the nation's physicians informing them that it had approved DES as a morning-after pill for emergency situations such as rape and incest. That bulletin was in error. FDA had not, in fact, given its approval and has not done so as of this writing three years later. FDA never corrected its error. Therefore, physicians have been acting since 1973 on the assumption that DES has been conditionally approved.

(Only four months after its erroneous bulletin, FDA made the same "mistake" concerning Depo-Provera, another potentially dangerous contraceptive. In both cases, without taking responsibility for approving controversial population control drugs, FDA spurred physicians into using them.)

FDA spokesperson Wayne Pines informed me in July 1976 that FDA would probably approve the morning-after pill for emergency situations as soon as it receives an acceptable application from a drug manufacturer.

* "Quality of Health Care—Human Experimentation," Hearings before the Subcommittee on Health of the Committee on Labor and Public Welfare, U.S. Senate, February 21 and 22, 1973, Part One. See "Health Research Group Report on the Morning-after Pill" and Fact Sheet by Kay Weiss, pp. 193–212 and 300–315. U.S. Government Printing Office, Washington, D.C.

Because of several highly unusual deviations from normal FDA procedure, that manufacturer will not have to conduct any studies on DES to demonstrate its safety or efficacy as a postcoital contraceptive.

Approval of the morning-after pill would normally go through the Generic Drug Division of FDA's Bureau of Drugs. But Dr. Marvin Seife and Dr. Vincent Karusaitis, director and medical officer respectively in that division, refused to give approval. Because DES was a drug that had caused cancer, they wanted the manufacturing drug company to perform studies showing its safety in its new use as a morning-after pill. Their superiors in FDA, whom they did not identify, overruled them.

"In all my [ten] years with the FDA, this is unique, this is the first time in my experience that a drug has been published for a new use in the Federal Register without any study, without any investigative new drug application for a totally new indication," Dr. Seife testified at Congressional hearings in 1975.*

While FDA is the chief villain in this piece, physicians have hardly been blameless. They have not confined their use of the morning-after pill to rape and incest cases but have been prescribing it much more broadly, Dr. Greenwald found in his New York State survey.

The 1974 study in Ann Arbor, furthermore, found that DES was being prescribed "with carelessness and casualness." Eight women obtained the pills, not for themselves, but for roommates or friends. Twenty-nine percent of the two hundred women in the survey said they had taken the DES pills at least twice within one year, suggesting that doctors were prescribing the drug, not as an emergency medication, but as a routine contraceptive.

Dr. William A. Nolen, author of the popular book, *The Making of a Surgeon*, exemplifies the casual attitude many doctors seem to have toward women on DES. In his June 1973 *McCall's* column, he responded to the question of whether a doctor should risk giving the morning-after pill to "Jane," an

---

* For a chilling description by Dr. Seife and Dr. Karusaitis of the abnormal procedures used to approve the morning-after pill without any precautionary studies, see *Regulation of Diethylstilbestrol (DES), 1975, op cit.*, pp. 26–32.

eighteen-year-old co-ed who had had unprotected intercourse: "In my opinion, and that of most doctors I know, yes. The risk in Jane's taking DES for five days is probably negligible."

Yet Dr. Arthur L. Herbst, who revealed the DES disaster, told a congressional hearing in 1971, "We do not have enough data or knowledge at the present time to say what the smallest dose or the shortest duration of exposure to this drug is that could cause trouble."

The foolhardiness of exposing "Jane" to the cancer risks of DES is compounded by the fact that she is probably not pregnant. Neither are the vast majority of college students and rape victims for whom the morning-after pill is prescribed. The estimated risk of pregnancy for a single, unprotected coitus is only four percent.*

* C. Tietze, "Problems of pregnancy resulting from a single, unprotected coitus," *Journal of Fertility and Sterility*, 11:485–488, 1960.

EPILOGUE

THE WOMEN'S
HEALTH MOVEMENT

THE WOMEN ON THE BUS BEGAN SINGING:

> They hold their hands up to their hearts,
> They sigh, oh they lie.
> They say they only care for us.
> We die, oh we die.

From a conference on women and health at Harvard Medical
School, the women were on their way to Boston's Prudential
Center to demonstrate against the use of DES in the morning-
after pill. Two thousand women had gathered in April 1975,
for this conference organized by female health consumers and
workers. During the assembly, ten women's health organizations formed a DES Caucus. They planned demonstrations in
five other cities. They called press conferences. They circulated
petitions. After the conference, the women rode to Washington, D. C. to lobby for a law curbing the use of diethylstilbestrol.

If physicians are experimenting on women's bodies with
population-control drugs, denying abortions, forcing sterilizations, usurping the childbirth experience and performing unnecessary surgery, women are no longer passively submitting.
Since 1969 they have formed at least a thousand women's
health organizations, twenty-five alternative women's clinics
and an uncountable number of small "self-help" physiology
groups. These groups exist in almost every major city and in
many rural areas. All of them make up the sprawling, vibrant
Women's Health Movement. Much work remains to be done
but the Movement has grown so quickly and accomplished so
much in its short life that it is impossible to report on it
without feeling exhilarated and hopeful.

Let's look briefly at the three aspects of the Movement.

HEALTH ORGANIZATIONS

The health organizations publicize problems in the delivery of woman's health care, educate themselves and other women about their bodies and guide consumers in finding the services they need. They run "Know Your Body" courses, explaining female anatomy and physiology in laywoman's terms. Some groups publish newsletters and health booklets, hold conferences, speak-outs and demonstrations. Others work politically to change the medical system into one which emphasizes preventive health services, eliminates profit-making in the healing of the sick, and shares decision-making with patients and health workers.

The earliest of the groups began by organizing around the abortion issue when that operation was illegal. Though it is difficult to trace the exact founding of the pioneer groups, the first one seems to have been formed in Chicago in 1969 to refer women to illegal abortionists. Members called the underground group JANE because in returning calls from women needing abortions, they always said, "This is Jane from Women's Liberation." When they discovered that their chief abortionist was not a doctor but a health worker, they learned to perform the operation themselves. By 1971, they were doing all the abortions and charging an average of fifty dollars per procedure. In the four years of its existence, 115 women belonged to JANE.

In the spring of 1969, when the feminist movement was just emerging, another group that was to become the influential Boston Women's Health Book Collective began meeting to discuss "women and their bodies." That summer, they researched topics that would help them learn about their bodies, discussed their findings in the group, and then wrote papers individually or in groups of two or three. In the fall, they used their papers to give courses to women in churches, schools and homes—wherever they could meet. The women taking the courses added their own experiences and ideas and some helped to rewrite the original papers. Later, the women bound the papers together, calling the resulting book *Our Bodies, Ourselves*. The New England Free Press (a political printing collective) and the women's group published it. Feminist consciousness-raising groups around the country purchased the newsprint books for thirty cents each and used them as springboards for discussion. Filling a great and previously unmet need, it sold 200,000 copies. In 1973, Simon and Schuster published the book and by March 1976 had sold an additional million copies.

Of all the health groups, two relatively new ones—one statewide and the other national—offer special promise.

In August 1974, various California women's, consumer, and minority groups joined together in the Coalition for the Medical Rights of Women. With the help of two public interest law firms—Public Advocates, Inc. and Equal Rights Advocates, Inc., both of San Francisco—the Coalition has filed numerous petitions and lawsuits to hold drug companies, medical professionals and the state government responsible to female health consumers.

The Coalition concerns itself with unnecessary surgery, IUD safety, the quality of Pap smear screening, the needs of DES daughters, and the health rights of women in mental institutions and prisons.

Its first action was to petition the California Department of Health for new regulations on intrauterine devices which would require adequate premarket testing. For over a year, its IUD Committee worked on the rules and had several negotiating and writing sessions with health officials. The Health Department approved the stringent new regulations early in 1976, giving the Coalition a dramatic victory.

The Coalition definitely has clout in California. Shortly after its formation, the Chief of the State's Office of Maternal and Child Health and the Director of Health began soliciting input from it on all health matters relating to women and children. The California Medical Association has also negotiated seriously with these organized consumers. It sends lawyers and physicians to respond to its petitions.

Women from around the country have asked the Coalition how to form similar organizations in their own states so in 1976 the Coalition prepared organizational guidelines. (See "Resources for Change" in Appendix.)

On the national level, leaders of the Women's Health Move-

ment joined together in June 1975 to form what may well
become the most potent of all the organizations, the National
Women's Health Lobby Network.* To finally make the voice
of women heard on health issues, the group will support—
when they are financially able to do so—a lobbyist in Washington, D. C., monitor FDA and the National Institutes of
Health, inform women when Congressional and FDA hearings
are to be held and provide expert feminist witnesses for those
hearings. It will publish a newsletter on pending health legislation, and work with women in their own communities in
organizing to protect themselves against hazardous drugs and
medical practices. The Network will also link female health
activists around the country so they can share resources.

In December 1975, the Network held its first official event.
On the steps of FDA's Maryland headquarters, it conducted a
memorial service for women who had died from hormone-
related therapies such as the Pill, DES and estrogen-replacement treatment.

WOMEN'S CLINICS AND
BIRTH GROUPS

The twenty-five or so women's clinics provide services in
institutions where workers and consumers share in decision-
making. Beginning in 1970, the clinics sprang up around the
country. The Emma Goldman Women's Health Center opened
in Chicago and the Elizabeth Blackwell Women's Health
Center in Minneapolis. Clinics sprouted in Plattesville, Wisconsin, New Bedford, Massachusetts, Gainesville, Florida,
Eugene, Oregon, Burlington, Vermont. They appeared in
Iowa City, Colorado Springs, Detroit and Seattle.

Most give standard gynecological exams, pregnancy and Pap
smear tests and contraceptive services. They also perform abortions.

* The founders were Belita Cowan, medical editor of *her-self* newspaper and
a health-care instructor at Washtenaw Community College in Ann Arbor,
Michigan; Barbara Seaman, author of *The Doctor's Case Against the Pill* and
Free and Female; Dr. Mary Howell, a Maine pediatrician and former Associate
Dean of Students at Harvard Medical School; Phyllis Chesler, author of *Women
and Madness;* and Alice Wolfson, a health activist and member of D. C. Women's
Liberation in Washington, D. C.

Viewing women as active participants in their health maintenance, the clinic workers teach as they give care. They explain everything they do during exams, encourage questions and provide full information on treatment options so the woman herself can make the decisions.

The clinics emphasize preventive health care for well women. Besides medical services, many of the clinics offer health-education courses, self-examination demonstrations and workshops for women approaching, or going through, menopause.

Female paramedics provide much of the routine care.

In Los Angeles, the Feminist Women's Health Center pioneered the "participatory clinic." Approximately six women come for their clinic appointment at the same time. They do not have the typical experience of women seeking gynecological care: sitting for an hour or more in a waiting room, being examined alone by a hurried male doctor, and leaving with more questions than with which they came. Instead, the group of women meets with a female physician and three health workers for approximately two hours. They fill out their medical forms together and discuss them. Each woman explains the reason for her clinic visit. Then, with the help of the physician and paramedics or nurses, the women examine each other and complete the tests and laboratory work necessary for each woman's care. The women learn about their bodies as they receive care.

Finding the current childbirth services offered by obstetricians unacceptable, at least five groups have organized to help women deliver their babies at home. One of these is the Birth Center in Santa Cruz, California, established by Raven Lang, a childbirth educator.

While serving as a labor coach, Lang witnessed dangerous obstetrical practices in a hospital. She then determined to help any woman who wanted an alternative to hospital birth. When some mothers in her natural-childbirth classes asked her to stay with them as they delivered their own babies at home, she agreed.

In early 1971, lay midwives and childbirth-preparation teachers began meeting, at Lang's instigation, to support and educate each other. Local doctors were refusing to give prenatal care to women who wanted home births, so in March 1971, the group of midwives and teachers opened a Birth Center to provide that care. They also gave classes in exercise, nutrition, relaxation, breathing, labor, birth and care of the newborn.

Sometimes, a mother would ask a midwife at the Center to attend her while she gave birth at home and the midwife would do so. In three years, the eight midwives at the Center attended more than three hundred births. According to a study by Lewis Mehl, a fourth-year medical student at Stanford University, the death rate for infants around the time of birth was 3.2 per one thousand births at the Birth Center. The national rate was 27.1.*

SELF-HELP GROUPS

Carol Downer, a California health activist and mother of six, developed the third prong of the Women's Health Movement: self-help groups. In April 1971, after eing an IUD inserted in another woman following an abortion, it occurred to her that she might learn about her body *from* her body. So she took a plastic speculum from the abortion clinic. Later, using the speculum to separate her vaginal walls, she shined a flashlight on a mirror placed between her legs and first saw her own vagina and cervix. She invited other women to look too. They became as excited as she.

The women got their own specula. Small groups began meeting to learn about their bodies through self-examination.

In November 1971, Downer and Lorraine Rothman, another prime mover in the self-help group, gave demonstrations in twenty-five communities, among them Wichita, Kansas; Cedar Rapids, Iowa; New York City; New Haven, Connecticut; and Washington, D. C.

Self-help groups sprang up wherever the pair had been. The women would learn how to do pelvic exams to locate the position of the uterus and check for any lumps or inflammations of ovaries or fallopian tubes. Some groups concentrated on

* For more details on the study, see Lewis Mehl (M.D.), et al., "Complications of Home Birth," *Birth and the Family Journal*, Vol. 2, No. 4, Fall/Winter, 1975–76.

specific areas, such as menopause, researching the topic and sharing information and experiences.

The self-help groups form and dissolve at irregular intervals so it is impossible to estimate the number that exist. Some meet for a few weeks, others for years.

The groups are important because in them, a woman dispels her ignorance of her own body—an ignorance that makes her vulnerable to unnecessary surgery and population-control experiments. Cowed by medical terminology and trained to believe that her body is a complicated apparatus only a physician can understand, she had previously accepted the doctor's treatments without question. But with the knowledge regular observation brings, the self-help woman stops being a passive recipient of whatever care gynecologists choose to give. She is familiar enough with what he or she is examining to ask questions and insist on answers.

Let's visit a demonstration of one of these remarkable groups at a National Organization for Women conference in Atlanta, Georgia in June 1973.

On a hot summer night, thirty women, chatting and laughing, troop into the darkened motel room of Joan Edelson, a forty-year-old nurse from Jacksonville, Florida.

She pins a sheet to the wall and sets up a projector as the women settle down on couch, tables and floor. Within minutes, they are watching slides of a self-help group in California.

Jabbing the air with her finger, Edelson explains how women can examine themselves internally and, in the process, demystify their bodies and "medical science."

"A mirror. A flashlight. A twenty-five-cent speculum. That's all you need to meet your cervix," she says.

Through regular observation of herself and others, Edelson explains, a woman can learn to recognize infections early. She can detect the sores of syphilis. She can observe the changes in the cervix during the menstrual cycle and learn what is normal for her. She can learn how to take Pap smears for cancer detection.

"You can learn it!" Edelson tells the women. "You don't need a fancy degree."

During a gynecological exam, Edelson explains, the doctor

sometimes clucks his tongue and says, "Oh, you have a tipped uterus," and makes the woman feel there is something really strange or dangerous about that. What becomes obvious in self-help clinics, is that many women have uteri which are tipped a little backward and there is usually nothing abnormal about it.

"But doctors sometimes con those women into having a 'corrective' operation. Some women are told they won't be able to have any children without it," she says.

She shows a slide of cervicitis, a slight inflammation of the cervix.

"In some women, cervicitis is a normal part of the cycle. It comes before menstruation and then goes away just as facial blemishes do on some women. Some doctors cauterize (burn away) the inflammation immediately even though there may be nothing abnormal about it."

When women learn about their bodies, she noted, they can prevent that kind of medical treatment.

The slides over, Edelson and two young women from Atlanta demonstrate a self-examination. They strip from the waist down, lie on the bed and insert specula. They lie near each other so the women can compare three different cervixes and see what variety there is among the normal.

"Every cervix, like every nose, has its own unique appearance," Edelson says.

The women crowd around them. Taking turns with the flashlight, they look at a cervix—most, for the first time. They are fascinated.

"Vicky has an IUD," one woman explains. "That's her feature attraction. Roberta's featuring a double os." (The os is the opening into the uterus.)

Robert lies back, her hands behind her head, and chats comfortably with the women who are looking at her cervix.

"Can you see both os?" she asks one viewer.

"Is that what's on top of the cervix?" a woman answers, squinting as her eyes follow the flashlight beam.

"Get closer so you can see," someone suggests.

"Does the speculum hurt?" a woman asks.

"Not at all," Roberta answers. "If it feels uncomfortable, you just get a smaller one."

The questions come faster: Is that little opening the os? Does the color of the cervix change when you're pregnant? Why? When you have an infection, how can you tell what kind it is? Is that a tipped uterus?

The women grin at each other as they pass the flashlight and ask questions. There's an air of excitement in the smoky room. They know something revolutionary is happening.

Always before, the pelvic exam had been something undergone alone, draped, in stirrups, in a sterile chrome-and-white room. A man examined a part of a woman she had never seen. Sometimes he was rough, having learned, in medical school, to perform the exam on uncomplaining subjects—anesthetized women and prostitutes. Because he often ended the exam with, "You're fine," and ignored her questions, she knew very little about her body and so, felt helpless. She depended on him to tell her if anything was wrong.

But at the end of this exam, each woman took a speculum away with her. She would be the first to know what was happening in her body.

Women's efforts to gain control of their bodies have been unsuccesfully challenged in court. In September 1972, ten policemen and a detective in Los Angeles raided the Feminist Women's Health Center. It had been under surveillance for six months. The lawmen issued arrest warrants for Carol Downer, the originator of the self-help concept, and Colleen Wilson, a clinic worker. Wilson pleaded guilty to fitting a diaphragm. She was fined $250 and put on two years' probation. (Fitting a diaphragm, Downer believes, is like fitting a shoe, only one fits it to a different part of the body.)

Downer was charged with practicing medicine without a license. She had practiced medicine, the police alleged, by helping a woman insert a speculum, by observing a vaginal infection, and by helping to apply a home remedy—yogurt—to relieve the discomfort. (During the raid, the police tried to confiscate some yogurt as evidence but released it when a woman protested that it was her lunch.)

Downer went on trial November 20, 1972 at the New Courthouse in Los Angeles. Money for the defense and telegrams of support poured in from women around the country. Feminist Robin Morgan, referring to the police, telegraphed, "If they think they can burn witches and midwives again, they will be taught a bitter lesson."

As the trial progressed, feminists publicly asked for a definition of medical practice. Was it giving an enema? Was it diagnosing measles? If you decided yogurt might cure a cold or a sore and you put it in your mouth, would that be a crime? Then why did it suddenly become a crime when the yogurt was applied to the vagina? Is it a crime to tell a woman she has a sore on her lip? Then why is it a crime to tell her she has a sore—cervicitis—on her cervix? Is it criminal for a woman to look at her own vagina?

On December 5, after two days' deliberation, the jury found Downer not guilty.

"Women in California now have the right to examine their own and each other's bodies," feminist Deborah Rose commented, ". . . amazing to me that we have to win that right."

Women also had to win the right to give birth without a physician. In Santa Cruz, doctors had warned midwives at the Birth Center not to "catch" babies because that was practicing medicine without a license. The midwives ignored the warning, asserting that a woman delivers her own baby and has a right to do so wherever she wants.

On March 6, 1974, officials from the State Department of Consumer Affairs, the District Attorney's office, the state police and the sheriff's office raided and closed down the Birth Center. They arrested one midwife there and two others in a private home, charging them with the unlicensed practice of medicine.

At their arraignment, the midwives refused to plead either guilty or not guilty. They demurred, arguing that the charge made against them—attendance at a normal physiologic function—did not constitute a crime. In January 1976, the Federal Appeals Court in San Francisco agreed. It ruled that pregnancy and childbirth were not disease states and that the midwives, therefore, could not have been practicing medicine. The court recommended that the state dismiss the charges. The prosecution is appealing.

Today, the Santa Cruz midwives continue to "catch" babies.*

* The Center itself closed in September 1975 as a result of internal pressures and of a great demand for services which the Center, with its largely volunteer staff, could not meet. The more experienced midwives still attend births privately.

In Florida, roles switched. The Tallahassee Feminist Women's Health Center sued physicians, charging them with harassing its staff.

The Center provides abortions for a thousand women each year at its Woman's Choice Clinic, charging from thirty to fifty dollars less than private physicians. The Center prospered until 1975 when it lost three doctors in four months as a result, it alleges, of intimidation by the medical community. The Center maintained local physicians harassed the clinic doctors by (among other tactics) questioning the "ethics" of any doctor who worked at a clinic that advertised. The feminists suspected that physicians simply disliked competition. On October 1, 1975, the Center filed suit against six local obstetrician-gynecologists and the executive director of the Florida Board of Medical Examiners, accusing them of violating the Sherman Antitrust Act by "conspiring to restrain trade and monopolize women's health care in Tallahassee."

As of this writing, the case has not been settled.

In April 1976, the Center learned that women's health groups around the country were being harassed by physicians. So it joined with seven other health groups to form WATCH (Women Acting To Combat Harassment). WATCH will help women's clinics finance and file antitrust suits.

Unretarded by harassment and legal assaults, the fledgling Women's Health Movement has been growing rapidly ever since it emerged in 1969. It still has much work to do in securing woman's control of her own body but that work could easily be accomplished if the rest of us were also engaged in it.

These, it seems to me, are the issues we must organize to deal with:

Maternity Care: Women currently have no voice at all in the maternity services offered us. We have to decide what we want and then work to get it. My preference is for the establishment of midwifery schools and birth centers, independent of physician control. Obstetricians would attend only abnormal and high-risk deliveries.

Routine Health Care: Many of us who need health care services are not sick. We need exams, cancer screening, fittings for diaphragms, prenatal care. Do we want physicians performing these services or female paramedics? If we want paramedics, we should lobby for appropriate training programs.

Abortion, Sterilization, Gynecological Surgery, and VD Care: We must devise methods of monitoring these services in local hospitals and women's prisons.

Health Policy-Making Boards: We should demand full representation of female consumers.

The Use of Unsafe Contraceptives on Unwilling Women: We need to establish joint pressure groups with women around the world to prevent population-control experiments on our bodies.

Medical Philosophy: The allopathic medical sect won out over all the others in 19th-century America. Are we content with it? I see it as an aggressive, masculine system in which diseases (and even normal states like pregnancy) are considered enemies to be conquered through drugs and surgery. I think healing needs to be feminized to include the gentler concepts of sects like homeopathy. Homeopathy concentrates on the whole patient—body, mind and spirit—rather than on the disease or on one isolated organ of the body. It strives to build up the person's strength so he or she can resist illness.

I would prefer an eclectic medical system—one which takes the best ideas from all the different sects.

The Exclusion of Male Medical Students From Obstetrics and Gynecology: When medical writer Barbara Seaman made this proposal at the woman's health conference in Boston in 1975,* it did indeed seem radical to me. It does not today. The truly radical proposals, I now see, were advanced in the 17th century when men took over midwifery, and in the 19th century when "gynecology" was created as a specialty in which only men—with very few exceptions—engaged. Women

* Barbara Seaman's speech on this subject was published under the title "Pelvic Autonomy: Four Proposals" in the Sept./Oct., 1975, issue of *Social Policy.* A reprint of that issue, which is devoted to women's health care, is available for $2.00 from *Social Policy,* Suite 500, 184 Fifth Avenue, New York, N.Y. 10010.

did not like that situation then, as numerous physicians of the time testified, and many do not like it now. If enough of us feel this way, we must decide what we will do about it. It may not be enough to simply increase the number of female gynecologists because, as Seaman points out, the few men remaining in the field will rise to the top, controlling hospital departments, research laboratories and population agencies. This has already happened in socialist countries where many, if not most, gynecologists are women.

We could deal with this and other health issues if each of us did one or all of the following:

1. Launched a local health group, using some of the "Resources for Change" listed in the Appendix.

2. Helped form a Coalition for the Medical Rights of Women, modeled after California's, in our own states.

3. Joined the National Women's Health Lobby Network.

By acting together, we can certainly take back control of our bodies. I see it happening now. And as I attend feminist health conferences, talk with committed activists like Doris Haire and Kay Weiss, and read the newsletters of various health groups— full of energy, outrage and fierce self-respect—I feel so proud of what we women are doing.

APPENDIX

RESOURCES
FOR CHANGE

HEALTH ORGANIZATIONS

National Women's Health Lobby Network
P.O. Box 24192
Washington, D. C. 20024
       or
National Women's Health Lobby Network
c/o Belita Cowan
556 Second Street
Ann Arbor, Mich. 48103

Coalition for the Medical Rights of Women
433 Turk Street
San Francisco, Calif. 94102
(Write here for guidelines on starting a Coalition for the Medical Rights of Women in your own state.)

Advocates for Medical Information
c/o Kay Weiss, M.P.H.
2815 Stanton
Houston, Tex. 77025
(Does medical library research and answers requests for information on proper medical procedures. Health professionals and consumers both belong to chapters in Boston, Hartford, Los Angeles, Atlanta, Ann Arbor and Madison.)

Medical Committee for Human Rights
Boston Chapter
P.O. Box 382
Prudential Station
Boston, Mass. 02199

Women's Health Alliance of Long Island
P.O. Box 645
Westbury, N. Y. 11590

National Women's Health Coalition
222 East 35 Street
New York, N. Y. 10016

Health Research Group
2000 P Street, N.W., Suite 708
Washington, D. C. 20036

The Grey Panthers National Health Service Task Force
3700 Chestnut Street
Philadelphia, Pa. 19004

Nurses NOW (National Organization for Women)
P.O. Box 5156
Pittsburgh, Pa. 15206

WATCH
c/o Feminist Women's Health Center
1017 Thomasville Road
Tallahassee, Fla. 32303
(A financial and legal resource for women's health groups experiencing harassment from the medical community.)

Committee to End Sterilization Abuse
P.O. Box 839 Cooper Station
New York, N. Y. 10003

The Association for Childbirth at Home
47 Ronald Road
Arlington, Mass. 02174

Birth Day
128 Lowell Avenue
Newtonville, Mass. 02160

H.O.M.E. (Home Oriented Maternity Experience)
511 New York Avenue
Takoma Park
Washington, D. C. 20012

WomanCare, Inc. Childbearing Clinic
1050 Garnet
San Diego, Calif. 92109

International Childbirth Education Association
P.O. Box 20852
Milwaukee, Wis. 53220

THE PUBLIC LIBRARY

The public library is an information resource for which you pay. It is often eager to provide the services and programs requested of it. You might form a health reading club and then ask the library to:

1. Publicize its medical resources through displays and lectures. (Many libraries own books like *Guide to Medical Terminology, Gray's Anatomy, Physicians' Desk Reference,* and *Dorland's Illustrated Medical Dictionary.* These books can help women who are just beginning to read medical journals and textbooks.)

2. Subscribe to the *American Journal of Obstetrics and Gynecology, The New England Journal of Medicine, Healthright, The Monthly Extract, her-self* and *Health Pac Bulletin.*

3. Work up bibliographies on specific health topics such as breast cancer or nutrition.

4. Provide speakers and movies on women's health issues.

5. Obtain copies of Congressional hearings on the Pill, DES, IUDs, Depo-Provera, Flagyl, etc., and keep them in a special section on women's health.

6. Give lectures on how to use a medical library.

WOMEN'S HEALTH CLINICS
AND PROJECTS

Santa Cruz Women's Health Center
250 Locust Street
Santa Cruz, Calif. 95606

Feminist Women's Health Center and Women's Choice Clinic
   (abortion)
1112 South Crenshaw Blvd.
Los Angeles, Calif. 90005
        and
429 South Sycamore
Santa Ana, Calif. 92701
        and
2930 McClure Street
Oakland, Calif. 94706

Feminist Women's Health Center
330 Flume Street
Chico, Calif. 95926

San Francisco Woman's Health Center
3789 24th Street
San Francisco, Calif. 94114

Haight Ashbury Women's Clinic
1101 Masonic
San Francisco, Calif. 94117

Women's Health Service of Colorado Springs
831 East Monument
Colorado Springs, Col. 80903

Gainesville Women's Health Center, Inc.
805 SW 4th Street
Gainesville, Fla. 32601

Feminist Women's Health Center and Women's Choice Clinic
1017 Thomasville Road
Tallahassee, Fla. 32303

Tampa Women's Health Center
P.O. Box 7350
Tampa, Fla. 33601

Options, Inc.
1825 Hendricks Avenue
Jacksonville, Fla. 32207

Emma Goldman Women's Health Center
1317 West Loyola
Chicago, Ill. 60626

Indianapolis Women's Center
5656 East 16th Street
Indianapolis, Ind. 46218

Feminist Women's Health Center
126½ North Sheldon
Ames, Iowa 50010

Emma Goldman Clinic for Women
715 North Dodge
Iowa City, Iowa 52240

Delta Women's Clinic
1406 St. Charles Avenue
New Orleans, La. 70130

Maine Feminist Health Project
105 Dresden Avenue
Gardiner, Maine 04345

New Bedford Women's Clinic
347 Country Street
New Bedford, Mass. 02750

Somerville Women's Health Project
326 Somerville Avenue
Somerville, Mass. 02143

Women's Community Health Center
137 Hampshire Street
Cambridge, Mass. 02139
   (This health center is compiling data on problems with conventional contraceptives. Women who have had side effects, complications or unexpected reactions to various birth control methods are asked to send details to Elizabeth Sommers at the above address.)

Community Women's Clinic
c/o Women's Crisis Center
306 North Division Street
Ann Arbor, Mich. 48104

Detroit Women's Health Project
18700 Woodward
Detroit, Mich. 48203

Feminist Women's Health Center
2445 West 8 Mile
Detroit, Mich. 48203

Women's Health and Information Project
P.O. Box 110 Warriner
C.M.U.
Mount Pleasant, Mich. 48858

Elizabeth Blackwell Women's Health Center
2000 South 5th Street
Minneapolis, Minn. 53404

Buffalo Women's Self-Help Clinic
499 Franklin Street
Buffalo, N. Y. 14202

Women's Clinic
341 East 12th Avenue
Eugene, Ore. 97401

Women's Health Clinic
3537 SE Hawthorne Blvd.
Portland, Ore. 97214

Elizabeth Blackwell Health Center for Women
112 South 16th Street, Suite 1012
Philadelphia, Pa. 19103

Philadelphia Women's Health Collective
5030 Newhall Street
Philadelphia, Pa. 19144

Women's Health Services, Inc.
1209 Allegheny Tower
625 Stanwix Street
Pittsburgh, Pa. 15222

Feminist Women's Health Center
368 East 6th Street
Salt Lake City, Utah 84404

Vermont Women's Health Center
P.O. Box 29
Burlington, Vt. 05401

Aradia Clinic
4224 University Way, N. E.
Seattle, Wash. 98112

Country Doctor Women's Clinic
402 15th Avenue East
Seattle, Wash. 98112

Fremont Woman's Clinic
6817 Greenwood Avenue N.
Seattle, Wash. 98103

Open Door Women's Clinic
5012 Roosevelt Way, N. E.
Seattle, Wash. 98105

SW Wisconsin Action Project, Inc.
432 Warner Hall
Plattesville, Wis. 53818

FILMS

Taking Our Bodies Back: The Women's Health Movement
Produced by Margaret Lazarus. Narrated by Barbara Seaman
Available from: Cambridge Documentary Films, Inc.
                 P.O. Box 385
                 Cambridge, Mass. 02139
                 Rental fee: $39

Self Health
by Allie Light and Kathryn Allen
Available from: Multi Media Resource Center
                 540 Powell Street
                 San Francisco, Calif. 94108
                 Rental fee: $40 ($20 for women's groups)

HEALTH PUBLICATIONS

Our Bodies, Ourselves
by the Boston Women's Health Book Collective
Simon and Schuster
630 Fifth Avenue
New York, N. Y. 10009
(Essential reading)

Healthright
Women's Health Forum
175 Fifth Avenue
New York, N. Y. 10010
(Newsletter for the Women's Health Movement)

The Monthly Extract
Box 3488
Stamford, Conn. 06905
(Newsletter for self-help groups)

her-self
225 East Liberty Street
Ann Arbor, Mich. 48108
(Publishes excellent articles on women's health)

Women's Health Care: Resources, Writings, Bibliographies
Edited by and available from:
    Belita Cowan
    556 Second Street
    Ann Arbor, Mich. 48103

Circle One Self Health Handbook
409 East Fontanero
Colorado Springs, Col. 80907

Women and Health Care, A Bibliography
by Sheryl K. Ruzek
Available from:
Program on Women
Northwestern University
619 Emerson Street
Evanston, Ill. 60201

Women & Health, A Bi-Monthly Academic Journal
Available from:
State University of New York
College at Old Westbury
Old Westbury, N. Y. 11568

Birth Control Handbook
        and
VD Handbook
P.O. Box 1000
Station "G"
Montreal 130, Quebec

How To Organize "Woman's Right to Health,"
  a Panel Discussion
Baltimore Chapter of the National Organization for Women
P.O. Box 21
Sunshine Avenue
Kingsville, Md. 21087

Health Pac Bulletin
17 Murray Street
New York, N. Y. 10007

Organizing for Health Care: A Tool for Change
Source Catalog 3
Write to: Source
    P.O. Box 21066
    Washington, D. C. 20009

Menopause Study Group Newsletter and
    Support Group Guidelines
Write to: University of Washington YWCA
    4224 University Way, N.E.
    Seattle, Wash. 98105

Prime Time
420 West 46th Street
New York, N. Y. 10036
(This feminist newsletter sometimes carries health articles
    of special interest to older women.)

Health Rights News
2251 West Taylor
Chicago, Ill. 60612

The New Woman's Survival Sourcebook
by Susan Rennie and Kirsten Grimstad
Alfred A. Knopf, Inc.
201 East 50th Street
New York 10020
(See "Health" section for many more resources.)

The Pregnant Patient's Bill of Rights
For a free copy, send a stamped, self-addressed envelope to:
    Committee on Patients' Rights
    Box 1900
    New York, N. Y. 10001

SOURCE NOTES

CHAPTER ONE

For information on the witch as healer, see:

Ehrenreich, Barbara, and English, Dierdre. *Witches, Midwives, and Nurses: A History of Women Healers.* Old Westbury, N. Y.: The Feminist Press, 1973. Highly recommended.

Forbes, Thomas Rogers. *The Midwife and the Witch.* New Haven: Yale University Press, 1966. See this book for details on the numerous regulations made by church and state to prevent midwives from engaging in witchcraft.

Mead, Kate C. H. *A History of Women in Medicine.* Haddam, Conn.: Haddam Press, 1938.

Michelet, Jules (1789–1874). *Satanism and Witchcraft, A Study In Medieval Superstitions.* New York: The Citadel Press, 1946.

Szasz, Thomas S. *The Manufacture of Madness.* New York: Harper & Row, 1970. Powerful book.

My knowlege of the popular health movement and the state of 19th-century medicine partially comes from the reading of *The Botanic Sentinel, The Health Record,* and *The Health*

Reformer, all 19th-century popular-health journals. They are available in the Francis A. Countway Library of Medicine at Harvard Medical School in Boston.

Other sources for the discussion of the early American medical scene were:

Brieger, Gert H., ed. *Medical America in the Nineteenth Century.* Baltimore: The Johns Hopkins University Press, 1972.
Shyrock, Richard Harrison. *Medicine and Society in America 1660–1860.* New York: New York University Press, 1960.
———. *Medical Licensing in America 1650–1965.* Baltimore: The Johns Hopkins University Press, 1967.
Stevens, Rosemary. *American Medicine and the Public Interest.* New Haven and London: Yale University Press, 1971.

Most of the sources for the story of woman's struggle to re-enter medicine are contained in the Elizabeth Bass Collection (EBC) at the Rudolph Matas Medical Library at Tulane Medical School in New Orleans. Others are in the Sophia Smith Collection (SSC) at Smith College in Northampton, Mass. A few of those sources were:

Chadwick, James R. (M. D.). "The Admission of Women to the Massachusetts Medical Society." Pamphlet printed in Boston, June 1882. (EBC)
Cleveland, Emeline H. (M.D.). "Valedictory Address to the Graduating Class of the Women's Medical College of Pennsylvania at the 16th Annual Commencement." James B. Rodgers, Printer, Philadelphia, 1868. (EBC)
Corson, Hiram (M. D.). "A Brief History of Proceedings in the Medical Society of Pennsylvania in the Years 1859, 1860, 1866, 1867, 1868, 1870 and 1871 To Procure the Recognition of Women Physicians By the Medical Profession of the State." Herald Printing & Binding Rooms, Norristown, Pa., 1894. (EBC)
Gregory, Samuel. "Letters to Ladies in Favor of Female Physicians for Their Own Sex." Published by the Female Medical Education Society, Boston, 1850. (SSC)
Harvey, Ellwood (M. D.). Valedictory Address to the Female Medical College of Pennsylvania, 1854–55. (EBC)
"Preamble and Resolutions of the Philadelphia County Medical Society Upon the Status of Women Physicians With a Reply by a Woman." Stuckey, Printer. Philadelphia, 1867. (EBC)
Preston, Ann (M. D.). "Introductory Lecture," Female Medical College of Pennsylvania. Printed by Anna E. M'Dowell, Woman's Advocate Office, 1855. (EBC)
Welsh, Lillian (M.D.). *Reminiscences of Thirty Years in Baltimore.* Baltimore: The Norman, Remington Co., 1925. (EBC)

White, Frances Emily (M. D.). Valedictory Address to the Women's Medical College of Pennsylvania, March 10, 1880. (EBC)

It has been contended that a medical education is wasted on a woman because she will only marry and leave the profession. In this chapter, I refer to six studies which have refuted that contention.

The first was conducted by Emily F. Pope, M. D., et al., and was reported in a paper read before the American Social Science Association, Sept. 7, 1881. That paper, entitled "The Practice of Medicine by Women in the United States," is printed in a pamphlet at the Sophia Smith Collection. Dr. Pope found that of 430 female doctors, 390 were engaged in active practice, 29 had practiced for some time and then retired and 11 had never practiced.

Clara Marshall, dean of the Women's Medical College of Pennsylvania, performed the second study in 1900. A report of her study is housed in the Elizabeth Bass Collection. Marshall studied graduates of her college and found that only eight of 189 had left medical practice because of marriage.

In the next study, dated 1938, the careers of female graduates of Johns Hopkins Medical School were traced over a forty-one-year period. It was concluded that the results were the same as would have been expected of a group of men of the same number. The study is reported in "Women Physicians," a 1945 pamphlet by the U. S. Women's Bureau.

The fourth study was conducted by Helen R. Downes, Ph.D., and reported in "Women in Medicine," *Medical Women's Journal,* 1946, and in the *Journal of the American Medical Association,* October 13, 1945.

Dr. Janet Travell conducted a study in the late 1950s. Of three hundred female doctors questioned, 91 percent were active professionally. See her book, *Office Hours: Day and Night.* New York: New American Library, 1971.

The final study was conducted in 1965 for the American Medical Association, the American Medical Women's Association, and the Association of American Medical Colleges. For details, see "Report of a Conference on Meeting Medical Manpower Needs; the Fuller Utilization of the Woman Physician," held January 12–13, 1968, in Washington, D. C. Copies may be available from any of the three study sponsors.

Interviews with Dr. M. Gene Black, Dr. Myra Shayevitz, Dr. Mary Howell and Dr. Alice Rothchild, all identified in the text, and correspondence with Dr. Judith Tyson, were helpful in preparing the sections on the status of female physicians today. Among the other sources were:

Campbell, Margaret. *Why Would a Girl Go Into Medicine?* Old Westbury, N. Y.: The Feminist Press, November 1973.

"Career Choices for Women in Medicine," Volumes I and II, printed by the American Medical Women's Association, 1971. Revealing the need to reconcile femininity with the "masculinity" of medicine, Dr. Elizabeth Vasiliki Coryloos writes in this pamphlet: "It (pediatric surgery) demands a great deal of patience and perseverance, which are more part of the feminine than of the masculine personality. It demands meticulous attention to details, which again is more suited to the female disposition . . . The work demands a high degree of manual dexterity and delicate handling of tissues—neither of which presents too great a problem to the average woman."

Center Scope, Boston University Medical Center, July/August, 1971. Special issue on female physicians.

Horner, Matina. "A Bright Woman Is Caught in a Double Bind." *Psychology Today,* November 1969.

Jenkins, Evans. "Women in Medicine Up Sharply." *The New York Times,* July 17, 1974.

Kaplan, Harold I. "Women Physicians: The More Effective Recruitment and Utilization of Their Talents and the Resistance to It— A Seven Year Study." Excerpts from the study are printed in "Discrimination Against Women: Hearings Before the Special Subcommittee on Education of the Committee on Education and Labor, House of Representatives, Session on Section 805 of H. R. 16098." June 1970.

Lopate, Carol. *Women in Medicine.* Baltimore: The Johns Hopkins University Press, 1968.

Norris, Frances S. Prepared statement, letters and supplemental material presented at the congressional hearings on discrimination against women in June 1970. For title, see information under Harold Kaplan's name.

Seaver, Jacqueline. "Women Doctors." *The New York Times Magazine,* March 26, 1961.

CHAPTER TWO

Blackman, Elizabeth. *Pioneer Work in Opening the Medical Profession to Women, Autobiographical Sketches.* London and New York: Longmans, Green, & Co., 1895.

Blackwell, Elizabeth and Emily (M. D.s). "Medicine As a Profession for Women." *The Feminist Papers,* Alice Rossi, ed. New York: Bantam Books, 1974.

Hunt, Harriet K. *Glances and Glimpses.* Boston: John P. Jewett & Co., 1856. (EBC)

Keating, Harriette C. (M. D.). Obituary of Dr. Clemence Lozier read before the New York County Homeopathic Society, June 14, 1888. (EBC)

Lozier, A. W. (M. D.). "In Memoriam—Clemence Sophia Lozier, M. D.," an address by Dr. Lozier in presenting a bust of his mother to the N. Y. C. Suffrage League, Nov. 1, 1888. (EBC)

Stanton, Elizabeth Cady. Tribute to Dr. Clemence Sophia Lozier delivered before The Women's League, June 7, 1888. (EBC)

Wait, Phoebe J. (M. D.). "Extracts from an Address Delivered at the Opening Exercises of the N.Y. Medical College and Hospital for Women," Oct. 1, 1888. (EBC)

CHAPTER THREE

Bullough, Bonnie and Vern L. "Sex Discrimination in Health Care." *Nursing Outlook,* January 1975, pp. 40–45.

Cleland, Virginia. "Sex Discrimination: Nursing's Most Pervasive Problem." *American Journal of Nursing,* August 1971.

Dolan, Josephine A. *Nursing in Society, A Historical Perspective.* Philadelphia: W. B. Saunders Co., 1973. For information on the use of nursing students as cheap labor, see pp. 259–262.

Donnelly, Gloria, et al. "The Anatomy of a Conflict." *Supervisor Nurse,* November 1975, pp. 28–38.

Ehrenreich, Barbara, and English, Dierdre. "Witches, Midwives and Nurses; A History of Women Healers." Old Westbury, N. Y.: The Feminist Press. 1973. Important.

Eichel, Larry. "Doctors, Nurses at War Here and Across U. S." *The Philadelphia Inquirer,* February 2, 1975.

"Firing of Nursing Director Sparks Demonstrations Over Who Runs Nursing." *American Journal of Nursing,* March 1975.

"Leadership: Problems and Possibilities in Nursing," A Symposium. *American Journal of Nursing,* August 1972.

Miller, Joe A., and Ferman, Louis A. "Welfare Careers and Low-Wage Employment." Institute of Labor and Industrial Relations, University of Michigan-Wayne State University; A Report Prepared for the Manpower Administration, U. S. Dept. of Labor, 1972.

Ostergard, Donald R., Broen, Elmer M., et al. "The Family Planning Specialist As a Provider of Health Care Service." *Fertility and Sterility,* July 1972.

Pool, Judith G., and Bunker, John P. "Women in Medicine." *Hospital Practice,* August 1972.

Reverby, Susan. "Health: Women's Work." *Health Pac Bulletin,* No. 40, April 1972.

Richards, Linda. *Reminiscences of America's First Trained Nurse.* Boston: Whitcomb and Barrows, 1911. (EBC)

Rothberg, June S. "Nurse and Physician's Assistant: Issues and Relationships." *Nursing Outlook,* March 1970.

Schaefer, Marguerite J. "Toward a Full Profession of Nursing: The Challenge of the Educator's Role." *The Journal of Nursing Education,* November 1972.

Stein, Leonard. "The Doctor-Nurse Game." *The American Journal of Nursing,* January 1968.

CHAPTER FOUR

Interviews with the following persons, all identified in the text, provided information for this chapter: Dr. Estelle Ramey, Dr. Mary Howell, Dr. William Smith, Dr. Linda Fidell and Ella McDonald. The following persons, who prefer to remain anonymous, also spoke with me: The director of an urban health center, a Massachusetts surgeon, and many female health consumers. Other sources included:

Anonymous. *Confessions of a Gynecologist.* New York: Doubleday, 1972. This gynecologist reveals one of his "most closely guarded secrets" about his practice: "that I frequently find women terribly funny—usually when they are being quite serious."

Brodsky, Carroll M. "The Pharmacotherapy System." *Psychosomatics,* 1971, 11, 24–30.

Campbell, Margaret A. (M. D.). *Why Would a Girl Go into Medicine?, Medical Education in the U. S.: A Guide for Women.* Privately published booklet. Now available from The Feminist Press, Old Westbury, N. Y. (1973)

Fidell, Linda, and Prather, Jane. "Mood Modifying Drug Use in Middle-Class Women." Paper presented at the Western Psychological Association Meeting, Sacramento, California, April 25, 1975. I obtained this paper, and others on the same topic, from Dr. Fidell at the Department of Psychology, California State University, Northridge, California.

Greenhill, J. P. *Office Gynecology.* Chicago: Yearbook Medical Publishers, Inc., 1971.

Howell, Mary (M. D.). "What Medical Schools Teach About Women." *New England Journal of Medicine,* August 1974.

Lennane, Jean K., and John R. "Alleged Psychogenic Disorders in Women—A Possible Manifestation of Sexual Prejudice." *New England Journal of Medicine,* February 8, 1973.

Ostergard, Donald R., Broen, E. M., et al. "Family Planning and Cancer Screening Services as Provided by Paramedical Personnel: A Training Program." *Excerpta Medica International Congress Series No. 246.* Advances in Planned Parenthood—VII; Proceedings of the Ninth Annual Meeting of the American Association of Planned Parenthood Physicians, Kansas City, Mo., April 1971.

Scott, C. Russell. *The World of a Gynecologist.* London: Oliver and Boyd, 1968.

Scully, D., and Bart, P. "A Funny Thing Happened on the Way to the Orifice: Women in Gynecology Textbooks." *American Journal of Sociology,* 78, 1973.

Seidenberg, Robert. "Drug Advertising and Perception of Mental Illness." *Mental Hygiene,* January 1971.

"Women Doctors Open Dispensary." New Orleans *States-Item,* June 2, 1905. I read this clipping in the Elizabeth Bass Collection at Tulane Medical School. The article revealed the distress poor women felt at being used as teaching material for young men. At the opening of the female-staffed New Orleans Dispensary for Women and Children in 1905, Jean Gordon of United Charities spoke for these women: "They cannot afford the luxury of the private sanitarium and to go to the Charity Hospital means that their physical infirmities must be exposed as a demonstration to a large class of men students. Many of the women refuse positively to be humiliated, and prefer to suffer on to the end, and no one can blame them. So this formal opening today means much to the young girls of this city. It means the opportunity to explain your troubles and pains to a woman as only a woman can speak to a woman."

CHAPTER FIVE

The Proceedings of the International Conference of Women Physicians, held September 15 to October 15, 1919, in New York City, were an important source for the attitudes of female physicians towards women's health issues. The *Proceedings* are in the Elizabeth Bass Collection, Tulane Medical School, New Orleans.

I gleaned much information on woman's health in 19th-century America from popular-health journals, all of which are in Harvard Medical School's library. Those journals, appearing largely in the 1830s and 1840s, included: *Botanico-Medical Recorder, The Botanic Sentinel, Thomsonian Manual, Boston Thomsonian Manual* and *Lady's Companion* and *The Health Reformer.*

Among my sources on 19th-century medicine were:

Brown, Isaac Baker. *On the Curability of Certain Forms of Insanity, Epilepsy, Catalespsy and Hysteria in Females.* London: R. Hardwicke, 1866. Available at the New York Academy of Medicine, New York City.

Cott, Nancy F., Ed. *Root of Bitterness: Documents of the Social History of American Women.* New York: E. P. Dutton, 1972. The section entitled "Sexuality and Gynecology in the Nineteenth Century" is fascinating.

Ehrenreich, Barbara, and English, Dierdre. *Complaints and Disorders; The Sexual Politics of Sickness.* Glass Mountain Pamphlet No. 2. Old Westbury, New York: The Feminist Press, 1973. Highly recommended.

Graham, Harvey (pseudonym for Isaac Harvey Flack). *Eternal Eve, The History of Obstetrics and Gynecology.* Garden City, N. .Y.: Doubleday & Co., 1951. For information on ovariotomies, clitoridectomies and the development of various other gynecological operations, read pp. 421–453.

Hersey, Thomas. *The Midwife's Practical Directory; or Woman's Confidential Friend.* Published by Hersey himself, Baltimore, 1836. Harvard Medical School library owns a copy.

Hollick, Frederick (M. D.). *The Marriage Guide.* New York: T. W. Strong, 1850. New York Academy of Medicine.

Mann, Kristin (M. D.). "A Woman's Movement for the Conservation of the Health of Women." 1919. (EBC)

Perkins, Charlotte Gilman. *The Yellow Wallpaper.* Old Westbury, N. Y.: The Feminist Press, 1973. A powerful account of the "treatment" women received for "nervous disorders." Perkins, a 19th-century economist and feminist, was herself subjected to that treatment.

Taylor, Walter (M. D.). *Counsel to Women in Health and Disease.* Springfield, Mass.: W. J. Holland & Co., 1871. New York Academy of Medicine.

Walters, Ronald G., ed. *Primers for Prudery: Sexual Advice to Victorian America.* Englewood Cliffs, N. J.: Prentice-Hall, 1974.

My sources on 20th-century medicine included:

Bender, Marylin, "Doctors Deny Woman's Hormones Affect Her As an Executive." *The New York Times,* July 31, 1970.

Gifford-Jones, W. (M. D.). *On Being a Woman.* New York: Macmillan, 1969. Written by a man; condescending.

Green, Thomas H., Jr. (M. D.). *Gynecology: Essentials of Clinical Practice.* Boston: Little, Brown, 1965.

Greenhill, J. P. (M. D.). *Office Gynecology,* 9th ed. Chicago: Year Book Medical Publishers, Inc., 1971.

Hayden, Trudy. "Punishing Pregnancy: Discrimination in Education, Employment, and Credit," Women's Rights Project, American Civil Liberties Union, October 1973.

Hutton, Isabel. "Women as Air Pilots." *Medical Women's International Journal*, June 1926. (EBC)

Kistner, Robert W. (M. D.). *Gynecology*. Chicago: Year Book Medical Publishers, Inc., 1971.

Novak, E. R. (M. D.). "Gynecologic Endocrinology and Hormone Therapy." *Davis' Gynecology and Obstetrics*, Joseph J. Rovinsky, Ed. Vol. 2, Part 2, Medical Dept., New York: Harper & Row, 1971.

Scully, Diane, and Bart, Pauline: "A Funny Thing Happened on the Way to the Orifice: Women in Gynecology Textbooks." *American Journal of Sociology*, 1973, 78, 1045–1049.

"What Constitutes Equality for Women in Sport?" The Project on the Status and Education of Women, Association of American Colleges, 1818 R. Street, N. W., Washington, D. C., April 1974 newsletter. A modern version of the woman-as-invalid theory runs this way: A female is delicate. Athletic activity might break her fragile bones, damage her reproductive organs and induce menstrual problems. These medical myths have no basis in fact but have nonetheless helped schools to justify spending almost all their athletic funds on males. For many examples of the unfortunate results, see this newsletter.

Wilson, Robert A. (M. D.). *Feminine Forever*. New York: M. Evans and Company, Inc., 1966.

CHAPTER SIX

The sections on past attitudes toward, and treatment of, VD are largely based on the following material:

Acton, William. "The Contagious Diseases Act: Shall the CDA Be Applied to the Civil Population?" Paper read before the Association of the Medical Officers of Health, December 18, 1869. London: John Church & Sons, 1870. Available at New York Academy of Medicine, New York City.

Acton, William. *Prostitution Considered in Its Moral, Social and Sanitary Aspects, In London and Other Large Cities With Proposals for the Mitigation and Prevention of Its Attendant Evils*. London: John Churchill, 1957. New York Academy of Medicine.

"Proceedings of the International Conference of Women Physicians." New York: The Woman's Press, 1919. (EBC)

Rant, Ettie. Letter to the editor of *American Medicine*, Vol. 20, No. 2, February 1925; and "Two Years in Paris," pamphlet published by Rant, London, June 1923. (SSC)

Rosebury, Theodore. *Microbes and Morals: The Strange Story of Venereal Disease*. New York: Viking Press, 1971.

The discussion of current VD problems is based on interviews or personal communication with the following persons: Thelma Bickenheuser, stepmother of the late Frank Bickenheuser, developer of Progonosyl; Uri Carpenter, administrative chief of the study of prophylactic contraceptives at the University of Pittsburgh Graduate School of Public Health in Pittsburgh; William M. Edwards (M. D.), chief of the Bureau of Preventative Medicine in the Nevada State Health Division; Ralph Henderson (M. D.) and Michael Rein (M. D.), both of the Disease Prevention Control Center in Atlanta; King K. Holmes (M.D.), VD researcher at the U. S. Public Health Service Hospital in Seattle; Milton Puziss (M. D.), of the National Institutes of Health; Lonny Myers (M. D.), clinician and vice-president of the Midwest Association for the Study of Human Sexuality; and Walter H. Smartt (M. D.), former chief of the Los Angeles County VD program.

The following papers, read at the First National Conference on Methods of VD Prevention, held at the University of Chicago in November 1974, were also helpful:

Cutler, John C. (M. D.). "Advantages and Disadvantages of Vaginal Prophylaxis Using Preparations Which Are Simultaneously Contraceptive."

Edwards, William (M. D.). "Vaginal Prophylaxis: A Critical Review of the Progonosyl Study."

Myers, Lonny (M. D.). "Attitudes Toward Sexual Behavior and Their Effect on the Prevention of Sexually Transmitted Infections."

Singh, Balwant. "Advantages of Prophylaxis Over Therapy In Curbing the Gonorrhea Epidemic."

Other sources included:

"The AMA Quick-Reference Guide" to the policies, positions and statements of the American Medical Association in regard to key health issues. Revised July 1974.

Brecher, Edward M. "Women—Victims of the VD Rip-Off." *Viva*, October/November 1973. Excellent article.

Cherniak, Donna (M. D.), and Feingold, Allan. *VD Handbook.* Montreal, Quebec: Montreal Health Press, Inc., 1972.

Handsfield, Hunter H., et al. "Asymptomatic Gonorrhea in Men." *The New England Journal of Medicine,* January 17, 1974.

Koba Associates, Inc. of Washington, D. C. "VD Control—A National Strategy Under Review," Executive Summary, Final Report, Contract No. HEW-OS-72-191; Submitted to HEW, August 1973.

CHAPTER SEVEN

Much of this chapter is based on material in the papers of Margaret Sanger and of the International Planned Parenthood Federation, and the Planned Parenthood Federation of America. All this material is available at the Sophia Smith Collection at Smith College, Northampton, Massachusetts. A few of those sources are:

Burch, Guy Irving. A letter to Dr. Arthur J. Barton dated January 23, 1934.
Kahn, Morris H. (M. D.). "A Municipal Birth Control Clinic." *New York Medical Journal,* April 28, 1917.
Kamperman, George (M. D.). "The Birth Control Movement." *The Journal* of the Michigan State Medical Society, September 1932.
Pierson, Richard N. (M. D.). "Victories for Planned Parenthood." Speech delivered when Pierson was president of Planned Parenthood, sometime between 1939 and 1943.
Rose, Kenneth D. "How Community Support for Planned Parenthood Has Been Developed." Paper dated May 12, 1942.
Sanger, Margaret. "The History of the Birth Control Movement in the English-Speaking World." Speech delivered to the Fourth International Conference on Planned Parenthood in Stockholm, August 1953.
————. "Fifteen Years Growth—1924–1939." Speech delivered in Philadelphia, December 4, 1939.
————. "International Aspects of Birth Control." Proceedings of the Sixth International Neo-Mathusian and Birth Control Conference, 1925, The American Birth Control League, Inc., New York, 1925. Edited and with an introduction by Sanger.
————. *Motherhood in Bondage.* New York: Brentano's, 1928. The book consists of letters to Sanger pleading for contraceptive information. Heartbreaking reading. Many of the original letters are also contained in the SSC.

The SSC provided some material on the eugenics movement. Other information came from the following books in the Rudolph Matas Medical Library at Tulane Medical School in New Orleans:

Alrich, Morton A., ed. *Eugenics: Twelve University Lectures.* New York: Dodd, Mead & Co., 1914.
Rice, Thurman B. (M. D.). *Racial Hygiene.* New York: Macmillan, 1929.

Robinson, William J. (M. D.). *Practical Eugenics, Four Methods of Improving the Human Race*. New York: The Critic and Guide Co., 1912.

Saleeby, Caleb Williams (M. D.). *The Methods of Race Regeneration*. New York: Moffat, Yar & Co., 1911.

Sources from the Elizabeth Bass Collection at Tulane were:

"Proceedings of the International Conference of Women Physicians," Volume 6. New York: The Woman's Press, 1919.

"Summary of the Discussion on Birth Control," Medical Women's International Association Stockholm Congress, August 10, 1934.

Sources for the discussion of the population-control movement included:

Archer, Elayne. "The Birth of Conspiracy." *Health Pac Bulletin*, March 1970.

"Founder of FHF Admits Errors, 'But No Thefts.'" Baton Rogue *State-Times*, February 14, 1974. The founder of Family Health Foundation states that one result of FHF's contraceptive service was the decline of Louisiana's nonwhite birth rate by 13.4 percent since 1967, at a time when Mississippi's nonwhite birth rate had increased by 1.8 percent.

Osborn, Frederick. *Population: An International Dilemma, A Summary of the Proceedings of the Committee on Population Problems, 1956–1957*. Copyright by the Population Council, 1958. Princeton, N. J.: Princeton University Press.

————. *The Future of Human Heredity: An Introduction to Eugenics in Modern Society*. The passages I found most disturbing are on pp. 92–112.

Prospect for America, The Rockefeller Panel Reports. Garden City, N. Y.: Doubleday & Co., Inc., 1961.

Sharp, Jean. "The Birth Controllers." *Health Pac Bulletin*, April 1972.

General sources included:

Haire, Norman. *Some More Medical Views on Birth Control*. New York: E. P. Dutton & Co., 1928.

Jaffe, Frederick S. "Public Policy on Fertility Control." *Scientific American*, July 1973.

The discussion of recent sterilizations is based on interviews with Morris Dees of the Southern Poverty Law Center, an attorney for the Relf sisters, and with Annie Smart, Southern Regional Director of the National Welfare Rights Organization. It is also based on legal papers and on many newspaper stories. Among those sources are:

"Aide Says 11 May Have Been Sterilized." *The New York Times,* July 3, 1973.

"Clinic Defends Sterilization of 2 Girls, 12 and 14." *The New York Times,* June 28, 1973.

Hicks, Nancy. "Sterilization of Black Mother of Two Stirs Aiken, S. C." *The New York Times,* August 1, 1973.

Kindregan, Charles P. "State Power Over Human Fertility." *The Hastings Law Journal,* May 1972.

CHAPTER EIGHT

Among the general sources for this chapter were:

Cherniak, Donna, and Feingold, Allan. *Birth Control Handbook.* Canada: The Handbook Collective, 1972.

"Health Research Group Petition for New Regulations on Human Drug Experiments." Filed with the Food and Drug Administration, April 16, 1974. Contains horrifying information on experiments with new birth-control drugs.

Transcripts of the Senate Pill hearings were an important source for the section on oral contraceptives. I think women would find it an enlightening experience to read the full testimony and the studies on the Pill reprinted in the hearing appendixes. The transcripts are available free from your Congressperson. You could also request your public library to obtain copies for you either from Washington or on interlibrary loan. Ask for, "Hearings before the Subcommittee on Monopoly of the Select Committee on Small Business, United States Senate, Second Session on Present Status of Competition in the Pharmaceutical Industry, Parts 15, 16 and 17, Oral Contraceptives, Vols. I, II and III." The hearings were held in January, February and March 1970.

Other sources for the discussion of the oral contraceptive included:

"Hazards of the Pill (Cont.)." *Newsweek,* October 28, 1974.

Kistner, Robert W. (M. D.). *The Pill.* New York: Dell Publishing Co., 1969.

Mintz, Morton. *The Pill: An Alarming Report.* Boston: Beacon Press, 1969.

"Our Readers Talk Back About the Birth Control Pills." *Ladies' Home Journal,* November 1967.

Population Reports: Oral Contraceptives, Series A. Number 2, March 1975. Published by the Population Information Program, Science Communication Division, Department of Medical and

Public Affairs of the George Washington University Medical Center. Supported by the U. S. Agency for International Development.

Seaman, Barbara. *Free and Female.* New York: Coward, McCann & Geoghegan, 1972. See chapter entitled "A Skeptical Guide to VD and Contraception."

———. "The New 'Pill' Scare—Important Research from England." *Ms.,* June 1975.

Shapiro, Jane. "Standard Operating Procedure." *Ms.,* February 1975. Shattering.

Silverberg, Steven G., and Makowski, Edgar L. "Endometrial Carcinoma in Young Women Taking Oral Contraceptive Agents." *Obstetrics and Gynecology,* November 1975.

The most important source for the section on the IUD was *Regulations of Medical Devices (Intrauterine Devices),* Hearings before a Subcommittee of the Committee on Government Operations, House of Representatives, May 30, 31, June 1, 12, 13, 1973.

Other sources included:

"FDA Links Rise in Deaths To Birth Device." *The New York Times,* August 22, 1974.

"Intrauterine Devices." *Population Reports,* Series B, No. 2, January 1975. Department of Medical and Public Affairs of the George Washington University Medical Center.

"IUD Device Cited in Deaths of Four." *The New York Times,* May 29, 1974.

"IUD Safety: Report of a Nationwide Physician Survey." *Morbidity and Mortality,* Center for Disease Control, July 5, 1974.

Katz, Barbara J. "The IUD—Out of Sight, Out of Mind?" *Ms.,* July 1975.

———. "The IUD's Unnatural Birth." *The National Observer,* September 8, 1973.

Oppenheimer, W. (M. D.). "Prevention of Pregnancy by the Graefenberg Ring Method; A Re-Evaluation After 28 Years' Experience." *American Journal of Obstetrics and Gynecology,* 78:446–454, 1959. This is one of the two papers which population controllers used to justify the reintroduction of the discredited IUD. Oppenheimer asserts that in his study of 329 women, the IUD proved to be 25 times as safe as the diaphragm, an assertion no one would seriously support today. The very first sentence of Oppenheimer's paper reveals a population-control orientation: "At a time when so many countries are overpopulated, the prevention of pregnancy has become a consideration of increasing importance."

Sources for the discussion of Depo-Provera were:

Quality of Health Care—Human Experimentation. Hearings before the Subcommittee on Health of the Committee on Labor and Public Welfare, U. S. Senate, February 21, 22, 1973. Part One.

Schmeck, Harold M., Jr. "FDA Will Approve Controversial Injectable Contraceptive Drug for Restricted Use by Prescription." *The New York Times,* October 12, 1973.

Use of Advisory Committees by the Food and Drug Administration. Eleventh Report by the Committee on Government Operations, House Report Number 94-787, January 26, 1976. (See pp. 29–34 and p. 57.)

Use of Advisory Committees by the Food and Drug Administration. Hearings before a Subcommittee of the Committee on Government Operations, House of Representatives, 93rd Congress, March 6, 7, 8, 12, 13; April 30; and May 21, 1974. (See, in particular, pp. 332–385.)

Zwerdling, Daniel. "Risky Birth Control: Depo-Provera." *The New Republic,* November 9, 1974. Excellent.

CHAPTER NINE

Interviews with Dr. Andrew V. Schalley and Dr. Don W. Fawcett, both identified in the text, were helpful in preparing this chapter.

The section on temporary male sterilization is based on interviews with Dr. Mary Calderone, Dr. John MacLeod, Dr. John Rock, Dr. Sheldon Segal, and Dr. Mostafa S. Fahim. It is also based on correspondence with Dr. Martha Voegeli and on her personal correspondence with, among others, Dr. Clarence Gamble, Alice Price, Dr. Harrison Brown, Dr. David Pyke, Dr. Nelson Warren, Margaret Grierson, Dr. Calderone and Dr. Segal. Those letters are in the Sophia Smith Collection. Other sources included:

Fahim, M. S., Fahim, Z., et al. "Heat in Male Contraception (Hot Water 60 C, Infrared, Microwave, and Ultrasound)." *Contraception (An International Journal),* May 1975.

Robinson, Derek (M. D.) and Rock, John (M. D.). "Intrascrotal Hyperthermia Induced by Scrotal Insulation: Effect on Spermatogenesis." *Obstetrics and Gynecology,* February 1967.

Rock, John (M. D.), and Robinson, Derek (M. D.). "Effect of Induced Intrascrotal Hyperthermia on Testicular Function in Man." *American Journal of Obstetrics and Gynecology,* pp. 793–801. November 15, 1965.

Rovik, David M. "What's Better Than the Pill, Vasectomy, Celibacy and Rhythm?" *Esquire,* January 1975.
Voegeli, Martha (M. D.). "Contraception Through Temporary Male Sterilization." Unpublished paper dated March 31, 1954. (SSC)

CHAPTER TEN

Information on the physician's reluctance to perform abortions was obtained from the following sources:

Brody, Jane E. "States and Doctors Wary on Eased Abortion Policy." *The New York Times,* February 16, 1973.
Hall, Robert E. (M. D.). "Abortion: Physician and Hospital Attitudes." *American Journal of Public Health,* Vol. 61, No. 3, March 1971.
King, Wayne. "Problems Persist in Getting Abortions." *The New York Times,* May 20, 1973.
Tietze, Christopher, M. D., Jaffe, Frederick S., et al. "Provisional Estimates of Abortion Need and Services in the Year Following the Supreme Court Decisions." A Report by the Alan Guttmacher Institute, Planned Parenthood Federation of America, New York, 1975.
Walter, G. S. (M. D.). "Psychologic and Emotional Consequences of Elective Abortion." *Obstetrics and Gynecology,* 36:483, 1970.

The section on abortion is based on interviews with Jimmye Kimmey and a Massachusetts physician who prefers to remain anonymous. It is also based on interviews with "Janice R." and with many women who had illegal abortions. A few of the other sources were:

Cisler, Lucinda. "Birth Control—Unfinished Business." *Sisterhood Is Powerful,* Robin Morgan, ed. New York: Vintage Books, 1970. See this essay for a more complete discussion of abortion.
Gold, Edwin M. (M. D.), et al. "Therapeutic Abortions in New York City: A 20-Year Review." *American Journal of Public Health,* July 1965. Pp. 964–972.
Gurtner, George. "Womb Is A Bank Vault; Tomorrow Stored There." *Clarion Herald* (New Orleans), October 4, 1973. Catholic newspaper article opposing abortion.

The sterilization sections are based on interviews with Dr. Sidney Wolfe of the Health Research Group; Betty Gonzales and Evelyn Bryant, both of the Association for Voluntary Sterilization; "Judy," who had difficulty obtaining a sterilization; and "Dr. C," chief of surgery at a Northeastern hospital. Personal communication from "Dr. C," dated May 15, 1973, also provided information for this chapter. Other sources included:

Caress, Barbara. "Sterilization: Women Fit To Be Tied." *Health Pac Bulletin*, January/February 1975.

Cobb, Carl M. "Students Charge BCH's Obstetrics Unit With 'Excessive Surgery.'" *The Boston Globe*, April 29, 1972.

Kihss, Peter. "'Noncompliance' Seen on Sterilization." *The New York Times*, April 14, 1975.

Rosenfeld, Bernard (M. D.), Wolfe, Sidney M. (M. D.), et al. *A Health Research Group Study on Surgical Sterilization: Present Abuses and Proposed Regulations*, October 29, 1973.

"Speakout Rage." *Second Wave*, Vol. 2, No. 3, p. 11.

For further information on sterilization, see the last section of source notes for Chapter seven.

CHAPTER ELEVEN

This chapter is based, in part, on the memoirs, diaries, letters and papers of Dorothy Reed Mendenhall. All the papers are in the Sophia Smith Collection at Smith College. A particularly important source was the manuscript of "Midwifery in Denmark," a report published by the U. S. Children's Bureau in 1929.

Also helpful in the preparation of this chapter were interviews with Doris Haire, Peg Beals, Paul Baier, Naomi Mayer, Dr. Abraham Towbin, Dr. Berry Brazelton, Dr. Yvonne Brackbill (all identified in the text), and a number of childbearing women.

Other sources included:

Arms, Suzanne. *Immaculate Deception, A New Look At Women and Childbirth in America*. Boston: Houghton Mifflin Company, 1975. Every American woman needs to read this book.

Baier, Paul. Brief of Amicus Curiae, expressing the views of the International Childbirth Education Association in the case of Bob E. Hulit, M. D., vs. St. Vincent's Hospital and Ob-Gyn Group of Billings, Montana in the Supreme Court of Montana.

Bishop, Edward H., et al. "Obstetric Influences on the Premature Infant's First Year of Development, A Report from The Collaborative Study of Cerebral Palsy." *Obstetrics and Gynecology*, 1965, 26, 628–635.

Bowes, Watson A., Jr., et al. *The Effects of Obstetrical Medication on Fetus and Infant*. Monograph published by the University of

Chicago Press for the Society for Research in Child Development. Serial No. 137, 1970. Volume 35, Number 4.

Brazelton, T. B. "Effect of Maternal Medication on the Neonate and His Behavior." *Journal of Pediatrics,* Vol. 58, No. 4. 1961.

Caldeyro-Barcia, Roberto. "Some Consequences of Obstetrical Interference." *Birth and the Family Journal,* Vol. 2, No. 2, Spring 1975.

Fields, Harry. "Complications of Elective Induction." *Obstetrics and Gynecology,* 15:476–480, 1960.

Haire, Doris. *The Cultural Warping of Childbirth.* A special issue of *ICEA News,* the journal of the International Childbirth Education Association, 1972.

Hirsch, Lolly. "Proceedings of the First International Childbirth Conference," June 2, 1973. Published by New Moon, Box 3488 Ridgeway Station, Stamford, Conn. 06905.

Liu, Yuen Chou. "Effect of an Upright Position During Labor." *American Journal of Nursing,* December 1974.

Newton, Niles. "Childbirth and Culture." *Psychology Today,* November 1970.

Optimal Health Care for Mothers and Children: A National Priority. A report of five conferences held during 1967 by the National Institute of Child Health and Human Development; National Institutes of Health; HEW. Available from Superintendent of Documents, U. S. Government Printing Office, Washington, D. C.

Shearer, Madeleine H. "Some Deterrents to Objective Evaluation of Fetal Monitors." *Birth and the Family Journal,* Spring 1975.

———. "Fetal Monitoring: Do the Benefits Outweigh the Drawbacks?" *Birth and the Family Journal,* 1:12–18.

Sweeney, William J. III (M.D.) with Stern, Barbara Lang. *Woman's Doctor.* New York: William Morrow and Co., Inc., 1973.

Towbin, Abraham. "Central Nervous System Damage in the Human Fetus and Newborn Infant." *American Journal of Diseases of Children,* June 1970.

———. "Latent Spinal Cord and Brain Stem Injury in Newborn Infants." *Developmental Medicine and Child Neurology,* 1969, 11, 54–68.

———. "Mental Retardation Due to Germinal Matrix Infarction." *Science,* April 11, 1969.

———. "Organic Causes of Minimal Brain Dysfunction." *The Journal of the American Medical Association,* August 30, 1971.

———. "Spinal Cord and Brain Stem Injuries at Birth." *Archives of Pathology,* 77:620–632, 1964.

Windle, W. F. "Brain Damage by Asphyxia at Birth." *Scientific American,* October 1969.

Worrall, Margaret. "BACE Hears Experts on Obstetrical Management." *BACE (Boston Association for Childbirth Education) Newsletter,* May/June 1974.

CHAPTER TWELVE

Atkinson, Donald T. *Magic, Myth and Medicine.* Cleveland and New York: The World Publishing Company, 1956.

Boston Thomsonian Manual and Lady's Companion, Vol. 5, 1838–1839. Also see, *Companion,* Vol. 3, Number 8, "Midwifery," by Dr. W. K. Gardner, 1836. Both volumes are located in the Harvard Medical School library.

Chadwick, James R. *The Study and Practice of Medicine by Women.* New York: A. S. Barnes and Co., 1879.

Edmunds, James. "The Introductory Address Delivered for the Female Medical Society," October 2, 1865. (EBC)

Haggard, Howard W. *Devils, Drugs and Doctors.* New York: Blue Ribbon Books, Inc., 1929.

Hersey, Thomas. *The Midwife's Practical Directory: Or Woman's Confidential Friend;* Designed for use of Botanic Friends in the United States. Baltimore, 1836. Published by its author. Available at the Harvard Medical School library.

Horton, Howard. *An Improved System of Botanic Medicine,* Volume II. Scott & Wright Printers, 1836. Harvard Medical School library.

ICEA News, Newsletter of the International Childbirth Education Association. Winter 1973.

Klemesrud, Judy. "The Return of the Midwife." *Woman's Day,* June 1973.

Mead, C. H. Kate. *History of Women in Medicine.* Haddam, Conn.: Haddam Press, 1938.

Mead, Margaret. Personal communication dated February 18, 1976. Dr. Mead, an anthropologist who has observed childbirth practices in many different cultures, believes that men sometimes reveal jealousy over woman's ability to give birth. In her letter to me, she wrote: "We find the myth of the island of women all over the world; the myth that expresses men's fear that women could give birth without them. In the myth, a man finally lands and teaches the woman how to give birth properly. In the obstetrician, this male desire to take control of childbearing is expressed."

Reiner, Eric. Movie of Lee Slavin's home birth. Shown at a childbirth conference in Stamford, Connecticut, June 2, 1973.

Singer, Charles, and Underwood, Ashworth E. *A Short History of Medicine.* New York and Oxford: Oxford University Press, 1962.

Thoms, Herbert. *Our Obstetric Heritage, The Story of Safe Childbirth.* Hamden, Conn.: The Shoe String Press, Inc., 1960.

CHAPTER THIRTEEN

Information on Flagyl was obtained from interviews with Dr. Jane Hodgson, assistant clinical professor in the Depart-

ment of Obstetrics-Gynecology at the University of Minnesota
and St. Paul-Ramsey Hospital; Anita Johnson, an attorney for
the Health Research Group; and spokespersons for the Food
and Drug Administration. My main source, which contains
many of the documents relating to the Flagyl controversy, was:

*Preclinical and Clinical Testing by the Pharmaceutical Industry,
1975.* Joint Hearings before the Subcommittee on Health of the
Committee on Labor and Public Welfare and the Subcommittee
on Administrative Practice and Procedure of the Committee on
the Judiciary, U. S. Senate, July 10 and 11, 1975.

I strongly urge women's health groups to obtain free copies
of these hearings from congressional representatives and read
the fascinating testimony. Also see a report on those hearings:

Burnham, David. "Drug Maker Is Accused of Falsifying Test Reports." *The New York Times,* July 11, 1975.

The section on menstruation and menopause is based on interviews with Dr. Mildred Gordon, reproductive biologist at
Yale Medical School, and Paula Weidegar, author of *Menstruation and Menopause: The Physiology and Psychology, The
Myth and The Reality.* Other sources included:

Austin, Donald F., Chief of the California Tumor Registry. Personal
communication dated January 14, 1976.
Brody, Jane E. "Coast Study Finds Sharp Rise in Uterine Cancer."
The New York Times, November 1, 1975.
Dalton, Katharina. *The Menstrual Cycle.* New York: Warner Paper-
back Library, 1972.
"Estrogen Is Linked to Uterine Cancer." *The New York Times,*
December 4, 1975.

Sources for the section on breast cancer treatment included:

Aug, Mary Ann. "A Report to the Profession from the Breast Can-
cer Task Force." National Cancer Institute press summary, Sep-
tember 30, 1974.
Crile, George. "Breast Cancer: A Patient's Bill of Rights." *Ms.,*
September 1973.
Frankfort, Ellen. *Vaginal Politics.* New York: Quadrangle Books,
Inc., 1972.
Kushner, Rose. *Breast Cancer: A Personal History and an Investiga-
tive Report.* New York: Harcourt Brace Jovanovich, 1975.

The section on unnecessary surgery is based on the following
material:

Bunker, John P. "Surgical Manpower: A Comparison of Operations and Surgery in the United States and in England and Wales." *New England Journal of Medicine,* January 15, 1970, pp. 135–43. For a more complete discussion of Bunker's study, see Barbara Seaman's *Free and Female.* New York: Coward, McCann & Geoghegan, Inc., 1972.

Diddle, A. W., et al. "Gynecological Surgery in Five Non-Teaching Hospitals." *Obstetrics and Gynecology,* February 1953.

Doyle, James C. "Unnecessary Hysterectomies: Study of 6,248 Operations in Thirty Hospitals During 1948." *Journal of the American Medical Association,* January 31, 1953. Doyle found that 30 percent of the women aged 20–29 in the study had no disease when their uteri were removed. He also found that 39.3 percent of the operations were subject to criticism and that in 12.5 percent of the cases there were no indications whatsoever for the hysterectomy.

Graham, Harvey. *Eternal Eve, The History of Obstetrics and Gynecology.* Garden City, N. Y.: Doubleday & Co., 1951. This book provides a history of gynecological surgery.

Gross, Martin L. *The Doctors.* New York: Random House, 1966. Excellent.

Miller, Norman F. "Hysterectomy: Therapeutic Necessity or Surgical Racket?" *American Journal of Obstetrics and Gynecology,* 51: 804, 1946.

Rogers, Joann. "Rush to Surgery." *The New York Times Magazine,* September 21, 1975.

Rosenfeld, Bernard, et al. *Health Research Group Study on Surgical Sterilization: Present Abuses and Proposed Regulations,* October 29, 1973.

Williams, Lawrence P. (Pseudonym). *How To Avoid Unnecessary Surgery.* Los Angeles: Nash Publishing Company, 1971.

Letters from DES mothers and daughters to Kay Weiss, cancer epidemiologist, were an important source for the section on DES. Correspondence and interviews with two DES mothers and one DES daughter provided more information. This section was also based on interviews with Weiss, and with Dr. Peter Greenwald, director of the Cancer Control Bureau in the New York State Health Department. Personal communication with Dr. Arthur L. Herbst of the Registry of Clear-Cell Adenocarcinoma in Young Women was extremely helpful.

Other sources included:

Greenwald, Peter, Nasca, Philip C., et al. "Prenatal Stilbestrol Experience of Mothers of Young Cancer Patients." *Cancer,* March 1973.

————, Barlow, J. J., et al. "Vaginal Cancer After Maternal Treatment With Synthetic Estrogens." *The New England Journal of Medicine*, 285, 390–392. 1971.

Herbst, A. L., Ulfelder, H., et al. "Adenocarcinoma of the Vagina: Association of Maternal Stilbestrol Therapy With Tumor Appearance in Young Women." *The New England Journal of Medicine*, 284, 878–881. 1971.

————, Rabboy, Stanley J., et al. "Clear-cell Adenocarcinoma of the Vagina and Cervix in Girls: Analysis of 170 Registry Cases." *American Journal of Obstetrics and Gynecology*, July 1, 1974.

————, et al. "Prenatal Exposure to Stilbestrol." *The New England Journal of Medicine*, February 13, 1975.

Scott, Joseph W., Seckinger, D., et al. "Colposcopic Aspects of Management of Vaginal Adenosis in DES Children." *The Journal of Reproductive Medicine*, May 1974.

Stafl, D., Dattingly, R. F., et al. "Clinical Diagnosis of Vaginal Adenosis." *Obstetrics and Gynecology*, 43:118–128, 1974.

Weiss, Kay. "Epidemiology of Vaginal Adenocarcinoma and Adenosis: Current Status." *Journal of the American Medical Women's Association*, February 1975.

————. "Vaginal Cancer: An Iatrogenic Disease?" *International Journal of Health Services*, Spring 1975. This article provides important information for DES mothers and daughters.

Sources for the section on the morning-after pill (DES) included:

"Health Research Group Report on the Morning After Pill," December 8, 1972. Available from the HRG, 2000 P Street, N. W., Washington, D. C. 20036.

"Morning After Contraceptive To Get Approval in Some Cases." *The New York Times*, February 21, 1973.

Regulation of Diethylstilbestrol (DES) and Other Drugs Used in Food-Producing Animals, Twelfth Report by the Committee on Government Operations, House of Representatives, December 10, 1973.

Regulation of Diethylstilbestrol (DES), Hearings before a Subcommittee of the Committee on Government Operations, House of Representatives, Part One (November 11, 1971), Part Two (December 13, 1971), and Part Three (August 15, 1972).

Regulation of Diethylstilbestrol (DES), 1975, Joint Hearings before the Subcommittee on Health of the Committee on Labor and Public Welfare and the Subcommittee on Administrative Practice and Procedure of the Committee on the Judiciary, United States Senate, First Session on S. 963, February 27, 1975. Wash., D. C.: U. S. Government Printing Office, 1975.

Schmeck, Harold M. "FDA Is Charged With Delays in Banning Hormone." *The New York Times*, December 11, 1973.

Use of Advisory Committees by the Food and Drug Administration, Eleventh Report by the Committee on Government Operations, January 26, 1976. U. S. Government Printing Office, 1976.

Use of Advisory Committees by the Food and Drug Administration, Hearings before a Subcommittee of the Committee on Government Operations, House of Representatives. Wash., D. C.: U. S. Government Printing Office, March, April and May 1974.

Weiss, Kay. "After Thoughts on the Morning After Pill." *Ms.,* November 1973.

————. "Fact Sheet on the Morning After Pill." *Quality of Health Care—Human Experimentation,* Hearings of the Committee on Labor and Public Welfare, U. S. Senate, 1973. Part One, February 21 and 22, 1973.

EPILOGUE

I gathered information for the Epilogue by attending self-help clinics in New York City (November 1972), Atlanta, Georgia (June 1973), and Baton Rouge, Louisiana (November 1973). I attended a childbirth conference in Stamford, Connecticut in June 1973, and a women and health conference in Boston in April 1975 and in Old Westbury, New York in October 1975. To learn about the Woman's Health Movement, I also took an eight-week "Know Your Body" course given at the Women's Health Center in New York City.

Pamphlets and questionnaires from most of the women's health clinics provided additional information and interviews with the following health activists were also helpful: Jenny Jennison of the Coalition for the Medical Rights of Women; Linda Curtis, a director of the Tallahassee Feminist Women's Health Center; Kate Bowland of the Santa Cruz Birth Center; Pam Booth of Healthright, Inc.; Lolly Hirsch, editor of *The Monthly Extract;* Carol Downer and Lorraine Rothman of the Feminist Women's Health Centers in Los Angeles; and Kay Weiss of Advocates for Medical Information.

Personal communication with Jody Norsigian of the Boston Women's Health Book Collective and Belita Cowan of the Women's Health Lobby Network also provided me with valuable information.

Other sources included:

Coalition News (Newsletter of the Coalition for the Medical Rights of Women, 433 Turk Street, San Francisco, California, 94102).

Issues dated April 15, 1975; July 1975; December 1975 and February 1976.

Downer, Carol. "Covert Sex Discrimination Against Women As Medical Patients," address to the American Psychological Association, September 5, 1972.

Healthright (A quarterly newsletter of the Women's Health Movement, available at 175 Fifth Avenue, New York, New York, 10010.) Summer 1975–Winter 1976 issues.

The Monthly Extract, An Irregular Periodical, August 1972–January 1975 issues.

INDEX